Also by Lourdes Odette Aquitania Ricasa

Unguarded Thoughts
Excerpts from Life
Pieces of Dreams
Running with Echoes of Desire
Touching the Wind

Love Echoes...Share and Inspire

LOURDES ODETTE AQUITANIA RICASA

authorHOUSE®

AuthorHouse™
1663 Liberty Drive
Bloomington, IN 47403
www.authorhouse.com
Phone: 833-262-8899

Published by AuthorHouse 12/18/2020

ISBN: 978-1-6655-0939-8 (sc)
ISBN: 978-1-6655-0938-1 (hc)
ISBN: 978-1-6655-0940-4 (e)

Library of Congress Control Number: 2020923945

Print information available on the last page.

Edited by Carolyn Norback
Walpole, New Hampshire U.S.A.

Front cover:
Yemen, Cover design by Rica Rudio

Includes paintings and sketches by the author.

Selected short stories and interviews with Filipinos, others living abroad.

Selected poems and articles translated to Spanish.

Dedication

FOR:
Rick
Rica and Joe
Richie and Christine
Robert and Chrissy
Riley
Rachel
Lucy
Kai Christopher

And my parents, Sixto and Luz

Our hunger to live
See the world with love
Eagerly holds my ardent soul

Introduction

LOURDES ODETTE AQUITANIA RICASA was born in the bustling city that never sleeps of Quiapo, Manila, Philippines,

A ceaseless experimenter, she describes her feelings and emotions attending festivals, commune dining, travel shenanigans with never a dull moment.

Her first and foremost priority is Love for Family. For without family, we are nothing.

She began solo travel when there was no internet, no cell phones. She used to manually write experiences in stenography notebooks, later collected to books. She curbs enthusiasm for finding ulterior meanings everywhere. During her interviews around the globe, there are no filters, never fearing to voice her opinion. She is a content creator.

Her mission is to seek out and encourage others to travel and step out of their comfort zone. As an artist her aim is to see the rainbows in parks, doodle in pencil, use paint brush with bright colors to remember the moment.

The world is a kaleidoscope of colors. Equally to be sensed are the smell of garlic, onions, curries in cuisines and the perfume fragrances of rose petals, plumerias and jasmine flowers. Touch the face of a Punjab girl, a Pakistani boy reading the Quran.

Wandering from one moment to the next from Lahore, Pakistan to Amritsar, India and then perhaps she will be back to Kerala, India, sometimes with a sudden crisis of the heart, in which she does not act or react. Some unconscious choices how a particular individual behaves, leading to a drama of psychological inclination.

During her travels she enrolls in painting classes, in Mission Renaissance Art School in Pasadena, California, Biarritz, France, Alicante, Spain, Bishkek, Kyrgyzstan. The most recent painting she did was in Solomon Islands. She has over one hundred paintings/works of art on display at in San Clemente, California.

She has traveled to 295 countries which include sovereign nations and territories per the Travelers Century Club list (www.travelerscenturyclub. org). She has been featured in several newspaper articles including the Samarkand, Uzbekistan Business Review, the Botswana Post, the San Clemente News, the Philippine Times News, the Holy Spirit College News, the Information Technology Division News of the Los Angeles Unified School District and the Servas magazine.

Television interviews include: The Encore, Los Angeles, California, Top Matin Show, Brazzaville, Democratic Republic of Congo, Radio Zaragoza Frequcncia .99.

Motivational Speaker: San Clemente High School, Prince Andrew School St Helena Island, Kamenge Youth Center, Bujumbura, Burundi. Frist Prize winner at Toastmasters Areas and Division contest.

Love Echoes…Share and Inspire is a clear exercise of her talents, a special type of poetry, short stories and interviews, experiences with locals in the country and Filipinos living abroad.

For without love, without poetry, we become squeezed in social conventions.

The thrill of bowing to the Dalai Lama in Ulaan Bataar.

She quips and captures stories and poetry that illuminate our minds.

To name a few of the more far-flung amazing places she has been include:

Timbuktu, Comoro Islands, Easter Island, the Galapagos Islands, Azores, Montserrat, Jersey Islands, Siberia, Guinea Bissau, Andaman

Nicobar islands, Island of St. Helena, Lakshadweep islands, Fernando do Noronja, Juan Fernandez and Robin Crusoe Islands, Chatham Islands, Norfolk Islands, Timor Leste and Nauru.

Exciting...she prefers to stay at the palaces, Paradores of Spain, chains of Palaces in Santiago de Compostela, Leon, Ducal Palace of Lerma, Trujillo and the Posada Dos de Evora in Portugal. These places immortalize yesterday, where the past emerges when Kings and royalty stayed here. There were times, she stayed in dorm beds in Iceland and Lake Baikal, Siberia. It was so much fun. I made a lot of friends.

From the streets of Pakistan, the jebel of Yemen, Las Geel caves in Somaliland, the smallest island nation of Nauru, the kasbahs of Algeria...unstoppable, giving classic poetry a fresh face.

Yemen, with villages perched steep on the hills, hanging precariously, clinging like eagle's nest to the sides of cliffs. Family homes on top of giant boulders. The underground villages of the Berbers in Tunisia, featured in the movie Star Wars. Frozen in time rock churches of Lalibela Ethiopia, the fascinating islands of the Maldives, Solomon Islands, Kiribati in the Phoenix Islands entices you to book a flight tomorrow.

Love cannot remain by itself – it has no meaning. Love has to be put into action. Not all of us can do great things. But we can do small things with great love.

Currently, her total travel is believed to be calculated at more than three million miles.

As of February 2020, she traveled to the Kingdom of Saudi Arabia, newly opened for tourist visas. ☺

Having traveled to two hundred ninety-five (295) countries, islands and territories, her book is a premiere show case, the world on pages of journeys.

Letters of Appreciation

You are so amazing! I don't know where to begin, such a unique talented, grateful, happy, warm person, full of life! You lift up our spirits. You give us such vivid description of your travels, so poetic, magnificent writer! I can feel the joy in your heart. I understand why people are drawn to you when you travel. You have that magnetic personality & you can share so many exciting stories for you carry a library of knowledge. Thank you for reliving your travels & sharing it with us. It is so great!

Alice P. Cuento, Los Angeles, California

You describe the beauty of each place and the people. You are a positive individual, seeing the good that surrounds you! It brings us to more places with splendor, majesty & overwhelming goodness.

Joseph & Ana, Trujillo, Spain

To me this charming account of your time on Norfolk Island, Odette epitomizes 5W. It resonated with me how, we cross cultural boundaries so easily when travelling and learn so much about local people. If we are open to receiving their thoughts and receptive to them.

I felt like visiting the place immediately. Yet I have never been there and I have travelled widely, certainly not to as many countries as you!

Marie Gracey, Sydney, Australia

You are my soul and inspiration.

Diane Labombarbe and Bobby, Ontario, Canada

Contents

Chapter 6 :   Our Minted World

Chapter 7 :   Eyes Beaming with Joy

Chapter 8 :   Make Hay While the Sun Shines

Chapter 9 :   Day to Dawn

Chapter 10 : Holding Glasses and Clinking

Chapter 11 : Entering a Reverie

Chapter 12 : Warm Newsletters

Chapter 13 : Apparent Spontaneity

Chapter 18 : Sailing in the Wind

Chapter 19 : Like Mirroring a Sky

Chapter 20 : Whatever is Hilarious

Chapter 21 : We Give Back to the Community

Chapter 27 : Don't Waste, Live It

Chapter 28 : Without Pause, Choosing You

Chapter 29 : Splash and Mosaics

Chapter 30 : Family is Priority

Chapter 1

In Our Contained Galaxy

Yemen, a Picture-Perfect Story Book

Year 2003 - Yemen, the best kept secret of the Middle East. A trip to Yemen is dating back to some 3,000 years ago. Sana'a, the old capital is a living museum. The scenery is like a ***story book - picture perfect***! Description by words is beyond expression. I never stopped saying "Wow!"

Our imagination was fueled by tales and folklore. Called the birthplace of all of our lives, the sons of Noah knew it as the land of milk and honey, the secret of eternal life.

It is an experience long lost to the modern world, free of commercial values, a picture of a ***different age.*** At the crossroads of spice and incense routes, Old Sana'a was ***frozen in time***.

In that era, teams of adobe, masons and stone, layers must have roamed the countryside, erecting these ***icing–cake*** houses on principles of elegance, the most dramatic feature of the country. Windows with white arches on top, triangular trims were cut in acute angles to emphasize the edges.

The north face basked in the maximum of sunshine. The east windows in geometrical patterns made of alabaster panes, framed the sunrise. The west turned toward the sunset. From the outside at night, it was magical to see all these windows play a kaleidoscope of colors, emerald green, gold, bright red and blue, all lit up.

Many houses are over 600 years old. Five or six floors story buildings grow out of the brown land, like huge square vegetables. Each one belongs to a large family with eight or ten children.

The sandy pink adobe stones belonged to an era of romanticism.

In the silent thickness of the stones, just behind the old plaster, I could hear the neighbors stirring, children shrieking gleefully, the trolley cars grinding on the narrow cobbled streets, the old taxis clanging at the corner, a wood burning stove, an oil lamp in the furnace. All these brought a tidal movement that made my eyes misty and my jaw drop.

We stayed at the Burj Al Salam hotel in Old Sana'a. We started the day at the Souq. Nothing can prepare you from the moment you enter the gates of the Bab al-Yaman. I was electrified, felt my adrenaline rush to the point of getting lost and losing concentration, weaving through the crowded alleys and dead-end corners of this enormous work of art.

Sellers stood on makeshift stools, waved their hands, and boisterously proclaimed their wares to attract our attention. One can find thousands of Iranian or Yemeni carpets, belts, shoes, yards of embroidered material, toys, and tiny packets of toothpick or giant sacks of sultanas.

The *qat* (stimulants) market was frenetically busy, the mounds of spices were an oriental fantasy brought to life. The small cellars where blinkered camels walked round and round in circles crushing sesame seeds to make oil was a glimpse into a bygone age.

The next day, we passed along wadis with verdant almond and walnut groves, myrrh, frankincense, tamarisk, acacia trees, and the *ilb* tree known as the crown of thorns of Jesus Christ. Yemeni terraced coffee plantations and *qat* (non-addictive leaves that men chew all day).

Mountains were lined by fields of golden summer hay, barley, beans, and lentil. Suddenly a rumbling waterfall would come into view. Fresh stream water flowed from these rocks running for millions of years. From the lowliest shrub lands to the sophisticated trees of Commiphora and Junipers, extra ordinary rock formations, a pack of landscape design, we stood in awe of the handiwork of generation after generation of farmers.

More impressive than the fields were the villages, perched steep on the hills, hanging, clinging to the sides of cliffs. Entire villages sat on top of giant boulders. Many appeared to be in the most incredible and dangerous positions. Abodes were built in a form of fortified housing with the walls of homes pressing each other. Architecture atop unconquerable peaks overlooking the green terraced fields was a panorama of unique beauty.

Add to this, the history of the village springing to life that all play a part in making Yemen the cradle of the Arab world. The heat played on the road caused mirages to form, then disappear, then wound its way, hugging the edges of cultivated valleys up to the very summit atop the striking Haraz Mountains, a picture postcard beauty.

The clouds embracing the slopes, followed us from village to village. Every turn was a complete surprise!

Local people are as colorful as their homes. The men dress to kill though not literally. Large, classical, curved, silver daggers are the Yemen equivalent of the necktie, while Kalashnikov rifles are carried with cell phones. The knives are often heirlooms made from the horns of rhinoceros and can cost as much as US dollars $200,000. The way it is worn (slanted to the side) indicates the rank of the judge in his class.

Men wore a long white one-piece robe with buttons on the chest. A decorated shawl is also worn. Can you imagine walking through crowded streets with a sea of men and their daggers hanging on their belt? Most women were covered from head to toe in black garb, some with flowery designs, with only their eyes showing.

The women formed a line along the cisterns, and carried precious jugs of water. The climb was challenging to a series of rocky stairways that split the mountains. They shyly talked in Arab and invited us to stop at her home for tea and sample her gracious hospitality.

Qat is another unique feature of the country. A coca leaf used as a stimulant, *qat* is chewed every single day. The whole country seems to be propelled by this legal drug, with most of the population chewing it up to 5 hours a day. Afternoon or evening *qat* parties are a part of daily life where groups of men, gather on the top floor of a house, or in a café. They lean on cushions, drink cola, smoke, chat and chew the *qat*. Leaf by leaf, they stuff their faces until their eyes are bright, their blood pressure is up, their conversation is wild and their cheeks bulge taking the shape of an orange.

We had lunch at the Al Harajah restaurant in the small town of Manakha. Plates and bowls of attractively laid-out foods covered every inch of space, near the steaming dishes. We sat on the floor and silently dipped our right hand, which we had washed in an adjoining room, into the savory foods.

The mouth-watering aroma floating from the *salta* (Yemeni's national dish, it is Hulba a whipped fenugreek condiment, the base is a brown meat stew called Maraq), the *chapatti* (big round flat bread), *thareed* (meat stew with vegetables) and Fattah served with yogurt and milk, served with lamb) fitted well into the atmosphere as we feasted on this ancient land from whence hailed the Queen of Sheba.

It seemed that we were living in one of the stories found in the *Arabian Nights*.

We danced the *jambiya*. We hopped and jumped, our feet soaring wildly into the air while clutching daggers and machine guns in hand, sinking into the exaltation of a bond between tribal members.

A silver feathered Arabian wax bill flew across the blue sky as we carried on a conversation, mixed with myths, legends and comedy. .

Goats, sheep, and chickens wandered the street. The most significant style of art music in Yemen is based closely on poetry, a solo singer with the accompaniment of percussion instruments to highlight the rhythms in expressive ways. The music is compelling, at the same time uplifting.

Past the first of many checkpoints, pyramids of yellow-and-green striped melons spilled along the road. The landscape takes on winding mountain passes in full powerful form, rising on either side of the road in jagged emerald peaks.

This is the kind of scenery that inspires silence—first, because it takes so much attentiveness to absorb the diversity of flora and the scale of the slopes, but also because the hairpin turns require intense concentration on the part of a driver.

At times, mists rolled into blanket everything, and then vanished. An ideal place for a pastoral life of quiet contemplation, the mountains surrounding the arch of the city darken into black silhouettes in the deep blue sky, as a cluster of stars winked overhead.

The abiding memory of this quest is _Old Sana'a's town, icing-cake houses_ and the dreamy mosques. Walking the streets as the evening prayer call rings out across the rooftops is a deeply exotic experience.

Timbuktu, the End of the Earth?

The most rhythmical of African names
Synonymous with Africa's mysterious inaccessibility
An end of the earth allure

Us Travelers
We just had to reach

Trembling with excitement
Nomads driving the cattle
Mud brick palace of the *imam*

Whirring ceiling fan
Embracing Allah for a few electric minutes
And then the sand dunes

During teen-age years
Dreamed of walking the edge of the Sahara
Foot prints track and blown
Stories of deserts and rivers
Lucrative trade

Sacred Muslim texts eminent scholars
From Cairo, Baghdad and Persia

Teachings of Islam
Astronomy, Mathematics, Medicine and Law

Madrasahs (schools and universities)
Served as wellsprings of Learning

Old homes with incomparable character
Hand littered manuscript
Stored in caves and cupboards

Live poetry composed in Spain
Centuries old essays
The Golden Age

Astronomy optics
Medicine ink concocted from black oil
In the market
Myriads of salt slabs
In tablet form or weighed on scales
To fatten the animals

Koranic schools
Antique memory aid for learning algebra
Students sing out equations

We bucked into town
In our dusty Humvee
Zigzagged across the dunes

Wealthy terminus of camel rides
Caravan route
West Africa and the Mediterranean
Encampment for Tuareg nomads

Elder women
Tended the animals
The town became known as Timbouctou.
A trading center

Echoed in mud and timber Dyingereyber Mosque
A forest of one hundred sturdy pillars
Interconnecting rooms with holes in the walls

Sidi Yahiya mosque
Main gate will not be opened
Until the end of the world

Sankore Mosque and University
Wooden framework into the mud walls

Thirty-three saints lived in Timbuktu
700,000 manuscripts
A shadow of its former glory
Mysterious black magic
Door that cannot be opened
Evil spirit will be released to the world

A journey on a slow boat
The Grand Niger
Waterways that provide the country's lifeblood

My T-shirt shows
I went to Timbuktu
And back

Americans, Okinawa, Japan

Hitting a tropical climate
Bus drivers wore sky blue Hawaiian shirt as uniforms
Busses painted in bright colors written "Happy?"

Population known to be
One of the longest-lived people in the world

Okinawa city - to the Ryuku islands
Bus stop at Makishi

Rewards the traveler's intrepid spirit
For now, I am a *tabinchu* (traveler) in the blue yonder

Rainbow colored reefs fun loving islanders
Empire of the rising sun
Bygone Ryuku kingdom

Kosetsu Ichiba market
Lending flavor to music
Shansin three string banjo buzzing
Wrapped in snake skin
Infectious, enchanting, enticing and energetic sound

Deep fried donuts, pork belly in sweet spicy soy sauce
Stalls into an unassuming doorway
Lead to a carnival of delightful and grotesque butcher shops
Fishmongers, octopus and pickle sellers in giant pots
White pink- eyed pig, faces stared down from the racks

A storm was brewing beneath the clouds
Rain poured for an hour
Then, bright sunshine once more

A Japanese woman caught my attention
She insisted that I try *chanpuru* (stir fried)
bitter melon with tofu and egg
She looked good with her bright red scarf
A hibiscus flower on her silver hair despite her spidery blue veins

Sunset beach in the Mihama American Village in Chatan town
Starbucks Coffee, Pizza Hut and Tony Roma's restaurant
American Depot creates a cultural blend
Carnival with a Ferris wheel

Taco rice with red hot sauce pickled like wasabi
King Taco is famous here
Jahana Kippan sweets fit for the royal court
Winter melon, sugar cane, and *kippan* (citrus fruit)

Kokusai-dori Street, an eye popper street for people watching
A place that carries a certain charm
Crew cut American military to teeny boppers and octogenarians

Pickled pigs ears and high proof snake liquor
Rafute (braised pork belly), steamed rice and wheat noodles

Guarding fortresses, homes and entrances
Shisa figurines lion-dog creature
Giant ceramic sculptures to plastic trinkets

Koza Gate 2 American military base
The Philippine store, Manila Bay Café and night spots
Bungalow restaurant serving *pancit* (noodles)
and fish *lumpia* (egg rolls)

Endearing writings on the walls in cafes with greasy spoons
Steaming pots with dumplings and luncheon spam meat

Wave-like opening Jomon pottery and the presence of shell axes
Black Harlem with ten thousand long playing soul records
Chilled out to Marvin Gaye

Rode the monorail to Shiro-ju Castle
Up and down the gray stones under the sweltering heat
Sprawling grandiose seat of the ancient Ryuku kingdom
A marvel for the eyes with bright red roof tiles
Vast stone courtyards massive gray walls

Sonoda local pubs (*izakaya*) and cafes
Nonda bus stop
Blue Seal ice cream shop
Tried *beni imo* (purple yam)

Edible kelp with *moyashi* (bean sprouts)
Flaked fish and dried eel
How about some snake sea soup

Stopped at the Lawton Station Convenience store
Refreshing Cold tea with milk

O. Ricasa Vibrant Spain Charcoal on Paper 1998

Vibrant, Romantic Spain

The concept intrudes my imagination
The impact this vibrant land has on me
The vividness of its colors so inviting

At Besalu
Church bells of Sant Pere tolled
Some story book myths

Spanish women wore their brightly embroidered mantillas
Veils of lace flowed
Tall ivory combs adorned their hair
Sang as if they were in a cathedral
Took each note seriously
Voices blending to powerful songs

Sun doped, I swung my legs
On a sparking swathe of concrete
Near the Romanesque bridge of the El Fluvia River

Studied the arcaded streets and squares
A restored *mikveh*, (a ritual Jewish bath)

Loud tourists drifted eagerly
Children's shrieks transformed to hysterical birds

Men weighed each word for appropriateness
Joy echoed when a joke was told

Medieval troubadours coughed horse laughs
Amplified by slaps on each other's shoulder

Twirling my red and yellow scarf with letters "Viva España"
I pretended not to hear at first
A male voice whispered
"Quieres tomar un vino?" (Do you like wine) ?
He broke a smile

I felt something tall collapse slowly inside me
As though I was walking into a wind
A usual trap
I clapped my hand over my mouth and giggled
"English, No Spanish"

A few meters away
I heard the drums beating, the cymbals whirring

Soon the procession began
Somewhere amid the almond and orange trees
The too proud band leader with a black velvet jacket
And candy apple red pants
Pointed his baton at the violinist

It was a simple invitation
Ferocious as a comet
Hurtling towards the day
Calling for friendship
I pretended I cannot speak Spanish

If you care about surviving the night
He boomed

"Sin duda Besalú es la ciudad más bella de España"
("Without doubt, Besalu is the most beautiful city in Spain")

Vibrante, Romantico España

El concepto se entromete mi imaginación
El impacto de este vibrante tierra tiene sobre mí
La viveza de sus colores muy atrayentes

En Besalú
Las campanas de la iglesia de Sant Pere de peaje
Algunos mitos del libro de cuentos

Mujeres españolas llevaban sus mantillas bordados de colores vivos
Velos de encaje fluyeron
Peines de marfil adornadas Tall su cabello
Cantó como si estuvieran en una catedral
Tomó cada nota seriamente
Voces de mezcla de canciones de gran alcance

Dopado por el sol, Saqué las piernas
En una franja chispas de hormigón
Cerca del puente románico del río Fluvia
Estudió las calles con soportales y plazas
A mikve restaurada, (un baño ritual judío)

Turistas ruidosos flotaban ansiosamente
Chillidos de los niños transformadas para pájaros histéricas

Los hombres pesan cada palabra para conveniencia
Alegría hizo eco cuando se le dijo una broma

Trovadores medievales tosían risas de caballo
Amplificado por palmadas en el hombro de uno al otro

El giro de mi pañuelo rojo y amarillo con las letras " Viva España"

Fingí no haber oído al principio
Una voz masculina le susurró
"Vino sin QUIERES Tomar ?"
Rompió una sonrisa

Sentí algo colapso de altura poco a poco dentro de mí
Como si yo estaba caminando en un viento
Una trampa habitual
Yo aplaudí mi mano sobre mi boca y reí
"Inglés, No Español"

A pocos metros de distancia
Oí el batir tambores, los platillos zumbando

Pronto comenzó la procesión
En algún lugar en medio de los almendros y naranjos
El líder de la banda demasiado orgulloso
Con una chaqueta de terciopelo negro
Y los pantalones rojos de la manzana de caramelo
Apuntó con su bastón en la violinista

Era una simple invitación
Feroz como un cometa
A toda velocidad hacia el día
Llamada para amistad
Hice como que no puedo hablar español

Si usted se preocupa por sobrevivir a la noche
Él tronó
"Sin Duda Besalú es la ciudad más bella de España"

Angkor Wat, Cambodia

Rising slowly in diminishing circles from the moat
Wondering if I am in a fantastic dream
Caught up into the heavens
I entered Angkor Wat

Like an exotic island discovered
After months at sea
Eyes sunk in tiered Temples
Galleries with columns, vaulted roofs, towers
Windows of stone turned to wooden rosettes

Immense pagodas and stupas in dark gray stone
Smelled of fresh jasmine
Up above, the wizened orange sun
Pierced my soul

Is this the universe in replica of sandstone?
Epics of Hindu mythology blocks
Asparas, nymphs churning the ocean of milk
Trying to discover an elixir render us immortal

A bare footed frail woman pounded my chest
Her wrinkled but strong fist
Heard the loud thud of my awe struck heart
In the narrow Hall of Echoes
I felt the first Epiphany of my life

An array of divinities riding elephants
A former empire of centuries ago
Still palpitating with life
Heard them chant and cry

Bayon temple exhuming grandness in every scale
Dwarfed by this colossus, I turned to an exploring bee
Crawling on the fifty-four immense pedestals

Giant four faced towers with curved lips
Eyes with shadows by the lower lids
Bore the smile of Angkor's *Svakum*, "Welcome"

Down and around the Siem Reap River
We traveled the dusty streets

No names, no numbers, sparse lamp posts
Coconut stands with leaning bamboo sheds
Cheerful faces proud of their heritage

Our Cambodian driver, Rota
With a bright flash of the eye
Raced with families piled in a single motor bike

Babies carried in mother's arms
Bright colored skirts rustling with the breeze
Four passengers, no safety belts, no helmets

Inscriptions in Khmer and Sanskrit
Temples startled in splendor

Heart almost bounded to my mouth
Viewing King Jayavarman founder of Angkor
Shiva, God of Wisdom and Vishnu

Miles of intricately sculptured lace walls
Transmitted heat like a burning furnace
Walked under a red and white parasol
Crossed the pond filled with lotus plants while
Dragon flies fluted through cocoa and areca palms

Children ate bowls of rice
Ensuring a bountiful harvest

Voices like scented oil
Gave patronage to Hinduism and Buddhism
Spirits so potent, I was exorcised

Ramayana legends in adventurous tales
Supernatural forces protective or destructive

Majestic Gods and ferocious demons
Sacred and profane reincarnation
Swept my body as I roamed the pillars

Serpent balustrades with scaly bodies
Spread its many heads
Formed the shape of a fan
Blew my hair in the arid wind

Joy rippled through all my bones
Alas! Shrouded in the jungle
Ta Prohm in a romantic setting
Twisted and convoluted trunks of banyan trees

Nature destroyed or consoled
Gigantic roots over, under and between terraces
Probed the walls, split the carved stones
Branches and leaves intertwined
A shanty roof balanced on rocks

Velvety mosses curbed
Dangling roots converged on my face
Most delicate tendrils sung
Emanating a conflict of moods
Inside my now sensitive soul

Terrace of the Leper King
Gallery of a thousand Buddhas with composure
Brutality and torture or ascension to paradise
Am I in limbo or in heaven?

Pitching Tents, African Safari –Year 1992

Pitching tents not Adam and Eve
Paradise on earth

I met an old man, Gideon, all eyes and ears
Hands trembling rowing our boat
He pointed to four sleepy eyed hippopotamuses
Fumbling the ropes tied to the shores
His world, not for me

Two eagles perched on a giant rubber tree
And watched him go, fast for his age

We winked and clinked our drinks
Under the bridge of the Zambezi River
Over the thousand stars of our tents

Scouting for rhinoceros, giraffes, tigers
Riding our safari jeep, Melvin driving
Larger grounds we feared our hearts

Running cheetahs, impalas so wild
The night falls, it is time for *sadza*
Gem squash, hot white maize porridge

Flushed and tired James collects our tents
Folding chairs, tables and kitchen wares

Through infield morning dew we board the bus
South of the equator like birds fanning wings
Replenished our safari supplies at Bulawayo

Winners and losers we all were
At night playing our game

Climbing the tree house, darkness prevailed
Not to utter a word
Thus the lion roars, the elephants trumpet

From Matobo hills to Masvingo
Kopje studded terrain weird balancing rocks

Some quiet entrance to Kruger Park
No accident of being here
As if my diary was written

Hail this peace of acres calm
Camping at ranger post Punda Maria
My purpose yet honored

Strange conical towers historic Zimbabwe ruins
Who carved your cones with spears?
Echoing bushmen, where are you now?

This ground's measure is to be learned
Paintings on rocks, spreads on woods
This day, this town, this wind, this cave
Will be written in a song

Cecil gives a smile
Yet holds his diamond heart for all to see
A warm friendly thank you
"It's a pleasure"

O. Ricasa A Quiet Place in the Pyrenees Oil on Canvas 1992

A Quiet Place in the Pyrenees

I felt in my blood
The scent of all the world's flowers
Blue iris, ancient Rosemary, red horned poppies
Of birch, maple, cedar and pine trees

The intoxicating smell of the earth
Fresh with torrential rains
That runs the river Garrone

Looking down from Andorra
Crying for sight
Recounting the northern parachutists
Gliders of air balloons in gigantic baskets

Walking under lifting mists in Spain
Where Panticosa sleeps in solitude
And Ordesa park over the clear lake

On the late French town of Luchon
We conquered the Bohemian dusk
Toasting champagne, clinking crystal glasses
Cutting foie grass like rolled curls of shredded wood

While in our hands the earthen bread burns
Upon the firewood in quiet peace

The skiers of Beñasque at chills of night
King Ferdinand's army men

From door to door in secretive voice
Their eyes are calm
Their looks are questioning

The last bells of the evening toll for St. Cecile
Shadows of Sant-Lary in the Aure Valley comes down
Looking for fate at dawn
Silvery weather upon the ground

Winds piercing our pale faces
We race over the slopes like children
With power in our hearts to win
Kaleidoscope magic of the pure white snow

O. Ricasa Sun Bathing, Nude in Jamaica Oil on Canvas 1998

Sun Bathing, Nude in Jamaica

White witch of Rose Hall
Slaves were her lovers
Murdered when she got bored

Doctor's Cove Beach
Panama lady with a basket of fruits
Perched on her head
Braided my hair
Intertwined with red and yellow beads

Watching the sunset at Negril
Pulsating sounds of reggae
Jamaican unrelenting good humor
Genuine welcome

Gliding in the falls of Ocho Rios
Caught a fire at the festivals
Dancing to the beat of reggae

Gentle ice cream man
Stood under a coconut palm
Detecting the charm and freewheeling spirit

The Naked truth is crescent shaped
Wind caressing our hammocks
Devoted to the pursuit of pleasure
Dreams of catching a prince

Went wild for a week

Sunbathing for one hour
One time short experience swimming in the nude

Chapter 2

Meditating in the State of our Universe

O. Ricasa My Soul Sings White Villages,
Costa del Sol Oil on Canvas 1999

Swiss Coffee White Villages of Costa del Sol

Overwhelmed with happiness
More awake than any one
We party until dawn

To go to bed before
Three o'clock in the morning
A personal dishonor

Riding on horseback
Riding on donkeys
Fireworks or processions
Fiestas of patron saints
Regional pilgrimages and funfairs

Romerias up to a venerated shrine
Driving covered wagons
Sensual costumes pirouette through
Throngs of comical caricatures

Thousands of people on the street
Exuberant circuses and competitions
Unpredictable blue or green hooded-eyed Cordoba
Flamencos, castanets clap incessantly

Tapas, jamon, cheese, wine and turron
We eat, drink and dance
Burn olive tree branches
Shoot guns in the air
Festival of Cristianos y Moros

A loose bull or two stampeding
Rolling hills of Andalucia

Covered with grapevines, orange trees
Whitewashed walls on every corner
Sierra Nevada quietly watching

Nerja, Malaga and Motril
A hundred church bells toll
For whom does it toll

Quite a phenomenal site
In these villages of white

Musee du Louvre

Startling beauty wealth of Paris
Masters fused
Orchestration of light and dominant colors
Culminating point of genius

Leonardo da Vinci, Mona Lisa
Albrecht Durer's Self-portrait
Veronese's sumptuous Wedding at Cana
Picasso's Guernica

The Birth of Venus, Botticelli
Grand statue Venus de Milo
The Persistence of Memory, Salvador Dali

David of Michelangelo
Rembrandt, The Night Watch
Johannes Vermeer's The Lace Maker
Winged Victory of Samothrace

Adoration of the Shepherds, Luca Gordano
The Grape Harvest, Francisco Goya
Giant Sphinx from the valleys of Luxor
Symbols of Life and Death

Shackled obsession
A tribute to powers of vision
Intelligence in all forms

There is no end
As I stand in awe
Comprehending memorable works
Preserved and passed onto tomorrow

Profound expression of secret details
Clinging to destiny
A revelation of techniques

Pangs of hunger for art
A certain softness or strong features
Feast for a lowly artist

Flamboyant Seville

Jasmine grows in profusion
Sharing the orange tree filled squares
Strolling old lanes
Haunted by Moors

Up and down the ramps of La Giralda
A line of horse drawn buggies awaited

In the night of a smoke-filled room
People squeezed like sardines in a can
Hands clapped harder and harder
ONE-two-three, ONE-two-three
ONE-two-three, dominated and thundered

Electricity was building
The crowd grew wild and fanatic
Cheered hysterically, bombarded
AN-selmaa! AN-selmaa! AN-SEL-M-A-A-A!!!

A charismatic dark haired lady
Dressed in velvet black
Wearing giant hoop earrings
Bracelets and rings on eight fingers

Glittering with diamonds and emeralds
Fleeted around with tapering red fingernails
Motioned everybody to keep silent

Lights turned off, candles blazed
Faced the altar of Our Lady of Rocio
Garlanded with silver flowers
Virgin and protector of the *marismas* (wet muddy area of land)

Miguel, a passionate Flamenco guitarist
Manolo with his ribboned tambourine
Solemnly bowed their heads
Crossed themselves at five points

Anselma blurted with grace
El Rocio es pa vivirlo
(The Lady Rocio is for us to live)

Sevillanas twirled their hands in the air
Proudly turned their heads left and right
Stomped their high heels
Raised their skirts up their thighs

Ecstatic on the dance floor
Mantilla tassels swayed
Touted their buns
Teased the *borrachos* (drunkards)

Barrio Santa Cruz, a lustrous gem
Narrow streets, tiny squares, white walls
Tiled roofs, wrought iron grilles
A thousand pigeons scattered
Where balconies hung colorful laundry

Crossing the Rio Guadalquivir
Sierpes, Tetuan, La Maestranza
Extremely animated on a bar crawl
Wine glasses in hand
With tapas and sherry

Basilica of the Sacred Virgen La Macarena
Soon I will leave you, Virgen

A miracle, crystal tear fell below your eye

The Thinning Crowds of Barcelona, Catalunya

I saw you walking among the thick crowd
Now scurrying in Las Ramblas
Then disappearing in Calle Boqueria
Into the serpentine old town

It was my fate to follow you at Placa Catalunya
I heard a boisterous band playing
I opened the balcony
There you were admiring the flutist

Dunking churros in hot chocolate
Opposite Gran Teatre Del Liceu
Our eyes met again

Dreaming, two souls lost in the night

Wandering and wandering
Through Gaudi's warrior-like chimneys
Stunning Modernista *La Pedrera*
I followed you like a spy

Continued walking to Calle Hospital
Paroquia de Sant Josep

My heart skipped
Almost run over by a trolley
I had to catch you
Lest you be gone again

The crowd is thinner now
I don't see you anymore

How lonely and desolate I feel
When will I see you in my dreams again?

Sidi Bou Said, Tunisia

Up and down the hill
We strolled on cobbled stone streets
An artist's colony
Set high on a cliff
Overlooking the Gulf of Tunis

Studded wooden doors
Gleaming whitewashed walls
Dotted with ornate window grills
All painted deep blue

Arab script interspersed with floral relief
Colorful arched doorways
Opened into small courtyards
Filled with magenta bougainvillea

Women in black dresses
Walked gracefully
I was transfixed in serenity
Oblivious to the crowd

Stepping into a huge marble paved mosque
Men greeted each other
With a peck on the right and left cheek

The *mihrab* (a niche in the wall of a mosque)
Were built facing the direction of Mecca

On the top of a steep path
We sipped sweetened hot tea
Sprinkled with pine nuts

I saw your face hidden
Among the olive trees
Phoenicians were your ancestors
I wish ancient ancestors were holding me now

The Underground Palaces of Moscow

Dazzling opulent decoration
Muscovites with cavernous spaces
In the Metro I got lost

Asking for directions
I approached a Russian in uniform

He led me to a room with security bars
Pulled the drawer of his desk
Took out an English dictionary!
I thought I will be in jail for a violation

Descending underground by staircase
Golden chandeliers and sculptured archways
Passageways glowed with gilded glass
Kievskaya Station an elegant drawing room

Pantheon of the Revolution
Palatial in décor I was mesmerized
Bronze figures of muscular men and women

Marbles of many colors from quarries
Music of the spheres, colorful panels
Gleaming floors, illuminated ceilings
I was hundreds of feet underground

Baroque with a proud glitter
Oval mosaics depict
Drawing lines of desire

Soviets in the sky

Mystical Bali Beach

Seeking esoteric enlightenment
Island with infectious charm
Flowing brooks like tiny pebbles
Women in orange, blue and purple Batik dyed dresses

Wearing a blue sarong with a pink sash
Meditating at Pura Uluwatu
Kneeling across covered tables

Tingling of the Gamelan bells
Hands flying in the air
Smiling Legong dancers
Palm leaf boxes filled with flowers

Monkey forest sanctuary
Faster than lightning
A mother monkey
Snatched the bananas from my hands

Laying on a straw mat
Sun bathing at Kuta beach
Balinese lady rubbed oil
Soothingly massaged my back

Temple of the Earth in the Sea
Sad Kabyangan changing colors
With every turn of the sunlight
A radiant outcrop of rocks

Tirtha holy water splashed
On my head and face
Wet rice grains pressed to forehead

A pink hibiscus placed
Behind my right and left ear

Sipping juice *campur* and coconut juice
Spring source of energies

Twelve Days in Toulouse, France

A room in the attic of an old fortress
In a rose tinted fortified town
Along Place Victor Hugo

Or, on top of a cliff overlooking the river Aude
Visigoths, feudal lords hanging on the walls

Each night palaces are different
A citadel, a book of stone in which to read history
The history of passion in the form of
Each column represented by love

Riding a golden chariot passing castles
Built on top of ninth century architecture
That reveals many of its secrets
As numerous as the stars in the sky

A loved princess I feel
Heart could melt
Unchained
All resolutions squeezed

How magical Les Jacobins looks at night
By moonlight we enjoy a nocturnal whim

Going to the concert or riding a sail boat
Heart captured by
Coming out of the moon

A Cinderella in dreams
Appears a prince's face

His eyes the color of olives picked from a tree
Gazing at me, holding me tenderly

The speed of my heart almost to a stop
Awakened to reality

Philippines Calling

Around the city, we rode the jeepneys
Or the *calesa* (a horse driven carriage)
When business became prosperous
He bought a 1954 Ford sedan
A gigantic car, as big as an armored tank

During summers he drove us to
The province of Nueva Ecija
Where we attended town fiestas
Virgin Mary met Jesus in a caravan of flowers
Procession of candlelight

Our district, Quiapo's fiesta
Was held every ninth day of January

Auntie Remy would arrive the night before
Cooking *pancit, adobo, lumpia,* and roasted pig
She was concocting recipes in massive quantities
Enough to feed an army

The district procession consisted of
Fifty bands parading playing Spanish songs

Then came the Statue of Jesus of Nazareth
Born on the shoulders of a sea of parishioners
Men with towels wrapped around their necks
The swelling crowd so dense
We dared not to go outside

All doors were closed
As we watched through our balcony window

Every now and then
One or two men walked on top of the heads
Of the swarm of people

To reach Jesus, they touched his face
Crossed themselves at five points
Walked back on top of the heads of the crowd

During Holy Thursdays
All offices and schools were closed
We had to go on a "Visita Iglesia"

At four o'clock in the afternoon
We visited seven churches
One church after another
Asking for penitence

Every Friday before Lent
And on Good Fridays
We were not supposed to eat meat

Christ died at three o'clock in the afternoon
From then on we were not allowed
To take a shower until the next day
Because the water might contain the blood of Jesus

Holy Saturday woke us up
With the loud tolls of church bells
We jumped gloriously
Christ has risen from the dead

Easter Sunday was a festive day
We visited grandpa and Grandma Nelly
There was always a spread of food
Bibingka (rice cake*), relleno,* (sausages), *leche flan* (custard)
We ate endlessly

When I reached High School
I had the good fortune of meeting a classmate
Linda, a niece of Philippine President Magsaysay
She lived in Malacañang Palace

Thus, dad spread the news to the whole town
I was always at the Presidential Palace

Dad believed in good education
Although we did not have enough money

For College, he enrolled me in a prestigious school
Assumption Convent in San Lorenzo Village
Located in a subdivision for the rich and famous

My classmates were the daughters of Vice President Pelaez
Or Senator Kalaw or Congressman Cojuangco
Up until that time
He religiously drove me to and from school
Making sure that I was on top of my studies

The day of graduation came
My brother, sisters, uncles and aunts
Were all present in the graduation ceremonies

At the convent's lawn
The graduation march played
Tears rolled down his cheeks
As with my mother's

He did not graduate from high school
It was his dream that I finish College

Time moved on
I got married

Immigrated to America
Mother and Dad followed

Filipino custom is
Mother and father live with their children
Thus, they stayed with me in Eagle Rock

At age fifty-six, he was eager
America was a land of opportunity
He landed a job as a parking attendant in West Hollywood

He developed camaraderie with friends
Occasionally they would eat *chicharron* (fried pork skins)
Drinking the Filipino wine bottle

On weekends
He took care of my children
Often buying them presents and surprises
With the same *cariño* (affection) that he doled on me

After a few years of working
Dad had a mild stroke

I took him to the best doctor in Beverly Hills
He was given medication
Exercises and therapy

But the series of strokes kept coming
I saw him become weaker and weaker
His muscles atrophied
Time came when he could no longer walk

Small that I am
I faithfully carried him in my arms
Up the stairs to the doctor's office for check ups

He used to say:
"Salamat anak."
"Thank you, dear daughter."

Little did he know
One day I would become a writer
Publish a book
The world will know about his kind virtues

At age sixty-two
Under a cloudless morning, he passed away

A day I will never forget
When my love was cut off physically
But stayed connected and lingered emotionally

No more dad to make *"Amen"*

"Nasa langit ka na daddy
Pinagmamalaki ka naming lahat"

"You are now in heaven, dad
All of us are proud of you."

Chapter 3

Magical Gifts of Expression

Notes from My Mother, Luz

Her father died when she was eight
Her mother when she was five or so
Born between Saturday and Sunday
Half way in the middle of the night
In 1917?

Two brothers and two sisters
She could turn to
Whatever battle she had to face
Not for me to trace

Bravery, her greatest trait
To know how to survive
A tennis player and swimmer she was
How best to tell her happy childhood

Life began in Lavanderos, Sampaloc
A street where women laboriously pounded clothes
Daily washing on the stone steps
Averting the sirens of the Second World War

Mother used to go there without shoes
Sit under a guava tree
Her face *cara de caimito* (white complexion)
Round and bright green fruit
Pure white milk inside

A bamboo house on wooden stilts
Tropical Island on the Philippine shores
Mangoes like apple tree yards
Bantay, her watchdog sniffs

Kerosene lamps and kerosene tanks
Water pumps, torn up streets, clay roads
Mosquito nets, sleeping mats, hot summers
Rice wrapped in banana leaves and shrimp *bagoong* (fish paste)

Novena masses, vows and pledges made
Rosary beads, long walks on her knees to the altar
Genuflecting, crossing herself three times

Faces staring in completion
Jesus of Nazarene in his crimson robe
Shrine of the Infant of Prague holding the globe

Father, he was one of sixteen children
Grandfather had three wives
All at the same time

Tomorrow is *Que. sera, sera* (whatever will be)
He must have struggled to keep his head up
A poor family, raised as a great thinker

Commerce and businesses he tried
Manufacturing pianos, sewing machine cabinets
Even all sizes of wooden crosses
Land deals of a dreamer negotiated here and there
Over Café Batangas on Ermita Street

One spring day two persons became one

First came my brother, then me
Who wanted to write, keep writing
In the old days, going to college was not for women
But mother tutored all my homework

Playing mahjong her favorite past time
Taking dancing lessons with Baduy
She was a graceful dancer

To father she would say
It's good exercise and justify

Soon came three more sisters
Nicknamed *Tatlong Maria* (three Marias)
Going to different schools
Long sleeved brown and white starchy uniforms

Family portraits
Comadre Georgina was the owner
X-or Studios in Escolta, Manila
We wore our Sunday best dresses

Sampaguitas, jasmine, sounds and colors
Lavender butterfly orchids, *waling-waling*
Of flowers, fruits and gleeful faces

Coming to America was her dream
The airplane ride her first
Is this the land of opportunity?
Where are the dollars that grows on trees?

Gave up mysterious future of success
Stayed home, took care of all my three children
Whole world of ideas far and beyond her
Mechanics of daily life she followed

Widowed, she led a good life
Laughing with senior citizen friends

Dancing with Bill and Maynard
"I have an American boyfriend", she would brag

Trips to far away Lourdes, France and Fatima, Portugal
Miracles happen everyday
Our thanks to the almighty God

At 74 she survived a delicate brain aneurysm
She never lost the desire to live

Now at 82, in her cotton duster
Her eyes clouded
She sits by the window
And asks, "Who are you?"

My heart sinks feeling sad and torn
Turning away, the day goes on

** Luz, beautiful mom died at 89 years old.

With the Dalai Lama in Mongolia

Sain baina uu (hello) from Mongolia, where there is no population explosion. Located on a plateau between China and Siberia .

The whole population of Mongolia is only 2.8 Million. A big land mass maybe six times the size of California. Very simple people, most are nomads. They prefer not to own a home because the mountains are all theirs, everybody's land. From the window of the airplane, the Gobi Desert looked so green and peaceful, stretches of miles of desert.

This is the coldest city in the whole world. It goes down to Minus -50 degrees Celsius or Minus -100 Fahrenheit during the winter!!!

Attended an afternoon show at the coliseum where the fourteenth Dalai Lama spoke. I got excited because I never heard him. It was a hot afternoon. The place was jam packed. I did not understand anything he said, it was Tibetan language. There was ritual chanting.

.

Caught in a trance, I was almost hypnotized!

Dinner at the Silk Road Restaurant overlooking the Boghd Khaan (Palace of Joy). Mongolian cuisine: dumplings filled with lamb and goat, bread with liver paste, fried mutton, drunk Chinggis Khan beer.

In search of simplicity combined with a romantic allure to the mountains, I stayed at the Terelj National park . The stunning view of the picturesque valley put a soft spot for the pastoral life in my soul.

In the shelter of a ger camp decorated with Mongolian national red, orange and yellow traditional patterns, the earthen stove was placed in the middle. A *ger* is a yurt in the middle of carpeted greens, meadows, pine and birch trees under sunny blue skies, almost a picture book.

There is some kind of inner peace here, a place less traveled, not commercialized. No telephones, no television, no cell phones, no computers. I called the maid with a wireless call tinkling bell.

Our charming guide's name was Bayarmaa (means Happy Mother). She had straight long black hair with bangs that complemented her oriental onyx eyes. In Ulaan Baatar, we stayed at the Khaan Palace hotel on Peace Avenue .

Night skies were clear with dazzling stars. I gazed at the Big Dipper and Milky Way. Viewing the meteor life and the movement of the planets, I almost saw Jupiter and Mars. Feeling directly connected to the land, I sang my bluesy lungs even though I was out of tune.

Visited the Buddhist University temple, great *ger* library Gandantegchinlen, the largest monastery that houses 5,000 monks. Along the left wall are the volumes of Kanguir penned in the fourteenth century penned in gold ink on black paper.

Walked along Sukhbaatar Square and the Vajradhara Temple made of earth and bricks, the top decoration is gilded gold. The 13th Dalai Lama lived here.

Scooted in a circle around the Turtle rock. Wind swept deserts to the breathtaking heights of the Altai mountains or the evergreen landscapes of the Khentii. Semi desert and mountain forest steppes, the highest peaks permanently snowcapped covered with glacier.

Flora: coniferous taiga forest, lichens, mosses, fungi. Animals: eagles, ground squirrel, an abundance of wolves and snow leopards, wild bear, elk, lynx and brown bear, gazelles, camels and Przewalski's horses.

Costume: men wear *deel* - calf length tunic with a brightly colored sash or *terleg* worn by men and women.

Mongolian nomads move several times a year by ox cart. They can dismantle a camp in a half hour and erect it back in one hour. Most families own goats, cows and horses. They believe that a man without a horse is like a bird without wings.

Music: Laments about the open steppe, long songs musical instrument horse fiddle represent the movement and sound of a horse. Blowing Ganlin horns to dispel bad spirits

Sports: Wrestling is the most popular. The reward is not money but nationwide popularity and fame.

Then, I flew to Irkutsk, Siberia to explore Lake Baikal, the biggest and deepest fresh water lake in the world, a UNESCO World heritage by itself.

Village of Olkhon in Siberia -- . **Oymyakon**, Siberia - itself is well-known for desolation and cold temperatures. The tiny town of **Oymyakon**, which is home to about 472 souls, is the coldest inhabited spot in the world.

Why do I Write?

Was it a dream when we trudged the mountain range, the caves?

Yacimientos (rich fossils, shoals) de Atapuerca?
Remains of the oldest Europeans have been found
800,000 to 1.2 million years ago, impossible to comprehend

"Burgos has the best roasted lamb"
Then we will discover that other part God has created

Now, were these objects to see?
No, no, it is the emotions building fire

Our dreams lay beyond the fields, the forests
We love suspense, something new
The magic moment

Are we wise and generous going to the mountains?
The mists and the paths we walked together
Changed our lives forever

You seem to know everything about Spain
Your eyes were shining
You looked wonderful

You have sprouted wings
In a heartbeat ready to roam the world
Some of your letters mailed from France, Belgium
Spoke of God

Then you entered the seminary
Dedicated a life to prayer

I wrote you back
I want freedom

At first, I stayed in a cave
Fearful of losing those magic moments

You wrote more letters
Painted vividly in words what you saw

Always saw me marching in the clouds
The sunset that made me happy

The conquest of the power of the stars
Do not let difficult times interfere

Do not lament
Believe in miracles

Go see the world
People will realize this
They will read your writings
Before life's magic moments pass by

So, I write in solitude

Yearning, longing to remember
What the flames have written
Feel the planet's heart beating

¿Por qué escribo?

¿Fue un sueño cuando caminamos penosamente
por la cordillera, las cuevas?

Yacimientos de Atapuerca?
Se han encontrado restos de los europeos más antiguo
800.000 a 1,2 millones de años atrás
Imposible de comprender
"Burgos tiene el mejor cordero asado"

Entonces descubriremos que la otra parte que Dios ha creado
¿Ahora eran estos objetos para ver?

No, no, son las emociones construyendo fuego
Nuestros sueños se encuentran más allá de los campos, los bosques

Nos encanta el suspenso algo nuevo
El momento magico

¿Somos sabios y generosos yendo a la montaña?
Las nieblas y los caminos que caminamos juntos

Cambió nuestras vidas para siempre
Pareces saber todo sobre España

Tus ojos estaban brillando
Te veías maravillosa
Te han brotado alas

En un latido del corazón listo para viajar por el mundo
Algunas de sus cartas enviadas desde Francia, Bélgica
Habló de Dios

Luego ingresaste al seminario
Dedicado una vida a la oración

Te escribí de Vuelta
Quiero libertad

Al principio me quedé en una cueva
Temeroso de perder esos momentos mágicos

Escribiste mas cartas
"Pinta vívidamente con palabras lo que ves"
Siempre me ves marchando en las nubes

El atardecer que hizo felices
La conquista del poder de las estrellas

No dejes que los tiempos difíciles interfieran
No te lamentes

Cree en los milagros
Ve a ver el mundo
La gente se dará cuenta de esto
Ellos leerán tus escritos

Antes de que pasen los momentos mágicos de la vida
Entonces, escribo en soledad

Anhelo, anhelo de recordar
Lo que han escrito las llamas

Siente los latidos del corazón del planeta

The Forest was Mine, Then the Northern Lights

My Swedish friends invited me to visit them. Bengt Enbuske lives in Overtornea, a locality in the Norbotten county and Gunar Bjork in Risudden, the Lapland forest. Taking us out into the forest, slathered in several layers of mosquito repellent with mosquito hats on our heads.

With sleepless nights due to anxiety, itching body parts as a result, we're hunting for the Arctic's very own gold? Oh! No, no we are here for the second time to hunt for the elusive *Aurora Borealis* Northern Lights.

It's because I also remember the forest glade illuminated by a ray of sun, the silence and the picnic basket with reindeer sausage sandwiches and hot cappuccino that we sit on top of a tree stump. And how proud I was of the riches in my red thickened down jacket. Once we got back home the scent was that of ancient forest sweetness.

In Sweden, there are people who say that you can hear the northern lights. Some say they whoosh like the wind. Others say they crackle like pine needles on a campfire.

After a week in the far north of the country, I still hadn't even seen the lights, let alone heard them. I kept hoping for a sign — any kind of whoosh or crackle would do — but apart from the gentle patter of falling snowflakes, everything was quiet.

Winter had come to Kiruna, the small, industrial city near the very top of Swedish Lapland, and a popular base for tourists hoping to see the northern lights. Arctic air had frozen everything, and the sun sent pale fingers of light across the icy streets for just a couple of hours each day.

Is it really true that anyone can walk around the forests and beaches of Swedish Lapland? Pick berries and pitch a tent anywhere? Yep, that's exactly what it's like in the democratic forest.

"Picking cloudberries with my parents might be my most boring childhood memory", quipped Gunar. Hunched down on marshland guarded by fir trees, not a gust of wind in sight and sweat pouring under my hat that offered, at best, protection against the mosquitoes. Wet socks sloshing around, was not a fun memory.

We went to the nearest store some forty five miles away, K-Market Ruoka-Attia. Bought the cans of fermented herring *surstromming*. Never has rotten fish smelled so bad but it tastes good. The fermentation process continues in the tine "souring" : *(surstromming!)*

On my third day. Wowwowiee !!! Luck was on our side!!!

The **NORTHERN LIGHTS** a quintessential bucket list item. Seeing the impressive display swirling overhead while we watched, is an incredible experience !!!

Fortunately we had the rare opportunity to see the display as early as 9:30 pm last night - lights began with a white wisp then changing to bright yellow and green! So thrilled!!!

We were in and out of the house for 3 -1/2 hours to midnight. then woke up at 4:00am but no more lights in the morning. Don't know might appear again tonight YES!!! A BIG thank you "Tack" to Bengt Enbuske and Gunnar Björk for inviting us to see this geomagnetic storm, due to a "positive polarity coronal hole high-speed stream. Still feeling Electrified !!!

The Irony of Intellectual Life

Having been around the world

Free Expression sometimes
I became intoxicated with reality
Downloaded Netflix films
Whose work has turned to muffled taste

Indulged in kitsch
Included R-ratings
Manufactured surprises and laughter
Mega wattage

More relevant to youngsters
Express overt admiration

One night stands
Ecstasy pills for stimulation of minds

Video streaming
Animated features

On the other hand one time philosophy
Worthy and Adult believable films
Subjects that are circumscribed
Makes us adore spy movies, romantic ones

Western lifestyles, glorified Hollywood

Centered on people guided by social and moral values
Flocks us
Coddles us

Your Poetry Saved Me

I am Filipina by descent
A round face with slit eyes

I use eyeliner to make my eyes look wider
You called me "Chinita"

I am mesmerized whenever
Two roads diverged in a yellow wood
And sorry I could not travel both
And be one traveler, there I stood and waited

I took the one less traveled by
And that has made all the difference

One evening I imagined he was playing cards
with his friends at Bar Las Vegas
Afterwards dinner with family

Looking afar from the balcony
You were staring at three airplanes flying high
Ohhh…, was he thinking of me coming to visit?

All of a sudden, you were sweating profusely, felt terrible

In an instant, the lights went out
You went home finally

Stories morph into their own memory and shape
At night, I lay in bed, thinking and thinking

When I look at your photo, I try to find myself in it

He wears spectacles beneath his olive eyes
His hair is salt and pepper, his shirt is pink
Holding a glass of wine, a boyish smile

Pasiones and Alegrias
A language where words were organized
To convey feeling and meaning

The voice is intimate and commanding
Through his descriptive powers
I remember my own experiences

I am transformed into solitary thought
I take the richness and layers of meaning hunkered in the words

I suffer my own private loss
Tragedy makes us self-conscious

When desperate for tenderness,
I read volumes of books
Poems were a source of comfort
An act of generosity and devotion

Through the act of imagination
I find myself
I am included in the verses, I belong
I travel along its roads

The power of poems has an everlasting life
An after existence in my memory
Replaced the void I felt

Tú Poesía Me Salvó

Soy Filipina por descendencia
Una cara redonda con ojos cortados

Utilizo el delineador para hacer que mis ojos parezcan más anchos
Usted me llamó "Chinita"

Estoy hipnotizado cada vez que leo poemas
Dos caminos divergieron en un bosque amarillo

Y lo siento, no pude viajar tanto
Y ser un viajero, durante mucho tiempo estuve de pie

Tomé el menos viajado

Una noche me imaginé
Que estaba jugando a las cartas con sus amigos en el Bar Las Vegas

Después cenó con su familia
Mirando lejos desde el balcón

Estaba mirando a tres aviones volando alto
Mama mia! ¿pensaba que iba a visitarme?

Entonces de repente sudaba profusamente, se sentía terrible

En un instante, las luces se apagaron
Mi querida se fue finalmente a casa

Las historias se transforman en su propia memoria y forma

Por la noche, me acuesto en la cama, pensando y pensando en él

Cuando miro su foto, trato de encontrarme en ella
Lleva gafas bajo los ojos de olivo
Su pelo es de sal y pimiento
Su camisa es de color rosa, está sosteniendo una copa de vino
Una sonrisa de niño

Paasiones y Alegrias
Un lenguaje donde las palabras
Fueron organizadas para transmitir sensación y significado
La voz es íntima y dominante
Ya través de los poderes descriptivos

Leo mis propias experiencias
Me transformo en pensamiento solitario

Tomo la riqueza y las capas de significado en las palabras
Yo sufro mi propia pérdida privada
La tragedia nos hace autoconscientes

Cuando uno lee el camino no tomado
Una carretera es usada y tendida

Prefiero tomar el camino que es demasiado grande
Sombreado y mágico

Cuando están desesperados por la ternura,
Leo volumenes libros

Eran una fuente de consuelo
Un acto de generosidad y devoción

A través del acto de la imaginación
Estoy incluido, pertenezco

Viajo por sus carreteras
El poder de tiene una vida eterna
También tiene una existencia posterior en mi memoria

Se reemplazó el vacío que sentía
Sé que puedes oírme ahora

Chapter 4

Solitude and Spectacle

Do You Remember?

I study whenever I can and use what I learn in your handwriting
Of what I read
To help make sense both of my feeling so lonely

As I have four of the last letters you wrote
I find it requires more concentration

Since the day you entered heaven
Were there gold secrets between the written lines?

In Ejea de los Caballeros
Papa is watching you

Come see the snow

Dreaming, I will come next year

Still we decided to stay in touch without touch
At times, it is unbearable and yet we felt it was the right thing to do

I can still see the wild white narcissus corona trumpets
Flowers on the curved hills of Albarracin and Panticosa
We marveled at its beauty
Snowy blossoms with their secret gold stamens inside

How I wish I could have been with you
When you asked me this spring to watch them bloom

When we are together
Our lives are simple as the open soft petals of a red rose

Now we are far apart trying to maintain our connection
Over this immense distance which effort changes us deeply
Maybe even deforms us

Our original character is not lost
There is a science to this

Through all this transformation, our lives are changing
Our bond to each other are changing

Yet we are essentially the same
In my dreams for a long, long time

Do you remember this?

How was I to know you will leave me forever

How was it a dream?

¿Te Acuerdas?

Estudio cada vez que puedo y uso lo que aprendo
Para ayudar a tener sentido tanto mi sentimiento tan solo

Desde el día que entraste al cielo
¿Había secretos de oro entre las líneas escritas?
Ven a ver la nieve.

Que vendré el año que viene
Aún así decidimos estar en contacto sin tocar
A veces, es insoportable
Y, sin embargo, sentimos que era lo correcto.

Todavía puedo ver las trompetas corona de narciso blanco salvaje
Flores en las colinas curvas de Albarracin y Panticosa
Nos maravillamos de su belleza de flores
Nevadas con sus estambres secretos de oro dentro
Cómo desearía haber estado contigo
Cuando me preguntaste esta primavera para verlos florecer

Nuestras vidas son simples
Como los pétalos suaves y abiertos de una rosa roja
Ahora estamos muy lejos tratando de mantener nuestra conexión

Sobre esta inmensa distancia
Cuyo esfuerzo nos cambia profundamente
Tal vez incluso nos deforma

Nuestro personaje original no está perdido
Hay una ciencia para esto

A través de toda esta transformación
Nuestras vidas están cambiando
Nuestro vínculo mutuo está cambiando

Sin embargo, somos esencialmente lo mismo
¿Te acuerdas de esto?
¿Cómo iba a saber que me dejarás para siempre?
Como fue un sueño?

Can You Hear Me?

There's a rhythm on the shores of Palma de Mallorca
Waves make a slap roar sound
As it rolls back and forth the clear blue waves

My soul sighs I feel your feathery touch on my cheeks
My own sanctuary
With the rising sun that bathes me with golden light
From the hidden patio along a narrow lane
Where I once stood

Studying the stones for insights your smiling face surprises
Hurried to change to swimming suits run to el Cuevas de Drach
Background music Chopin playing the piano
in the caves as our boat glided

Your bushy eyebrows arched over your round face
I felt your heart leap warmly in my throat

Awakened by Secret amiable memories
I rested my nape on the edge of the corner sofa in Xabec, Can Pastilla
Fell into a revelry

Without a change of facial expression, stiff necked
An experience that will resonate long
After my second trip is over without you in my Dreams

¿Puedes escucharme?

Hay un ritmo en las costas de Palma de Mallorca
Las olas hacen un sonido de bofetada

Mientras rueda hacia adelante y hacia atrás las claras olas azules
Mi alma suspira, siento tu toque de plumas a mis mejillas
Mi propio santuario
El sol naciente me baña con luz dorada

Desde el patio escondido a lo largo de un camino angosto
Donde estuvo una vez

Estudiando las piedras para descubrir las percepciones
Que sorprenden a tu rostro sonriente

Nos apresuramos a cambiarnos a trajes de baño
Dirigidos a las Cuevas de Drach

Musica de fondo Chopin tocando el piano en las cuevas
Mientras nuestro bote se deslizaba

Tus espesas cejas se arquearon sobre tu cara redonda
Sentí tu corazón saltar cálidamente en mi garganta

Despertado por recuerdos secretos y amables
Descansé mi nuca en el borde del sofa
De la esquina de Xabec, Can Pastilla
Caí en un sueño

Sin un cambio de expresión facial
Con el cuello rígido
Una experiencia que resonará mucho

Después de que termine

Mi segundo viaje en mi sueno

Rare Books

A present For Me?

Day began to dawn
I had a sleepless night yet full of happy visions

Bending over
I took a tea bag
Prepared for some polvoron (short bread cookies)
Looking at them very closely

On account of the mist in the clear cup
I saw you
At Zurita restaurant Calle Zurita
Publicaciones Vidal Hermanos, (libros raros y viejos) rare and old books

We walked separately
Calle Baltasar Gracian
Plaza San Francisco Kiosk

Specialty in churros with chocolate
Toasted bread with coconut spread and honey

Sipping the boiled tea
My tongue burned

Swirling from the smoke
Framed with eyeglasses
Your naughty face pinched my cheeks

Was it a Dream?

Libros Raros

Un regalito para mí?

El día comenzó a amanecer
Tuve una noche de insomnio
Pero llena de visiones felices

Agachado Tomé una bolsita de té
Preparado para un poco de polvoron
Mirándolos muy de cerca

A causa de la niebla en la copa transparente
Te vi en el restaurante Zurita
Calle Zurita Publicaciones Vidal Hermanos, libros raros y viejos

Caminamos por separado Calle Baltasar Gracian
Quiosco Plaza San Francisco
Especialidad en churros con chocolate
Pan tostada con coco y miel

Sorbiendo el té hervido
Me quemé la lengua

Arremolinándose del humo
Enmarcado con anteojos
Tu cara traviesa me pellizcó las mejillas

Fue un Sueno?

From Now On

How I wish you could be with me now
This morning I opened the little trunk where I kept letters
My fingers softly opened a faded envelope

Your messages cheered me
Especially your enclosed picture
Holding a gigantic balloon
A puffed pink heart with your wide grin

How happy you were then
It is an astonishing gift

I sigh like a lost child

I am entering a new chapter of my life
We shall say the journey
Between a mouse and a teddy bear
Is a thumbs up for listening to life's events

Entranced by your whispers
A profound execution of large truths
Delivered across the thousands of miles
Arrived with much expectations

I was not set to see Jupiter or Venus
Rather I was set to see the ring around your universe

The everyday stories of your life
Dearer to me from this moment on
In my Dreams

De Ahora en Adelante

Cómo desearía que pudieras estar ahora

Tus mensajes me alegraron
Especialmente tu foto adjunta
Sosteniendo un globo gigantesco
Un corazón rosa hinchado con tu amplia sonrisa

Qué feliz eras entonces
Es un regalo asombroso
Ha sido mi mayor consuelo

Lloro poco
Entonces suspiro como un niña perdido

Ahora que te has ido

Estoy entrando en un nuevo capítulo de mi vida

Diremos el viaje entre un ratón y un oso de peluche
Es un aprobado para escuchar los eventos de vidas

Encantado por tus palabras
Una profunda ejecución de grandes verdades

Entregado a través de los kilometros
Llegó con muchas expectativas

No estaba preparado para ver a Júpiter o Venus
Más bien estaba listo para ver el anillo alrededor de tu universo

Las historias cotidianas de vidas

Más querido desde este momento
En mis sueños

Every Night I Pray

God bless your way

Every Morning
i see you winking

At the foot of my bed you fly
Your wings rapidly flapping like a butterfly

Almost every day I imagine you are by my side
This thought enlarged my life

Dark and mysterious Spain I knew it
I can hardly understand where I am now

How shall I explain it to you?

Try to imagine
In a daze I walk and walk without a destination

A speck of light tucked in the dark sky
Where the stars are entangled into the moon
Are in a dangling position

I am at the edge of the land
The boulevard of broken dreams stretching clear

Across towards the endless horizon
When I learned you finally went home

I felt excruciating pain, no one can imagine
I cried until my chest hurt

I am headed towards the highest peaks
Grand mountain range of the Pyrenees
Pic Aneto, where the low clouds will soon be lifted

There I will find you
I will give your telephone as an emergency to call you

Instead, I saw a newspaper clipping
Flapping doom in the wind

You were always in my dreams
I adored you for a long, long time

Today, snow covers the mountain top
The same spot that looked at me

How nice was all
Tender caresses, of course

Always in dreams

Todas Las Noches Rezo

Dios bendiga tu camino
Cada mañana te veo guiñando un ojo
A los pies de mi cama vuelas tus alas
batiendo rápidamente como una mariposa

Casi todos los días

Que ensanchó mi vida
España oscura y misteriosa lo sabía
Apenas puedo entender dónde estoy ahora

¿Cómo te lo voy a explicar?
Intenta imaginar las lágrimas
Aturdido camino y camino sin destino

Una mota de luz escondida en el cielo oscuro
Donde las estrellas se enredan en la luna
Están en una posición colgante

Estoy al borde de la tierra
El bulevar de sueños rotos que se extiende claro
Al otro lado del horizonte interminable

Cuando supe que finalmente te fuiste a casa
Sentí un dolor insoportable, nadie puede imaginarlo
Lloré hasta que me dolió el pecho

Me dirijo hacia los picos más altos
Gran cordillera de los Pirineos Pic Aneto
Donde las nubes bajas pronto se levantarán

Ahi te encontrare

Vi un recorte de periódico
Aleteo en el viento

Siempre estabas en mis sueños
Por muchos, muchos años

Hoy, la nieve cubre la cima de la montaña
El mismo lugar que miró siempre

Que lindo fue todo Tierno
Toque y caricias, por supuesto

Siempre en mis sueños

Chapter 5

Full of Laughter and Stories

Interview with Marilyn Gurobat, working in Rarotonga, the Cook Islands:

This is Marilyn Gurobat, married to Marcial Gurobat.

We arrived here in tiny Cook Islands in April 2013. It was our first time for us to go abroad.

At first glance, the lands looked like a province in the Philippines. Roads were not paved, dirt roads, gravel and sand with pot holes prone to erosion and flooding.

There were hundreds of tall coconut trees, its fronds swaying "Welcome!" It was very tempting to chop, cut off a coconut and drink its juice, but we did not have a machete. Red and purple bougainvillea, pink and yellow plumeria flowers lined the fences.

It only takes one hour driving to go around the whole island with towering waterfalls. We saw small mom and pop stores, larger grocery markets, a beauty salon and two bakeries.

We had to flag down public buses for transportation.

Our everyday routine as OFWs (Overseas Foreign Worker) is going to work, then to home, again going to work to home the next day. We go to the market weekly. We have been here more than six years.

My employer and the whole family are down to earth and extremely nice. The company is stable. The number of workers turnover is fast because of short term contracts.

I work as a Housekeeper and front desk receptionist at the MOANA SAND BEACH FRONT HOTEL AND VILLAS, Averua District. I love my work. I take the interested tenants on a tour to the vacant room and show the many amenities of the villa.

I enjoy customer relationship adding a little comedy to my showmanship.

My salary is A-ok. We get free housing, Medical care benefits and free transportation to and from work. We are paid every week. We get paid vacation leave, plus free round trip air tickets to the Philippines every two years.

There are many Filipinos here. We have a Filipino community with get together parties almost every weekend. There are Mass services every first Sunday of the month at a Christian church. We attend the 6:00 PM mass at CLSF (Christ the Livingstone Fellowship), where approximately ninety percent Filipinos attend ☺.

For night time entertainment, we have happy hour and disco dancing bars.

I send money every week to my kids and some family members in the Philippines. The truth is, we have been working here for six years, but we don't have much savings.

Such is life, our generosity comes from within to help others in need.

There are times I have the scenario in mind, we will go home to the Philippines for good. But it is postponed for the time being.

I am very thankful for my life here. I learned how to drive a motorcycle. I got my driver's license and got a car.

Our family is getting bigger. I filed petition papers for my sister who arrived two years ago. Then my brother arrived last year. Thank you Lord, for your abundant blessings.

Another blessing.

I am very lucky and thankful for: I met Ms. Odette Ricasa, the world traveler!

Ps. Thank you, Marilyn. It was February fifth (5), my exact birth date, when I visited your beautiful home.

You prepared a delicious island cuisine of golden brown fried chicken dipped in Islanders sauce. Fried noodles with shrimp and meat mixed with chopped fresh vegetables, vegetarian egg rolls and garlic rice. We said grace before meals.

Afterwards, I made a wish and blew the candles of my birthday cake. I was the lucky one to have met you and your husband, Marcial. You are a lovely couple.

Interview with Marilyn Gurobat, working in Rarotonga, the Cook Islands: in Tagalog Language:

Ako nga si Marilyn Mendoza Gurobat. kasal kay Marcial.

Ito ang unang pagaabroad namin magasawa dito sa maliit na isla ng COOK ISLAND, dumating kami dito APRIL 5, 2013 @6am island time.

Noong una akala ko nasa probinsya lang kami ng Pilipinas kasi ang paligid puro puno at ang kalsada baku baku. One hour lang kung mag around the island, ganoon lang kaliit, pero marami rin tindahan mayroon din Pilipino store, mayroon din Pilipino salon, Bakery.

Mayroon din falls Dito ang tubig ay walang bayad. Mayroon buses din.

Nakakatuwa dito kasi yong cycle ng life namin as OFW bahay-trabaho, market bibili ng mga kailangan for the whole week.. Iyon karaniwan routine pag day off. Six years na kami dito.

Mababait naman ang mga AMO friendly ang buong family stable ang company. Iyon nga lang palit palit ng mga trabahador Anyway ganoon naman talaga kapag contract worker ka.

Siya nga pala housekeeper ang work ko here @MOANA SAND BEACHFRONT HOTEL AND VILLAS. Averua District.

Mahal ko ang work ko natutuwa ako sa mga costumer at nag eenjoy ako lalo na kapag speaking of entertaining matuto ka talaga.

Anyway speaking of SAHOD maayos naman every week ang sahuran dito, libre din kami ng bahay, medical kapag ngkasakit ka at transportation going work and back home, libre din pamasahe pauwi ng Pinas after the contract.

Marami na rin FLIPINO'S dito meron din Pilipino community na minsan may mga gathering, may Pilipino MASS every 1ˢᵗ Sunday of the month mga christian churches.

Lahat na yata meron dito pati disco place mayroon - yon nga lang may oras ng bukas at sarado.

Mayroon kaming service na inaatendan every saturday @6pm CLSF Christ the Livingstone fellowship puro Pilipino.

Oo nga pala every week ako ngpapadala ng pera sa Pinas para sa mga anak At pamilya ko. Ganito na yata talaga kapag OFW ka sending dito sending doon.

Sa totoo lang six 6) years na kami dito, wala pa rin kami ipon.

Minsan naiisip ko nalang kailaan kaya ako uuwi ng Pinas FOR GOOD, but I am very thankful kasi dito kami napunta. Dito ako natuto magdrive ng motor at sa ngayon marunong na din ako magdrive ng kotse.

Oo nga pala pati driver's license dito rin at natulungan ko na rin ang aking sister na makarating dito last 2 years ago.

Sa ngayon kakarating naman ng aking brother last September 2019 kaya taos puso ang aking PASASALAMAT SA PANGINOON mahirap man sa una marami naman magandang ngyari sa pagpunta namin dito.

At dito ko rin nakilala ang traveller of the world na si mommy Odette. Thank you po!

Interview with Dr. Wesley Balneg, Dentist at Hargeisa, Somaliland

Somaliland lies in northwestern Somalia, in Africa on the southern coast of the Gulf of Aden. It is bordered by the remainder of Somalia (per international recognition) to the east, Djibouti to the northwest, and Ethiopia to the south and west.

Five Filipinos working at Abokor Artan Dental Center and Pharmacy. Hospital Road,

Woqooyi Galbeed, Hargeisa, Somaliland.

With Carlos Barrientos, Dr. Elmer Sicat, Dr. Jonathan Evora and Noel Gregorio

Our families have not visited Hargeisa ever since we arrived here. Life here is convenient. Everything we need is within walking distance. We stay at the fifth (5th) floor of the Artan Hotel atop of our dental office.

We go on vacation yearly, I myself would stay in the Philippines for two months and the rest of my team stays 40 days.

We are well treated here by our employer financially with good working conditions. All basic needs for a decent living including internet are free, except food, courtesy of our employer. These are the factors why we stay here for so long and keep coming back despite of the country is an unknown place Imagine sixteen (16) years and counting. Yaayh!!!

For me, I am planning to go for good next year and spend time with my family but the rest will keep going.

Our boss is an African American. The whole family are US citizens. He studied in the Philippines and graduated in dentistry at the University of Baguio. We met in Manila in the year 2004. He invited me go to Hargeisa because there were no available dentists then. So I came as a tourist and eventually engaged in dental works.

Now a days there are a lot of dental clinics around Hargeisa, two of these dental offices has one Filipino staff each, a dentist and a dental tech.

Once a month we get together with the rest of the Filipinos. All in all, we are eleven Filipinos here. We celebrate special occasions and holidays together with a bottle of whisky we brought from vacation. Of course the celebration will not be complete without karaoke singing. Hahahaha. It's a Filipino "Pinoy" trade mark anyway.

Thank you for interviewing me, M'am Odette. You are very blessed to travel around the world and interview our country men.

August 7, 2019 – I took a tour of the Las Geel Cave paintings.

Interview with Celia / Caesar Nunez - Papua, New Guinea

-

A BIG thank you to Caesar and Celia who hosted me for three (3) nights while the situation in Papua was considerably dangerous. Fortunately she has a live-in help in the household.

Name: Caesar & Celia Nunez

1) Married or single? Married with two sons.

2) How did u learn / arrive Papua. Eg thru a friend's recommendation ?

Through a friend and was hired direct by the employer.

3) Your present position:

Now retired but previously worked as a General Manager/Chemist with Bell Chemicals (formerly Belltek Chemicals Ltd.)

4) You are treated financially well? With benefits ? Days off? Good working conditions?

Working status as an expatriate with ALL BENEFITS and perks of being one.

5) How often do you go home to the Philippines?

At least once a year, 4 weeks for all family.

6) How long have you been in Papua?

Thirty six (36) years

7) Do you meet with co-Filipinos during birthday parties, baptism, good news.—

Port Moresby is a small place. Most of the Filipinos are close to each other. The Filipino Association of PNG (FAPNG) is such a wonderful organization, bringing most of the Filipinos together for important events such as Philippines Independence Day celebration, Christmas and other social gatherings. The FAPNG also brings in *"Hatid Saya"* (Delivering Happiness) from the Philippines.

8) Are you a member of Parish church - name of church? Serve in fund raising? Community service?

We are members of Couples of Christ Global Inc- a family oriented Catholic movement intended for the renewal and strengthening of Christian family life.

· 9) Do you send financial assistance to family/relatives to the Philippines? Do you support family brothers or sisters going to school?

Yes, we do support some members of the family who are in dire need of assistance e.g. School fees, medical and others.

·

10) Any comments you want to include: --

Overall we are so grateful to God that He has given us the opportunity to work in Papua New Guinea as an expatriate. We were so blessed that we were able to share the blessings to so many others. Praise God!!!

Interview with Joyce Paras
in Beirut, Lebanon

Name: Joyce Paras

Married with four children and one grandchild from the Philippines, forty one (41) years old.

Works as a DH Domestic Helper in Lebanon, more than ten years.

I was recruited in my hometown as a DH Domestic Helper in Lebanon. It's not easy to work in Lebanon because it was banned then and until now. I prayed hard. My papers had to be processed thru the Philippine Embassy in Beirut. As of now, my papers are legal.

My daily duties are cleaning the house, help in cooking and taking care of the children, now a nanny.

I do not go out often because our house is a little far from the city. My employer is super nice!

No problem with the salary and always pays on time. Free food ☺. I go on vacation every two years or so. My employer pays for my round/trip air fare and five weeks pay while on vacation.

During summer, we go to my employer's summer chalet I meet some Filipinos and go bonding with them on weekends, lunch dinner get together with dancing and singing karaoke. During my younger days, I was a member of our Parish Youth Coordinating Council. I am no longer active.

I send most of my monthly salary to the Philippines to support my four children and one grandchild. We are building a house. It should be finished soon. There are times I help my brother and sisters too.

I am not embarrassed to say I am a Domestic Helper / Nanny. I am proud because I can support my family and help others. I earn my own living. I am independent. I have abundant blessings. God blesses me all the time.

Thank you very much Madam Odette. I am so glad to have met you.

Interview with Joyce Paras
in Beirut, Lebanon
Tagalog language

Hello, I tried my best to answer. I am a (DH) domestic helper.

Name: Joyce Paras

1) I'm married

2) Sa lugar namin may nag re-recruit to work in Lebanon bilang isang domestic helper. It's not easy to come in Lebanon to work because it's banned and until now...dasal at tibay ng loob ang kailangan and thanks God dumating ako dito ng maayos. Sa ngayon legal na ako nag tatrabaho dito kasi iyong first na nagbakasyon ako dumaan muna sa Philippine Embassy Beirut at nagprocess ng mga papers upang maging legal na ang pag work ko dito.

3) My daily routine to clean the house, to help madam preparing our foods and to take care the kids (I'm a nanny)

4) I'm so thankful that my employer treated me so good...walang problema sa sahod on time at walang problema sa pagkain din hehehe

Hindi ako nag day off kasi magastos din pag lumalabas ahahaha malayo-layo din kasi ang bahay namin pero ok lang naman sa akin because weekly lumalabas at gumagala naman kami mag sisimba, pupunta sa mall at kumakain sa labas.

5) Every two (2) years, umuuwi ako sa Pinas mgbakasyon ng five (5) weeks at with Pay yong bakasyon ko...pag uuwi mag sama-sama lahat ng pamilya at mga kaibigan at syempre kainan, inuman, sayawan at kantahan hehehehe.

6) Thank God I'm more than ten (10) years here in Lebanon and hoping more years to stay in the same employer kasi mababait naman sila.

7) At summer time we stay in my employer chalet (north lebanon) I meet a lot of co-filipino nannies there.

8) When I was a teenager I'm a member of Parish Youth Coordinating Council but now hindi na.

9) I send my monthly salary to my family kasi apat iyong anak ko at hindi pa tapus yong pinagawa kong bahay namin. My brother and sister sometimes they ask help magbibigay naman ako.

10) Ooppss honestly hindi ako naka pagtapus sa pag aaral Im only 3ʳᵈ year high school.

11) Sa mga tulad ko domestic helper kailangan matibay, lakas ng loob at mag dasal lang lagi. Hindi ikakahiya na katulong sa ibang bansa dahil ito ay marangal at malinis na trabaho.

Thanks Madam Odette I really glad to meet you..

Take Care and God Bless!

Fri, Aug 30, 2019 1:14 pm

Interview with Noe M. Gallardo from Jeddah, Kingdom of Saudi Arabia

Name: Noe M. Gallardo

Status: Married with three children. All my children has finished their education, two nurses and one Information Technology Specialist.

POSITION : Cashier/ line leader at Boracay Restaurant located at Al Ballad, old Historical Jeddah. Duties: manage cash and sales transactions. Promoting services, taking orders of food to take away, improving customer satisfaction, answering inquiries, greeting customers and reporting to the restaurant owner.

The owner of Boracay Restaurant is a Yemeni married to a Filipina.

I did not get to meet her. She was arranging a banquet event. The restaurant occupies five suites. The main suite has two floors. We enjoyed a variety of authentic Filipino dishes in a warm casual ambiance that spells comfort from home. Many Saudis adapted to Filipino cuisine. They line up for the delicious buffet (all you can eat), lunch, served seven days a week.

Al Balad (The Town) recently is the historical area of Jeddah, founded in the seventh century. Many tourists pose for a picture at the entrance with color, a place where the buildings come with stories. There are crumbling developments, dusty streets, and swarming of cats.

Day off: only once a month.

Salary is OK.

Vacation: every two years.

I am here in Jeddah, Saudi Arabia since August 1992.

Yes, I send remittance to my family for a little support because all of my children already finished their education.

Interview with Eleanore Andres, Larnaca, Cyprus

Name: Eleanore Andres

Status: Single

I applied with a Travel Agency to be an Overseas Filipino Worker (OFW).

POSITION : Domestic Helper – work within the house. care for a family. Includes housekeeping, cleaning, household maintenance, cooking, laundry, shopping for food, other errands as needed.

Day off: once a week every Sunday.

Walk at the water front of Mckenzie beach, meet fellow Filipina workers at McDonalds, Burger King or other restaurants. Relax at the area of Finikoudes where bright orange trees line the streets, tourists and locals relax on their beach chairs. There are many street sellers of post cards, balloons, cotton candy, cold drinks, ice cream and snacks. I go to Metro Supermarket or the Alpha Omega for groceries for my employer. Also shop for clothes, other necessities.

Salary: 400. Four Hundred Euros per month.

Vacation: I went home to the Philippines, two times in 2016 and 2019.

Sunday masses at Terra Santa, near the Greek Orthodox church of St. Lazarus.

At St Catherine Catholic church - Every third Sunday, the Filipino Association Larnaca, Cyprus (FALC) our association, are the usherettes during the mass. We have volunteers to teach Catholicism.

After the mass, we gather the birthday and anniversary celebrants, pose for photographs. Around noon time, we take our lunch at a covered hall outside at the terrace. We exchange news about home, work, friends, jokes or just about anything and laugh. We also have a cheerful group of ladies from Sri Lanka.

I am currently based in Larnaca, Cyprus. I also worked in Nicosia, northern part of Cyprus, approximately 3 hours by bus. I have been working here for ten years. If we ever have problems, we go to the Consulate of the Republic of the Philippines in Nicosia.

Occasionally, I send money remittance for my family in the Philippines, to my mother and sisters. I enrolled in the Social Security System (SSS) of the Philippines. And the IMG Kaiser Health Group. For a small investment, I bought an empty lot in Tanay, Rizal, Philippines. Am saving money. Eventually my dream and hope is to be able build a house. When I retire, I have a pension to collect.

Over all, I have grown accustomed to the way of life of the Greek Cypriots here. They are friendly, welcoming and hospitable. I plan to work for a few more years, then retire in the Philippines.

Interview with Jamil Malang Pangcoga

(Jaypee Umpar Malang) – Jeddah, Saudi Arabia

I was looking for post cards. Nel, the receptionist at our hotel, the Rove Jeddah recommended the Afnan Bookstore, the Nobel bookstore and the Fursan bookstore. I took an Uber taxi to all these stores – so disappointed. No post cards at all for sale. Finally, a lady pointed us to Jarir Bookstore.

With a photo of a post card on my i-phone, I asked the Customer Service counter if they have post cards. He pointed upstairs. I climbed the stairs to the second floor - waited for someone to help. Saw a guy pushing carts with loads of books. It was Jaypee, who came to the rescue. Mentioned we are tourists from USA, with roots from the Philippines. He got so excited and showed us many post cards. He described his passion for archaeological sites. "I want to go to Mecca". He said we must be of Muslims religion. We became friends. We have kept in touch in our virtual world.

Interview:

I am Single since birth.

I applied for an agency manpower in our country through friends' recommendations and influence.

I am currently working in the biggest bookstore in Saudi Arabia the (Jarir bookstores) as a salesman in the English books department.

Jarir Bookstores, in its early years, dealt in used books and art sold by expats living in Riyadh, Saudi Arabia. Since then, it has grown to be the largest retailer of books and consumer electronics in Saudi Arabia. Their showrooms are world class. The staff are cooperative, friendly and very helpful like Jaypee.

Salary: 2,500-3,300 Saudi Riyals, depending on overtime pay. Approximate currency Conversion: US $900.00 NET per month – NO taxes withheld.

I send money regularly to the Philippine for financial support to my family and some other relatives.

Employee benefits include health insurance, commissions if we reach the target sales, yearly bonuses and yearly vacation. We have two days off per week. If we choose not to take the day off, we can select to work with overtime pay.

We have yearly vacation and yearly bonuses. This is the reason why most of the Filipinos and other nationalities in our company have stayed with us for a long time.

During days off, I go the Mall of Arabia or Red Sea Mall and meet friends, or go on a leisurely stroll with relatives. Time is precious. I make sure to exchange news and laugh with them. The specialty of Middle Eastern Nations are fragrances and perfumes. There are many perfume stores free samples and testers. We have fun spraying ourselves with fragrances of a rose, or a lavender or a plumeria, or a jasmine before we actually decide which perfume to buy or plain window shop.

I have been working in Saudi Arabia for nine years since year 2011 to present.

I am a Muslim. Mecca (Makkah) is a dream place to visit during the Hajj season and Umrah.

Umrah is a shorter version of the Hajj. A Muslim can perform the pilgrimage anytime of the year except during the five days of the Hajj.

Muslims all over the world share the same belief. It is one of our obligations to go on a pilgrimage. Selflessness is one of the noble qualities emphasized in Islam. The teaching is that there is only one God. Muhammed is a Messenger of God.

I have been to Mecca. It is the holiest site in Islam during the annual performance of the Hajj. - This is the time where pilgrims seek to wipe clean past sins and start anew before God. Time to deepen our faith. It is a Muslim pledge to make a trip to Mecca once in their lifetime, if financially capable.

I love Saudi people especially their culture and their government for being so kind to us expats. We are being paid enough for our salary - Without taxes.

I feel very lucky to be assigned here in Jeddah because I am close to my uncle, aunties and cousins. Location wise Jeddah is close to the two holiest cities in our Islam religion: Medina, 415 kilometers, four hour drive. and Mecca, 86 kilometers, one hour drive.

We have the tallest fountain in the world, King Fahd's Fountain. The fountain shoots water up to 312 meters high. It is beautiful when illuminated at night.

We have the best restaurant in Saudi Arabia – the Albaik – a major fast food chain that primarily sells roasted chicken and shrimp with a variety of sauces., chicken nuggets and fish. They also serve iconic Big sandwiches named Saj DeLite with its spicy counterpart, Lahaleebo Tawook and Shawarma sandwiches.

Interview with Joy Gundran-Snieders in Douala, Cameroon

My family moved to Cameroon in 2009 after our posting in Kinshasa, DR Congo, when my husband took on a new job as head of a microfinance institution in Douala. We lived on the fourth floor of the Apartment Marly building which was overlooking the port of Douala and had great views of the Mt. Cameroon at a distance.

We stayed four years in Douala, forming great friendships that continue till now and amassing wonderful memories with my husband Frank, my daughter Jolie and the friends we made and kept all these years.

Jolie was barely a year old when we moved to Douala so during this time I was a full-time stay at home mom and wife. Other than these motherly and wifely roles, I actively participated in the activities of the Douala Women's International Group (or DWIG), wrote the blog: mydouala, learned how to paint, bake and cook, explored Cameroon, its culture and offerings, and a whole lot more.

Through the DWIG and its coffee mornings, I met a lot of expat wives like me and was introduced to a Filipina who was married to the manager of the Le Meridien Hotel at that time. She introduced me to other Filipinas (Rovi and Reggie) who were already living in Douala for some time. With them, blossomed friendships that spanned years and continents, maintained through Facebook, Messenger and a few visits to their new homes after Douala.

Not far from Douala is Edea where the Rogationist Seminary was located.

Two Filipino priests – Fr. Willy and Fr. Philip built up this seminary and until now, it is still run by Filipino priests.

Some Sundays, my Filipino friends and I would organize a trip to Edea so that we could hear mass in English. Other times, Fr. Willy or Fr. Philip would celebrate mass in our homes on a rotation basis. Edea is also on the way to Kribi, the beach resort area near Douala. So an outing to Kribi would always mean a stopover in Edea to say hello to the priests or drop off some goodies for them.

In June 2012, a friend who I first met in Kosovo then later on reunited with again in Kinshasa, Democratic Republic of Congo (DRC), Mafe Leal, sent me a message that a traveller friend of hers was coming to Douala and would I be available to meet her.

Not only did I meet Tita Odette but offered her to stay at our place which was just a minute away from the hotel she was staying in. At that time I was seriously doing oil painting and was attending lessons with Etienne Maurice, a gifted artist who patiently showed me what oil painting and drawing was all about.

Learning that Tita Odette was also an art afficionado and did painting herself in most countries she visits, I introduced her to Etienne and with him, she created a beautiful painting similar to what I had painted with another painting teacher friend.

I showed Tita Odette the Douala that I know and introduced her to other ladies of DWIG and to Tita Reggie who invited her and a few others to lunch at her house. We also managed to fit in some games of mahjong at our place!

My husband who is hardly impressed by anything had only admiration for Tita Odette. In his words: for such a diminutive lady, it is amazing that she has conquered the world and at her age, is still going strongly at it!

We were very happy to have hosted her in our place and would love to host her again.

Unfortunately, she has already been to Myanmar, where we are based now. Perhaps another trip to the golden land could still be added to her list. We can do the Mogok trip together and explore the source of the world's best rubies, Tita Odette!

Joy Gundran-Snieders, Douala, Cameroon, 2009 - 2013

Chapter 6

Our Minted World

Interview with Grace Garcia in Sudan

Special mention to Mafe Leal-Lalonde who introduced me to her friends in the United Nations around the world, especially in Africa.

Mafe introduced me to many locals, Filipinos living abroad. To name a few countries: Sweden, Switzerland, Portugal, Haiti, Sierra Leone, Monrovia, Timor Leste, Papua, New Guinea, Accra, Togo, Cameroon. Burkina Faso, Ivory Coast, Swaziland, Mozambique and more.

I met Grace Garcia thru my good friend, Mafe Leal-Lalonde via Messenger. After introduction, we communicated the details of the weather, clothes to wear, wi-fi connections, sites to see, safety of walking on the streets and transportation. My plan was to arrive in Khartoum on September 2019. Tours included the Meroe pyramids, the Nubian culture, and more sites were arranged by Midhat Mahir Travel Agency in Khartoum. My visa was in the process. Early riots and protests were happening and spread rapidly. The agency advised us to postpone travel plans.

January 2020 – After exploring Saudi Arabia, I flew to the Philippines I had the chance to meet Grace in person. We met during the a fiesta FEAST celebration in the city of Angelese, STO. TOMAS, CITY OF SANFERNANDO, province of Pampanga, a city rich in history and heritage.

THE FEAST IS IN HONOR OF THE HOLY CHILD (STO. NINO) AND IS BEING CELEBRATED IN THE ENTIRE COUNTRY. The streets were packed with devotees holding a procession, celebrated with marching bands in colorful uniforms, swinging majorettes, music and dancing.

THIS IS A CULTURAL TRADITION THAT HAS BEEN CELEBRATED AS A FAMILY TOGETHERNESS AND SUMPRUOUS FOOD.

Grace AND FAMILY prepared a banquet table of Filipino cuisine, chicken adobo, fried noodles, ox tail with peanut sauce, skewers of barbeque pork, and an array of desserts, rice cake, cassava cake, leche flan, custard and meringue pie. She baked her specialty of chocolate chip cookies with less sugar. She was in the process of promoting her special cookies.

I met her husband, ERNIE GARCIA and her children, her brother-in-laws and other family members. We had a fabulous time, including karaoke singing, a tradition of Filipino parties. Filipinos love to send a care package of food after the party. Our take away / care package was a box full of her special chocolate chip cookies . Thank you, Grace.

March 17, 2020 - My second time to go to Sudan, Visa was issued. Then Covid-19 pandemic arrived. The Travel Agency advised to postpone the trip again, hopefully the pandemic ends soon.

Grace: Married with two children.

My husband is an Overseas worker (OFW) with a family status contract. He has been working with an International Organization, assigned in different countries where there is a need of emergency / humanitarian assistance.

Sudan was our last home-based country where we have lived for the past nine (9) years, before we decided to resign and retire in the Philippines on October 2019.

I have been a full-time housewife since I resigned from my work in Mozambique, Africa. We moved to Sri Lanka for our new post, then Sudan. As a full-time housewife, my priority was taking care of my family. I started learning to cook home-food, baking, and developed my passion for photography of sunsets, markets, churches and top sites.

Aside from the monthly salary of my husband, we were also enjoying other benefits of housing (electricity, water, cleaner services included), vehicle, children's education, Rest & Recreation every 3 months, and a home-leave entitlement.

Sudan is categorized as a hardship post. Therefore, we have the benefits to go to any place we want to, every 3 months for one (1) week, and a yearly home-leave for three (3) weeks to one-month.

We lived in Sudan for 9 years (2010-2019). Our children studied at the British Educational School (BES) in Khartoum. Our daughter (the eldest), attended her last senior year at the BES before she went to the United States of America for university. Our son (the youngest), attended BES from year 2005 to year 2019.

Filipinos meet on the weekends, after a week of work from Sundays thru Thursdays. There will be birthday parties, baptisms, weddings, and other personal celebrations which take place on weekends (Fridays thru Saturdays).

I was an officer (Treasurer) for the Association of the Filipinos in Sudan (AFS) (year 2015-2016). We held fund raisings like Bingo social, Bowling, Basketball leagues, Valentine's party with tickets as entrance and raffle draws.

I was also a Treasurer for the Filipino Catholic Community for the Saints Peter and Paul Church year (2015 – 2017) The church's fund raisings are: food bazaar, fun-run and caroling. We donate the funds to outreach charity and to different local Catholic parishes and its communities.

I sometime send financial assistance to some family/relatives in the Philippines when needed and necessary.

We help finance the schooling of nephews and nieces, for example: tuitions, students uniforms and other school-related expenses.

Add to interview:

In the early months of 2019, Sudan's economy collapsed. Shortages of fuel, the increase of prices in commodities and the local bread, sparked demonstrations in the East. Discontent over living standards, rage and anger spread rapidly to the capital, Khartoum.

Things were not getting any better in Sudan in the mid-part of 2019. Sudan's economy collapsed. Gasoline stations had long waiting lines of vehicles. The people religiously waiting for the supply lasting to a couple of days.

The professionals started the protests to the government which led to demonstrations, fire and riots all over the place. Some places were closed as they were burning tires, and gun shootings. Schools were also closed as students from the government schools were required to participate in the riots and demonstrations. Social media like internet connections were cut-off to avoid spreading the news outside the country.

The civilians were able to oust the President who was in position for more than thirty (30) years. For this reason, my husband and I decided to finish his employment contract in September 2019. My husband resigned but was requested to continue working until October 2019.

- END

Interview with Xandrea Fernandez, Dubai

Looking back in 2008, I had my humble beginnings here in Dubai, United Arab Emirates (UAE). I came across Dubai by the influence of my siblings who had been working here earlier than me.

I have been enjoying a great work and life balance for a decade since I started working, on top of that, I earn a decent salary. There is no income tax here so I enjoy my paycheck in its fullness.

Dubai is a modern melting pot of culture, and this allows me to work with people from all over the world. Despite this, I always have peace of mind as the government of Dubai has a strong political will in protecting its people's welfare. For several years running, Dubai is in the limelight when it comes to safety.

Among the seven emirates, Dubai is in the forefront of technological advancements and is the epitome of infrastructure projects, well-ahead even when pitted against its oriental and western counterpart cities.

Like a concrete jungle of skyscrapers, it is a work of art and technology where both leisure and fitness thrive together. You can always find a workout facility for all people to use.

Time and again, Dubai to me is an absolute beauty.

Living here is nothing less than a breathtaking experience.

Visiting Honorable Mr. Marcos A S Punsalang, Santiago, Chile

Santiago - feels almost European at times - loving it here near Plaza Italia and El Cerro Santa Lucía -- winding cobblestones and charming coffee houses.. Relaxing half a day touring museums in Santiago. I love bright colors.

Until a few years ago, I never spent any time during annual visits to Santiago, Chile, in the neighborhood of Lastarria, a well-heeled belle epoque-style residential district at the edge of downtown. I would gravitate instead to three central neighborhoods; a meal in Vitacura, a cocktail in Bellavista, and a stay in Providencia.

Lastarria, a triangular barrio partly closed to traffic by Santa Lucía Hill to the west and Parque Forestal to the north, was off my radar. Lately, though, with a half-dozen hotels having opened in Lastarria in the last two years alone, not to mention dozens of new shops and restaurants, it's where everyone wants to be.

Lastarria's regal architecture are a stark contrast to the glass-towered commercial districts to the east, where the majority of Santiago hotels are concentrated. It feels almost European at times, with charming coffeehouses like Colmado Coffee & Bakery, which added a full-service restaurant.

Nov. 2017 Embassy of the Philippines, Felix de Amesti Street Santiago Chile, located in the Las Condes Region, Metropolitana, Chile.(subway stop Metro Escuela).

Upon arrival, the steel gate was locked. A security guard met me and asked if I had an appointment. Then the wooden doors opened wide.

I was met by Ms. Pearl Camento with a wide smile. I was led to a room where the flags of Chile and the Philippine flags were displayed.

She introduced me as a writer who has written five books to Honorable Consul Mr. Marcos A S Punsalang, Ferlina, Jeffrey and Jenny.

The embassy includes consular services:

1) voter registration mobile field registration to vote during Philippine election time.

2) Women's health lectures – display announcements on bulletin boards.

3) Celebration of Philippine Independence Day, parade in traditional Filipino costumes, food banquet, singing and dances such as Fandango sa Ilaw, Tinikling.

4) Participate in Chilean activities

5) School children lectures

Thank you very much - *maraming salamat* (Thank you) for granting a most informative conversation / interview. I enjoyed every moment of it including comical jokes. I fly tonight back to Los Angeles *con buenas recuerdos y memorias* De Santiago. Come and visit me in Los Angeles www.sanclemente com. Mabuhay !

Nov 16, 2017 website: www.santiagope.dfa.gov santiago.pe@dfa.gov. ph embassy@vtr.net

Hi Madame, we also enjoyed your visit to the Embassy. Good that you wrote, because I could not find you on Facebook. God bless and more countries to visit Cuidate !!!

Interview with Pearl Santiago Stationed in Chile

Lastarria's coffee houses like Panaderia y Café Gabilondo, is where I had breakfast before going to the Philippine Embassy in Santiago, Chile.

The Philippine Embassy is located in the municipality of Las Condes in the Santiago City, Metropolitan Region, Chile. It is known for its chic hotels and lively dining scene, ranging from high-end Chilean and Japanese restaurants. After dark, office workers and locals gather in cocktail bars and traditional pubs.

Interview with Ms. Pearl Santiago, while stationed in Chile.

1) Single/Married: Single

2) How did you learn / arrive <u>Chile</u>. Eg thru a friend's recommendation ?

Arrived in Chile through work assignment.

3) Your present position: Embassy of the Philippines in Santiago, Chile. - giving assistance to Filipinos. For example: Process passport applications and visa applications, voter registration and issuing emergency travel documents.

4) We have very good working conditions and benefits.

5) How often do you go home to the Philippines?

Twice during my assignment

6) How long have you been in <u>Chile?</u>

<u>I have been living in Chile for seven years from Year</u> 2013 – 2020.

7) Do you meet with co-Filipinos during birthday parties, baptism, good news.

Not always, because busy at work.

8) I attend church services. Usually at the Parroquia de Santo Toribio in Del Inca, 10 – 15 minute walk from my home.

Other services are Parroquia de Nuestra Senora de los Angeles in El Golf.

Sometimes, during special occasions I go to the Santiago Metropolitan Cathedral located in Santiago Central and if I want an English mass I go to St. George church, attached to St. George College.

With the arrival of a Filipino priest in 2018, I attend church services at Nuestra Senora del Carmen Verbum Dei in Providencia.

9) Do you send financial assistance to family/relatives to the Philippines? Example: You support family brother or sister going to school.

Yes, i support my mother in the Philippines

.10) Do you enjoy living in <u>Santiago, Chile?</u>

<u>Yes.</u>

11) any outstanding / funny experiences?

Yes, at the location of: The Valle Nevado ski resort has some of the highest quality snow in Chile. Because of its location at three (3) thousand meters of height, it counts with modern infrastructure and the best equipment to give excellent service to its visitors that want to enjoy the summits of the Chilean Mountains.

This ski resort was created with the inspiration of French ski resorts and modern buildings, hotels and equipment, such as Andes Express ski lift. It is the most advanced in the southern hemisphere.

Living in Chile gave me a chance to experience snow for the first time in my life.

We traveled from Las condes to Valle Nevado, one and a half hour drive from Santiago, Chile. It is a road with many curves, it was recommended to drive with caution. Winters in Valle Nevado are rainier, when snow comes, it is advisable to use snow chains.

My colleagues and I (newly arrived) were full of anticipation and eagerness. Dressed in our winter clothes, we were feeling playful and acted like children. We were so excited that we took photos jumping/ posing/laying / sitting on the snow.

The irony of it is that, during that time, winter took so long in arriving. When the snow finally fell, it did not really cover the spot where we chose to stop. We wandered around for a little while. Finally, at the spur of the moment, we decided this spot was good enough. We played with the clumps of snow, rolled snowballs, gave high fives, slapped each other on the shoulders, gyrated our hips, yelled and chuckled with laughter. We took turns taking memorable photos.

At Las Condes - Life is very convenient where I need 30 minutes or less to go to my work. The internet speed was way beyond what I have experienced in the Philippines. The speed increases with the same amount that I paid throughout my stay with my phone subscription. It is faster and cheaper so that I have been able to maintain contact with my colleagues and friends and enjoy programs / apps on my phone.

It also gave me the opportunity to travel in some parts of Chile and South America and visited places found in the bucket list of some people.

Interview: Wilma Lorenzo Bayaua from Mozambique.

I met Wilma Lorenzo Bayuaua thru my friend Mafe Leal Lelonde in the year 2010. I stayed at the newly built M Residences in Maputo, close to the city center. Just a short taxi ride to Wilma's place are top sites and restaurants.

Begin story from Wilma:

I arrived Mozambique as a single parent.

I came to Mozambique through a friend.

Taught at the American International School of Mozambique

Though locally hired I was treated well with benefits such as free education for my kids and medical aid and with a retirement plan.

We go home yearly to visit my aging parents. I just lost my father last October.

I have been in Mozambique for 26 years now.

We meet as a community here and we have a strong community connection.

We go to a Catholic Church, the Holy Cross Parish Church.

I send money to my parents and family members who need some assistance.

I send my niece and nephew to school.

My kids are holders of two passports Philippine and Mozambique. Our stay here in Mozambique is lovely and less stressful because we don't get involved with politics. People in Mozambique are very respectful.

I have never met any arrogant Mozambican. My maids are like family. My kids love them. We eat together. They eat what we eat because we realize we cannot function well without them.

Our Filipino community in Mozambique is our support system when troubles or problems arise. As Filipinos we love to gather on social occasions like birthdays and Philippine Independence Day.

We really love it here because of the beaches and seafood and all fresh fruits.

My job pays well so I was able to buy my own house and a piece of land.

I was in the process of paying two condominiums.

When the fierce and selfish covid-19 came I lost my job. It is heartbreaking and devastating as my kids are still studying.

Now my condominiums are out looking for potential buyers.

Thank you, Odette Love, Wilma.

Interview with Roger and Lucy
Fabros – Efate, Vanuatu

THE FILIPINOS IN VANUATU:

Introduction:

Vanuatu is a South Pacific nation. Geographically, it is located

South of Solomon Islands, West of Fiji and Northeast of Australia.

Prior to its Independence on 30 July 1980, Vanuatu was Jointly Administered

By the French and British governments and was referred to as Anglo-French

Condominium. Vanuatu before its Independence was popularly known

As New Hebrides.

Historical Background:

It was in the year 1979 when the first group Filipino expatriates arrived in Vanuatu

Working in the Hotel Industry. Consisted of accountants, executive housekeeper and musicians.

Reasons for being in Vanuatu:

It was learned there are only a couple of reasons they are in Vanuatu.

These are the 2 L's – LABOR AND LOVE.

The first L – LABOR concerns their employment. The Second L, specifically for Filipino wives, their greater LOVE for their husbands.

Arrived in Vanuatu:

I came to Vanuatu on 30 November 1986 and worked as an Accountant with a Gas

Company, BORAL GAS, until July 2007. Now I own a Shipping Agency business since 2009 until present.

Though our family stayed in Vanuatu for 33 years we still go back to Philippines for a

Holiday every year to see our families.

VANUATU IS A TOURIST DESTINATINATION IN THE SOUTH PACIFIC WHERE LIFE IS SIMPLE, CRIME RATE IS VERY MINIMAL AND I THINK THIS IS THE PLACE FOR OUR FUTURE RETIREMENT.

Best regards,

Roger and Lucy Fabros

Chapter 7

Eyes Beaming with Joy

Interview with Riley Joseph Ricasa Rudio

(My grandson. We explored Spain and France two times).

I am Riley Rudio. I am twenty (20) years old and I am the older brother to my little sister Rachel from two lovely parents Joe and Rica Rudio.

I am currently going into my Senior year of college at Kansas Wesleyan University studying for my B.A. in Business Management with a minor in Computer Technology. At Kansas Wesleyan University, I am not only a student (with high honors on the Dean's List) but an ATHLETE as well. I am on the Kansas Wesleyan University Men's Soccer Team.

Soccer has been a passion of mine since I was 7 years old and has led to me being able to have the opportunity to compete at the collegiate level after playing many years of club and high school soccer. This upcoming season will conclude my 14 years of playing soccer. (YES!!! that's me, Soccer fired up!)

So far, my college experience has been full of many amazing memories that I have had the opportunity to experience. For example, during my Sophomore season (2018-2019) our men's soccer team at Kansas Wesleyan went UNDEFEATED in regular season on conference tournament with a record of 15-0 and an overall record of 17-4, we each earned a RING to signify our accomplishments that year.

Every time I look at my ring I am reminded of PERSEVERANCE and STRENGTH. We had non-stop spraying of champagne, fierce shouts of ecstasy, shrieks of laughter, pandemonium as we lifted and carried our coach that memorable day! This iconic ring takes me back to that particular chaotic situation.

Ending up to every season our team endures a rigorous training schedule consisting of two practices a day for one whole week. These practices are full of fitness tests, training with the soccer ball itself, and mental preparation (like Kobe Bryant's mental preparation for his basketball) for our upcoming opponents.

It is best that you come prepared before this "hell week" begins as your body will be tested physically and mentally.

Soccer has brought me countless memories.

However, one that I could not forget is the time that my family and I accompanied me to my tryout at the Kaptiva Sports Academy in Sant Cugat del Valles, Barcelona, Spain. I was able to tour the facilities, meet foreign students from Uzbekistan and Poland in their dormitories.

My family had snacks at the school cafeteria where a toasted *jamon serrano* (ham sandwich) with heavy mayonnaise dressing cost 2.50 Euros. Surprisingly the beer only cost 1.00 Euro. Whaoa!!!

The best part is I had a chance to play with the Kaptiva team. My selective language in high school was Spanish. So that when the coach shouted *"Patear la pelota con el pie izquierdo"* (kick the ball with your left foot)" I followed instructions with ease.

Barcelona will always have a place in my heart as my grandmother, Odette Ricasa, has taken me twice now, showed me her favorites places and given me the opportunity to experience the sport I love in another country.

When I was fourteen years old, she took me to different cities in Spain and the French border.

I will never forget the thrill and excitement of taking the *Le Petite Train Jaune* (Little Yellow Train) that run from Villefranche de Confient to Latour -de-Carol-Envetig in the French Pyrenees. The ride was 39 miles long, the trains powered by electricity runs to a suspension bridge. The line is a single track with passing loops. My lips melted the snow flurries. Below were myriads of majestic Alpine trees as far as our eyes can see with patches of glistening snow.

Talk about snow, Salina, Kansas where my school is, has long periods of snow specially in the month of January. Snow falls for three (3) continuous days and aggregates to six (6) feet high! I have had my share of hard working days scrubbing my black Toyota car, shoveling the snow!

Currently, I have one more year left in my collegiate career and I could have never predicted that soccer would have brought me so many opportunities throughout my life.

Yes, that's me the Defender. I live and breathe soccer, Obsessed, better terminology, POSSESSED with soccer.

My goal is to accumulate three Undefeated Champion Iconic rings. ☺

(My grandson. We explored Spain and France two times).

Interview with Cutie Rachel Ricasa Rudio

Interview with Cutie
Rachel Ricasa Rudio

I have amazing parents Joe and Rica Rudio. I am a junior attending San Marino High.

Throughout my high school experience, I have taken up learning how to become a better version of myself by joining my school's Link Crew program. Here they teach us how to be a leader.

As a little girl, I would sit on the side lines of my brother's soccer games and watch him play. Ever since then, I was inspired to be just like him.

I have been playing soccer since I was eight years old. Currently I play for the Social Blues 04 team.

This upcoming season I will be playing my 9th year of soccer. I hope to play in College soon.

I celebrated my 16th birthday at my grandmother's house by the beach in San Clemente pier. My mom drove a van for us four girls. During the 1-1/2 hour drive, we sat apart with social distancing and wore masks for protective covering. I have many friends but invited only three guests. We followed the Los Angeles County guide lines during this pandemic.

My mom baked pasta alfredo and grilled chicken with tossed kale salad on the side. For dessert, we had my favorite, chocolate mousse cake. Hooray! I made a wish and blew the candles and posed for picture taking. We had a blast!

My favorite color is white and sky blue. Most of my dresses and tank tops are white with minimal black lines or designs. I love small silver earrings, anklets, silver necklace and Louie Viton small pouch.

My grandma gave me a big surprise by buying the latest model of Apple laptop computer. Ohhh..I hugged her tight and kissed her many times. I love her dearly.

I like hanging out with my friends. Now that we are quarantined due to Covid-19 we send text messages often. This school year our classes are online.

I miss the social inter-action with my friends and family. Hopefully the quarantine ends soon.

Interview with Mick Aniceto: Taylor, MaKenzie and Gabriel

Taylor Rose "Ate" your typical teenage girl. Loves hanging out with her friends. She's bossy to her younger siblings but she means well. She loves to cook especially desserts. Takes care of her dad when he is not feeling well. Loves Christmas movies. -- Taylor Rose Aniceto age thirteen (13). Was on the school's academic team and won various medals in math and robotics

Makenzie Carmen "the feisty one" she is smart and loves all things astrology. She says her temper comes from the fact that she's an emotional Pisces. She is generous and kind. She loves animals and even saves bugs instead of killing them. The most responsible of all my kids. ---

- Makenzie Carmen Aniceto age ten (10) has been part of the gifted and talented program since kindergarten and is doing advanced math. She is also in extra-curricular activities such as school leadership and safety teams.

Gabriel Rey "the king" the youngest and no doubt the spoiled one. He's smart and awkward all at the same time. He's hard headed just like his dad and wants things done his way. He loves cars and is a risk taker. ---- Gabriel Rey Aniceto age eight (8). Being tested for advanced placement in math.

Odette's Speech at 75

75th birthday get together at Sanam Luang Restaurant in Old Town Pasadena, California. Date: February 25, 2020. Three weeks before the pandemic happened.

While Luchie Combate Juatco was playing the violin.

"Wow ! Thank you Lord I'm now 75 YES! Tonight I want to share the history of precious BFFS. First I would like to acknowledge is: Alice Roxas whom I have known since we were in grade eight (8). We were twelve (12) years old, makes sixty (60) plus years of precious friendship.

Next special mention to Goya Morelos, friends since 1971. Her husband, Jun Morelos is Rick's high school classmate, forty three (43) years, friends forever.

Then to Nancy Narvaez, we worked at the Los Angeles Unified School District (LAUSD) since nineteen seventy four (1974), forty (40) years.

Shortly followed by present here tonight: Tess C. Nufable, Carolina (Carole) Cotter, our secretary at Asian American Realty. Quickly, Carole rose up to become our top producing realtor. Then Nelly Neri Aquino, Olivia Lopez, Tata Eduarte and Nini Maldonado. Tita Palermo, Nieves Wilmot, Meg Gutierrez, Femy Wagas, Ruby Guerrero and Josie Inacay could not make it tonight. Surely all are precious friends, dear to my heart.

Over the years I may have made mistakes. I sincerely apologize whatever I may have done. When we are wise. we embrace the people around with love while on earth.

Thank you for your fabulous presence, gifts, singing and story telling. Good luck, Good health and God bless us all.

Zoom Interview by Regin Reyno of Philippine Global Explorers (PGE):

#Travel Conversations with Odette Aquitania Ricasa The most traveled Filipino: May 24, 2020 at 7:00 PM L.A. Time www.reginstravels.com.

Regin Reyno circumnavigated the world in 2019. Because of his feat, he was accepted into the **Circumnavigator's Club** whose members included General Douglas MacArthur, Neil Armstrong, William Howard Taft, and Harry Houdini. He named his journey around the world *Tuyok*, a Visayan word which means *ikot* in Filipino.

In the course of his historic journey, Reyno visited the **Seven Wonders of the World,** 12 territories, and encountered a brush with death he never expected.

Regin: What made you decide to visit every country in the world?

During the first 10 years here in USA, my concentration was on making a living, work, work, work. I lived in the Bronx, New York and worked in Manhattan. Short trips were to nearby Niagara Falls, Rhode Island, Washington DC and Virginia. After 8 months, we moved to Los Angeles.

I started to travel international, flying to Mexico city. Followed by a few organized trips with friends or sometimes solo, to more destinations, Madrid, Germany, Russia. My friend who belonged to Travelers Century Club (TCC) showed me a list of the countries she checked. I was not paying attention to the list, but decided to count the countries I have been anyway.

Surprise I have been to 76 countries. She said you can apply to be a provisional member. You meet the criteria of 75 countries. When you reach 100 countries, you will be an official member. I was challenged. From then on, before planning a trip, I would review the TCC list and decide on the next island or country to explore.

When did you decide traveling passionately?

I was born and raised in Quiapo, Manila, Philippines. In school, Geography was my favorite subject. I was fascinated by pictures of bright red apples trees, the spectacular beauty of the Grand Canyon, Rome, Scandinavia, Norway, learning about the Vikings, the heritage sites of Europe, the tundra of the North, the snow, the mountains where deer were crossing. I pledged to my dad: "Someday I will go to America".

So, you started traveling in 1983?

Yes. My first travel was to Mexico. I was invited by my sister-in-law's sister who lived in Mexico City. I took the bus to different cities, Taxco, Acapulco, Jalisco. I had a fantastic time discovering their traditions, dances, arts, listened to the stories of the locals - because I speak Spanish.

After two years, I joined an organized tour with Cosmos tours. We visited 6 countries in two weeks. Every other day, I would wake up and say "Ohhh I am in Amsterdam, change currency, money to gilders, then Milan Italy, change money to Italian lira, change money to German Deutschmark. Change money to Spanish peseta. We were given one hour to change money, shop and eat. What a fast track tour. There were no ATM machines, no cell phones. The tour guide used a microphone to gather us and explain the sites.

A year later, the next adventure was to Israel and Egypt. As a Roman Catholic, I had dreams of visiting the Holy Land, Nazareth, Jericho, the Wailing Wall, Bethlehem and Mount Sinai. We had a local guide in every city.

How was traveling back then specially without the internet and cell phones. What were some of the challenges? Any stories of difficulty of traveling before the internet age?

No internet? I went to the public library and read travel books. With any country in mind, I started by asking friends if they know somebody from example: in Norway. I sent letters of introduction and my short biodata to their relative or friend. I enclosed postage stamps. Those Days I went to the post office here in L.A – they sold stamps – I think it was called International Stamps.

For telephone calls, I'd go to the Post office or a Lottery/shop where I was assigned a Telephone Cabin with a clock timer. I paid the cashier by minutes used.

My first solo trip was to Madrid, as a courier. – Attending a party, I was introduced to a friend who worked with DHL Courier Express. Exchanging stories, I mentioned I love to travel. She said "If you are willing to travel alone, you can apply to be a courier with us". Your application once accepted, you have only 4 hours to confirm your free flight" Free? Yes, free, fly solo, you can only bring a hand carry luggage, no check-in luggage.

It was 1987, solo travel was rare especially for women. The first call I accepted was to Madrid. I was lucky because my boss gave me an ok for one week vacation with a very short notice. I met the DHL representative at the LAX airport. He gave me a manifest /package of documents. We checked in 16 huge bags as a courier. Upon arrival in Madrid, I was met by the DHL representative. After that I had a whole week to explore Spain.

A scary story to share: I stayed in the city center of Madrid, Plaza del Sol. The first evening, after taking tapas for dinner, I pressed the elevator to go up to my room. A Spanish *Pogi* (handsome) guy follows, his room is the same floor as mine? After a few minutes there were knocks on my door. My room had no telephone to call the Front desk. What to do? I did not open the door, continuous knock 10 – 15 minutes, not saying a word. Scared to death, I blocked the door with the desk and chair. Knocks finally stopped. Thinking now, I should have opened the door, Yes? Need a date? I am available. hahahaha.

In the eighties (1980's) DHL did not have their own planes. I flew by courier to Bangkok, Sydney, Tokyo, Singapore, on courier trips. No such thing today. DHL expanded and bought their own airplanes.

Surprise, having reached two hundred fifty one (251) countries I was invited for an Interview

- On Television show Brazzaville Republic of Congo
- Students Kamenge Youth Center, Burundi
- Radio interview Zaragoza, Spain

You have visited 295 countries and territories based on the Travelers Century Club count. May you explain what is this club all about Travelers Century Club?

Our tag line…..”World Travel.. the passport to peace through understanding.” We are more than simply a member. We are ambassadors of peace and love for the good of humanity. We meet four times a year. We hold international meetings every two years. Last year, our meeting was in Barcelona, Spain – 4 days of conferences, talks, dining and sharing. Our next meeting will be in Malta, year 2021.

My first Recognition award certificate was when I reached One Hundred Fifty (150) countries.

Recognition is given in increments of fifty (50) countries. Then, I got an award for two hundred (200), and two hundred fifty one (251) countries.

The list of islands, territories and countries goes up to three hundred twenty one (321) – crazy?! But the list satisfies my hunger for more learning –"The World is my classroom". The countries I have not explored are those that are at times dangerous like Libya, or hard to explore. Because I have a passion for remote islands, I gave it priority. For example: Home Island, Yap Island, Chatham islands, Kiritimati, Cocos island, Niue island, Lakshadweep islands, St Helena islands.

I saw your photo on FB with your backdrop as the vast sky at night with Aurora Borealis or Northern Lights. That must be an amazing moment. It is my dream and a lot of people I'm sure to be able to witness that . - can you describe to us that moment?

OH! Wow! Exciting! An aurora sometimes referred as polar lights is a natural light display in the Earth's sky. Auroras are the result of disturbances caused by solar wind.

A short background story:

When I was at the remote Christmas island in line with Gilbert islands in the Pacific, I was waiting at the gate for my flight. I heard two men talking in a different language. I smiled, asked: "Where are you from? Are you going to Christmas island? Not many people travel to Christmas island", They were from Sweden, going fishing for a whole week. Flights are only once a week. I did not have a hotel. When we landed I was looking for a taxi – none. Turns out you have to book a hotel in advance for the hotel to pick you up. I went with them and booked at the same hotel. Eventually we became friends, exchanged stories. His name is Bengt and his friend, Gunar. He invited me to the very north part of Sweden, on the line of the Arctic circle or Polar circle where he lives.

I got excited! I can see the Northern Lights? Yes, but be prepared, in January the snow covers six feet in height, weather is always below freezing minus 11 degrees Celsius. The sun seldom rises, twelve (12) to

(14) hours darkness. Bengt and Gunar were going to visit a friend in Los Angeles. "Ohhh come and visit me".

They did visit me, I showed them around Beverly Hills, homes to the famous stars, Hollywood, Universal Studios, Central Market in downtown, the Flower Market and the Union Rescue Mission.

My first attempt to see the Northern Lights was a stay at the famous Abisko guest house February 2017.

I did not visit Bengt because he was not home. Every winter he flies to Asia for four months to escape the harsh winter. My friend, Meg Pipo, son Vito, we waited and waited, played in the snow, played games, drove snow mobiles. We took tours "Chasing the Aurora". Nothing! Nada, zero no - Northern Lights, We were so disappointed.

The second time was September of 2017 – second attempt, with perseverance. Bengt invited me to stay at his home, because sometimes, the Northern Lights show earlier in the year. The closest airport to his village was the domestic airport of Kemi in Finland.

Bengt met me at the airport. He took us on a day tour around the villages. He lives in a very small village of Overtornea, Sweden. There are only eight (8) houses in the whole village. The closest grocery store is one and a half hour away. Whenever he needs something, (example: sugar) he borrows or barters with his neighbor.

Bengt is proud to say he has completed the 193 countries in the United Nations list. We had a dinner of moose and potatoes. He is a magical chef. We cheered, with wine welcome toast, exchanged more stories.

It was around 10:00Pm when Bengt was washing the dishes. He saw thru the window, shouted, "Go out! Go out! the lights are forming." We rushed outside. He lent me his heavy Siberian wool jacket and High legged boots, I could hardly walk, much run. And there it was!

It's hard to paint a picture of the emotional impact the Northern Lights has.

The aurora is a manifestation of space weather. It all starts at the sun. As the sun's magnetic field becomes stronger and weaker, it becomes unstable, resulting in solar flares and a coronal mass ejection. Basically the sun burps a piece of itself into space. The earth rotates us, under the aurora at midnight. As for the color that's indicative of what altitude the reaction happens at, which gas the electron hits. If it hits oxygen, you get green and red light typically. If it hits nitrogen you get blue light and so on, colors of rainbow dancing in the sky.

Watching the sky dance and come alive! It's almost like Heavenly Visual Music. Squinting and wondering if the small cloud might be the Northern Lights, an alien green ribbon unfurled from the sky. Sometimes the whole sky was moving and just impossible to photograph. Lights were moving and moving!

Pure luck! We would go outside for 15 minutes then run back inside the house for warmth on the fireplace. Again, outside for 10 – 15 minutes, photo shoot and go inside. We did this for more than 4 hours.

Absorbing it all. After 4:00AM the lights were gone.

You have to have a powerful camera for really good shots. My i-phone took some good and some blurry shots. My friend Bengt had powerful lenses, he gave me some of his spectacular photos. A night to remember!

Am fortunate to be stationed here in Hollywood, a city that celebrates diversity, the Entertainment Capital of the World. I have run into Jack Nicholson, Nicholas Cage, Sean Connery, Steven Spielberg.

Friends from all over the world are curious about Hollywood.

At the airport, smile. At a café, smile. Yes, each of us has been afforded the rare privilege to explore a greater part of the world, most people will never see. An action of love – SMILE.

You are currently short of 5 countries to be able to completely visit every United Nations recognized countries in the world. What are those countries?

I was not paying much attention to U.N. countries. I was more concentrated on the list of Travelers Century Club (TCC). I received my Recognition Certificate of having visited 251 countries, seven years ago in 2013. I was so hung up on exploring remote islands, not included in the U. N. List. Example: Chatham islands, Fernando de Noronja island, Lakshadweep islands, Isle of Man, Jersey and Guernsey, the island of Niue, St. Helena island and Home Island.

And what made you decide to visit them towards the end?

Every time I am ready to go, for example: to Iraq, there were high alert risks. Two months ago. I was very ready to go to near Erbil, Iraq. My friend, Susan Detera whom I met in Botswana, invited me to visit. We will go bar hopping, disco and have fun. There are many Filipinos working in Erbil. Some of them own restaurants, barber shops, small markets.

Experience the wafting of smells from food stalls

But, suddenly according to the news, the United States ordered the assassination of a high Iranian officer. My friend called thru Skype to cancel my flight. It was too dangerous to continue! There's intense bombing day and night near the military zones and the city!.

I changed plans and went to Doha instead (my third time) and continued to Manila.

I planned to go to Karthoum, Sudan. Last October, my Filipina friend advised the overthrowing of the President. Fire, riots and killing on the street were rampant. "Don't go!!". Then again this March, with approved visas, all set to go to Sudan, Chad… Uhh.. Ohh the pandemic happened.

God is with me. Protecting me. Four days before the lockdown, I cancelled all flights for the year. My target was to complete 300 countries, islands and territories by September. 2020. Ready to be awarded a recognition certificate of having traveled to 301 countries, including plans to explore the Austral islands from Papete of Raivave, Rurutu and Tubuai.

You are not just a traveler. You are also a pianist, an artist and an author, You have written 5 books. What are these books all about? Are these travel books?

Playing the Piano:

My father owned a small piano store in Quiapo, Manila, Philippines, the Century Music Store. I learned to play the piano when I was 12 years old. I remember practicing piano as soon as I woke up. But, every time my father was short of pianos to sell, he would bring the customer to our home at the upper floor and show the piano. If the customer liked the piano – Uhh ohh! There goes my piano. I had to wait a little while before my piano got replaced.

My piano teacher, Mrs. Monica Manalansan held recitals. During one recital, I fumbled on my piano piece, playing the measure again and again. Monica from behind the curtain, kept whispering softly. "It's ok, it's ok. End your piece and make a bow." With tearful eyes, I ended my playing and curtsied with a bow. My parents, family, friends clapped – "pala" (exerted applause) ! I cried the whole afternoon. I made a mistake Boo- hoo!

Travels and Writing books:

During my early travels, I carried Stenography notebooks. I wrote about the city, the people, the cuisine, their dresses and religious beliefs.

Noticing these, my friend said" Why don't you compile your notes and make it into a book?" Really? I got the idea. The friendly computer was beginning to be in the market. Languages were in Cobol and Fortran.

I learned to store my notes in the computer, eventually writing my book. I inquired about publishing. Voila! year 2000 – 20 years ago, my first book "Unguarded Thoughts" was released.

Since then, I have written a book every 2 or 3 years. The books are available at AuthorHouse.com; search books written by Odette Ricasa.

Each book is about 400 pages each, available in soft or hard cover. I designed / painted the Art cover of the second book "Excerpts from Life".

The third book cover is my picture in front of the Rajasthan in Uzbekistan. I was so fascinated by the ancient mosques, madrassas, buildings of Samarkand, the whole city is a UNESCO World Heritage site.

I wrote a poem "Samarkand the Garden of my Soul." It was published in the Uzbekistan Daily News.

I had a private tour for 16 days plus 2 days in Tajikistan.

The Fourth book, Running with Echoes of Desire – front cover is a picture I took of Yemen". I was fortunate to have traveled to Yemen before the civil war. Today, the heritage sites, the fortresses, homes built on top of a rock are all gone!! Centuries of history all gone because of a violent war!!

The books contain poetry written in free verse and also short stories. I wrote about my family, the fiestas in the Philippines, the particular events of the countries I visited.

Often, people would ask, "How are your books selling? Has it reached the best seller?"

I smile. Politely I answer " Money was not my goal in writing. I wrote these books primarily to remember where I traveled, what I did during my life time. My grandchildren will know what grandma did. When I turn 89 and have difficulty moving, I will reach out to my bookshelf and read the PRECIOUS MEMORIES in my books."

These books are my legacy to my family – it will be handed down to generations. My great, great grandchildren, down the line will have an Idea of what Wanderlust Grandma Odette did.

You have inspired many people to travel. What's even more impressive is you're still doing this passion at 75 years old.

"Do it while you can". Whenever you do something, give it your best, 110% percent enthusiasm. Inspire people. God created us to love and share.

What is your message to people out there, who are retired or over 60 years old and they would love to travel but is kind of like scared or hesitant because of their age?

Take one step at a time or take baby steps.

The internet has a wealth of information. Study solo travels, or organized tours whichever attracts you. For example: Websites Travel Zoo, Getyourguide.com and Makemytrip.com has tour suggestions that you can design / plan the way you want it.

Begin with one or two countries, in Central America, or Europe. It is advisable to stay at least six nights in a place, unlike my first organized Express tour with Cosmos – six countries in 14 days including flying time! No, no my advise is Do Not do this, do not rush your travels.

I have a deep love for humanity. Connecting with people everywhere is just more than a checked box in the list. As travelers our ability to connect with and love people around the world is our special opportunity to share. Keep sharing. Keep networking.

Reading the stories of travelers help us plan trips at the same time formulate our own stores and share to others.

Any tips while on the road?

Pay attention to scams: In Paris, Charles de Gaulle airport, I arrived very late. The train ticket machine was a far walk downstairs, the place was deserted. No police, no security late at night.

I was inserting my credit card ready to pay, when all of a sudden, a man from behind pulled out my almost inserted card from the machine. He said, "let me show you how to use your card faster - you can insert some bills and coins." I looked around, saw nobody, I gave him my money, he gave my train ticket. It was a fake ticket, I could not enter the station, the rolling stilts would not move.

Finally, a French lady came to my rescue. She used her ticket and we both squeezed n the rotating stilts to enter. Whew! What an experience. I could have gone to the police, but the scam guy disappeared, nowhere to be found.

Another time I was attending the Feria de Seville in Spain. I was driving the car with my friend. Our windows were rolled down about a one third space because the weather was so hot. Can you imagine, in an instant a guy inserted his whole head, his neck thru the window opening and asked for money. I could not step on the gas pedal, he will be rolled and carried away! He stayed there for five minutes or so, we were talking in Spanish" No dinero, no dinero." He said even" cinco pesetas no mas " five pesetas. We finally gave the money.

I was also afraid because if I rolled the window down, others might quickly swarm around us. Thank God, nothing happened, we slowly drove through the crowd.

I had my camera stolen at the airport of Botswana, my laptop in Barcelona. They are out there, trying to get the next victim!

At the Metro subway in Madrid, a guy pushed me in. We were packed like sardines. When I got out of the train, my purse was open, he was pulling my wallet but had no success. I learned to tie my money with a strong cord, with three safety pins to my vest, or my purse or pants :).

Out of approximately 1,000 cities and stops, these are just a small percentage of bad experiences while traveling.

The positive sides of meeting people, making life time friends, drinking hot lattes in coffee shops in quaint towns, drinking horse milk in Kyrgyzstan, savoring oven baked bread in Timbuktu, discovering dinosaur footprints from 63 Million years BC, in Gijon, Spain - outweighs the negative side of travel.

To make sure our travels are more meaningful, people do certain things. For example: we give back to the community, volunteer or take up ministries.

What is your current mission in your travels, nowadays?

Build an Art School, offer art classes to children / adults who cannot afford to take Art LESSONS.

151

My current mission during travels, is to interview Filipinos living abroad. Most often, we are seen as OFW workers working domestically with minimal pay of $400. US dollars per month.

When I was in Saudi Arabia, families were often accompanied by Filipino nannies. When they learned that I am from USA with roots from the Philippines, have written five books and traveled to 295 countries, they gasp! and, say "Wow!." They form a heart shape of praise with their fingers. As a souvenir, I give them my bookmark.

I have interviewed doctors, nurses, architects, engineers, business men. In Freetown, Sierra Leone there was a Filipina lady in charge of operations overseas and the financial reporting of a Diamond Mining company. I did not get to interview her but they said she earns US $14,000. per month I was very proud to hear that.

Your photo in our poster was taken in Robinson Crusoe Island. It has a tagline "Far away from it All". How difficult is it to get to that island?

Robinson Crusoe island is also known as Juan Fernandez Islands.

The trip was awesome, the trip of a life time. A PRIVATE JET experience, South of Santiago international airport.

I planned twice for this adventure. It took more than six months of waiting, Flights with Aerocardal airlines operate only from mid-November to early March. After this, the season is closed. Flights are only once a week. Depending on the wind factor, the time of stay can be cut short or extended to several days. When horizontal winds or cross winds occur, it is prohibitive to take off or land.

I arrived Santiago 2 days before the flight. As soon as I arrived, I had to call in to Aerocardal Airlines, check in and give my hotel information. On my airline ticket, is the diagram of the place I will check in. Easy, I studied it. I can walk from the international airport to the domestic airport. Uhh ohhh!!. Oh No! it is located way in the rear some 25 miles of driving The Uber driver had to call Aerocardal Airlines and ask how to get there. After a 30 minute ride, we found the office.

It is an impressive office with a check-in counter for private jets!

There are STRICT regulations on the weight. My baggage and I stood on the scale three times, making sure I met the requirements. After the wight was approved. I signed all the paper work and was given a seat number. The waiting area was striking and super clean. A spread of Danish cookies, muffins, juice, milk, cereal, chocolate candies and fruits were free!

The weather was showing it was not a good factor to fly, so we waited a bit more. By 1:00PM we were sent home. I was disappointed and at the same time thankful because weather factors were carefully reviewed. We will try again tomorrow. They had a limousine that took me back to my Airbnb.

The next day, I was picked up by the limousine. The same routine of weighing and seat assignment, waiting for the right visibility factor. I was sent home again.

The third day, I was getting frustrated but did not give up. – Armed with Perseverance - What do you know! Cheers erupted when we were called to board the flight.

It was a private jet with a capacity for 12 persons. Reclining seats, a bag of goodies, snacks, sandwiches and drinks. Every passenger who boarded took pictures, high fives and handshakes as we sat in. Six men from Brazil were on a fishing expedition. The pilot and co- pilot assured the weather was cooperative and on our side. The flight will be approximately 3 hours.

The private jet could only hold so much gasoline for fuel. After one hour or so, we stopped to refuel, the gas tank was on top of the plane!

An old step ladder was used to go up. The attendant pulled the long heavy gasoline hose like a fire hose manually. Ok more photos of these rare events.

After 2 hours, finally we arrived at the loading dock. There was a small immigration room with ten chairs, a rest room, a vending machine for water, sodas and fruit juices. We waited patiently for entry requirements to be checked. Our passports and boarding passes were finally stamped.

The loading dock was out of sight! The waves were crashing on black lava rocks. IN the DARK LAVA BEACHES, hundreds, thousands of fur seals, glided in with the waves. The fur seals vocalization sounds like a buzzing chain saw – - barking continuously - music to my ears. They dove through pounding surf with easy, graceful nonchalance and landed smoothly on the coastal rocks before me. It was a phenomenal site. We were crazy taking photos!!

Then, we had to ride a boat. The sky was bluer than blue, very clear with a few clouds. The cliffs often shrouded by mist inspired many writers who visited Robinson Crusoe. The boat ride took another 1-1/2 hour.

The island population: 600, number of cars: 25, number of motorcycles: 3, no stress, no pollution. No rental cars, no buses, no taxis. I had the best walking tour. Occasionally a delivery truck driver will stop and offer a ride. I politely say "Thank you, it's a beautiful day I would rather walk and explore every corner of the island" I walked everywhere. The island is famous for giant lobsters, each weighing more than 8 kilos. I feasted on too much lobster and had a slight indigestion.

I had a busy schedule - I even watched a soccer game "Cumberland vs Nocturno" -- the amazing thing is the play field is right beside the ocean and a view of the magnificent hills of Robinson Crusoe / Juan Fernandez islands. More sceneries. Colorful houses, mini markets, Isla Pacifico lodge.

Guillermo, my host at Isla Pacífico Eco lodge pointed to the church "la capilla de Robinson Crusoe" explaining further its history.

Walking along the main road everyone greets with a friendly Buenos días. I saw a house decorated in festivity with colored balloons flying on the front porch. I went up the steps and introduced myself as a writer from Los Angeles, California. Oohhh!, they were surprised! They invited me to join the baptismal party.

One of the advantages of traveling solo - many surprises along the way. The mother, Lydia, of the baby boy Joselito, eagerly recounted, proud to share the history of the island and why they chose to live in such a remote island. She quips, " here no stress, every day is your own pace. Nice!"

Life couldn't be sweeter here. *Hora de feliz (*Happy hour) at Cafe del Coral Negro Robinson Crusoe. Patricio, a composer and a famous guitarist entertained us with comical songs "*Cucooku Curooo* " mixing with the friendly locals Elizabeth, Lupita and Elsa. He proudly shows the paintings of his wife Cristina.

The marine mammals, Juan Fernandez fur seals I am observing - once covered these beaches in the hundreds of thousands or more. And then, starting in 1687, sealers came and methodically killed them. Season after season, they harvested the animals. By the 1850s, the Juan Fernandez fur seal was annihilated, considered extinct.

- end =

Chapter 8

Make Hay While the Sun Shines

IN MANILA

It is raining again
Rainy season is here

I am at Fort Bonifacio
Weather is hot and muggy

I have the blue umbrella you gave me
A green plastic raincoat

Streets are a little flooded
After two or three hours the sun shines

I see you all the time
At times I roam around
Attracted to the fluttering wings of a multitude of pigeons
Maybe one of them is you

My heart throbs
A Filipina selling flowers with a shack of purple hair
Offers bouquets of daisies, roses and sunflowers

Reminded, I am saddened
You called me "My sunflower"

In solitude, my life has two strands
Two months earlier
A strange pleasure of opening letters

Trying to imagine what I need to hear
In my dreams, a rounded image of your face with olive green eyes
Appears when I read them

You are with me side by side
My truest self

I want to show you everything
What I am seeing, thinking, feeling
But you are nowhere to be found

The other strand is to keep myself
Afloat with the daily routine of life

A colorful jeepney with ruffled curtains on the windows
Kept away the hot sun
It stops
I hop in transporting me to the real world

I am headed to the church of San Agustin
To the lively neighborhood of Intramuros
Spaniards conquered this city before I was born

I have your blood
It is true from a drifting point
We are connected by Blood from ancestry

En Manila

Está lloviendo otra vez
Llega la temporada de lluvias

Estoy en Fort Bonifacio
El clima es caluroso y húmedo

Tengo el paraguas azul que me diste
Un impermeable de plástico verde

Las calles están un poco inundadas
Después de dos o tres horas, el sol brilla

Te veo todo el tiempo, muerto de hambre
A veces deambulo
Atraído por las aleteo de una multitud de palomas

Tal vez uno de ellos eres tú
Mi corazón late como si fuera a explotar

Un vendedor de flores filipina con una cabaña de cabello morado
Ofrece ramos de margaritas, rosas y girasoles

Recorde que me llamaste
Me llamaste, Mi girasol

En soledad, mi vida tiene dos hilos
Dos meses antes
Un extraño placer de abrir cartas

Tratando de imaginar lo que necesito escuchar
En mis sueños,
Una imagen redondeada de tu cara con ojos verde oliva
Aparece cuando los leo

Tu estas conmigo lado a lado
Llenándome de deseo de abrazarte
Te ofrezco un beso de mi verdadero yo
Quiero darte todo
Lo que estoy viendo, pensando, sintiendo
Pero no estás por ningún lado
El otro hilo es mantenerme
Flota con la rutina diaria de la vida sin ti

Un auto bus pequeño, colorido con cortinas rizadas en las ventanas.
Mantiene alejado el sol caliente y luego se detiene
Salto transportándome al mundo real

Me dirijo a la iglesia de San Agustín
Al animado barrio de Intramuros
Los españoles conquistaron esta ciudad antes de que yo naciera

Tengo tu sangre
Es cierto desde un punto de deriva
Estamos conectados por la sangre de la ascendencia

Travels to Hargeisa, Somaliland

Amazing Laas Geel. Painting on the Rocks - The paintings cover an area of 10 rock caves, also known as *'alcoves'*.

Hargiesa, Somaliland: As we drive along on the thin layer of pock-marked asphalt that passes for a 'highway', a rusty, fading sign directs us in the general direction of 'Laas Geel'.

We are about 30 miles outside Hargeisa, the capital of Somaliland, a self-declared independent republic that the international community and the government in Mogadishu consider a part of Somalia.

With our tour guide, Mohammed Abdirizak and his Whatsapp cell phone: We go off the highway, and into the semi-desert environment that is so evocative of the African region. The dust covered Toyota 4WD has no trouble navigating the rock-strewn and gravel-laden track and, after bouncing about for over half an hour, we reach a 'checkpoint' in the middle of absolutely nowhere.

It's made up of old printed blankets thrown on top of standing wooden logs to make a canopy, with a yawning gunman seated on a plastic chair inside.

He is the tourism department's guy, and is basically in charge of an area several dozen square kilometers wide.

He takes us to Laas Geel, a complex of caves with ancient rock art in an excellent state of preservation.

The paintings cover an area of ten (10) rock caves, also known as alcoves. Stunning figurines depict wild animals such as giraffes, and decorated cattle, like cows and bullocks. It is believed the paintings, made in an erratic pattern, are the work of the herders who resided in these caves thousands of years ago.

Though most of paintings are of bovines, many also depict anthropomorphs, figures in ancient art resembling human beings. The thorax is wide, and dressed with a type of shirt showing vertically painted stripes. These characters sometimes carry a bow-and-arrow, sometimes just a stick. This indicates they were both hunters and herders.

At the foot of the rocks of Laas Geel is a confluence of two ancient wadis, which are now dry riverbeds.

The paintings look like they were made a few hundred years ago, but are, in fact, between five thousand (5,000) and seven thousand (7,000) years old. In the modern era, Somalia (and Somaliland) have been totally off the tourist map; as a result, there are few signs of any human damage in Laas Geel. The dry climate of the region has also assisted with the preservation.

Although it was known to the inhabitants of the area for centuries, astonishingly, the cave complex only came to the attention of the world in the year 2002, after being discovered during an archaeological survey by a team of French researchers.

In fact, they were actually there to document the historical period when a production economy appeared in this part of the Horn of Africa. They were guided by villagers who knew about the caves from stories told by their ancestors.

Back in Hargeisa, the carbon dating had shown the paintings go back to at least 3,000 BC. All we know about these caves is from the findings of the Frenchmen who undertook the excavation.

The people who made these stunning paintings lived in these caves. Laas Geel - which loosely translates to valley where you water your camels.

The high quality of material that was used to create this art is still a mystery for us. It is so unique that we are still not able to tell what kind of leaves they used to make that paint. Laas Geel is a true treasure trove. and recognized as a UNESCO Heritage Site.

Only a handful of tourists visit the caves in a month.– Laas Geel is slowly becoming a tourist magnet.

Prince Andrew School - St. Helena Island - Motivational Speech

The Saints of St. Helena Island, Motivational Speech and Comments

It's one of the most isolated and intriguing places in the world. It remains a British outpost smack in the middle of nowhere, deep in the South Atlantic.

You have to get a letter of invitation from a local "the Saint" or from a confirmed reservation of a hotel. A US $500,000 trip cancellation insurance is required, which you have to show at the airline counter before boarding.

Flights are only from mid-October to mid-March. Otherwise, you take a steam ship for three to four weeks. This is a place you definitely want to visit.

From the sky I could see the view of this charming island located between South Africa and Brazil in the South Atlantic Ocean. Arriving into Jamestown, I was met by Robert, a Saints. term used for locals born and raised in St Helena.

It was sweltering hot, immediately I was swept away to a tour of the city's outskirts. I got on first names with Locals.

Attended a Sunday mass at St. Paul's Cathedral, two blocks from my hotel. It was Mother's day. The choir with the piped organ sung angelic hymns. The children fashioned bouquets of flowers out of their gardens. I was honored to be given three bouquets with red ribbons.

Sightseeing: Plantation House in St Helena sits proud amid gumwood trees alive with chirps and whistles. It is the official residence of the Governor of the British Overseas Territories in the South Atlantic. I have not come to see the governor, nor the large brown hills which dot the pristine lawns.

I ventured here because to my surprise I was invited to give a talk to the student at Prince Andrew School. Also, I was going to take painting lessons with Teeny Lucy.

Hazel Wilmot at the iconic consulates hotel:

Dear Odette

At last - time to myself to just sit and catch my breath - so I can start again ! Hotel is a roller coaster of late - and never believe anyone who says island life is Life in the Slow Lane...

First I want to say how much I am looking forward to meeting you, and to thank you for offering to speak to the school students.

I had a word with Teeny Lucy from Creative St Helena this morning. She teaches art and music as well as ballet lessons. She is having an exhibition of the student's artwork soon, but sadly the exhibition finishes on Saturday 30th March. She has however agreed to leave all - in the museum, until you can see it on Monday morning - bless her. She is a very kind soul who hides her talents under a bushel.

I am awaiting feedback from Penny Bowers, at Prince Andrew School, as to Monday 1st April schedule for your talk.

May be cheaper for you in the long run as bank here is not shy to charge bank fees on incoming sums. Please remember there is a £20 fee for a entry permit, payable on landing.

Our representative will be at the airport to meet and greet - and will have a board with your name on to hand.

Kind regards

Hazel

Hello Hazel: I was actually going to change my room reservation dates to stay 3 nights only due to lack of time. Now that I received an in house offer - I will plan to stay Four nights :), will appreciate the one night in house.

Regardless of any offers I will be delighted and thrilled to talk to the students of Prince Andrew School. I have given motivational speeches to San Clemente high school. Won the first prize trophy during a Toastmaster Division Contest :) See photos You must have googled my name to know that I play the piano. I will firm up the dates of air tickets and apply for a tourist visa needed. Looking forward. - Odette

www.odettericasatravels.com

What an honor! I was invited to give a motivational speech to the students of Prince Andrew School.

From Ms. Penelope Bowers, Head to Hazel Wilmot, owner of Consulate Hotel.

Thank you.

We are looking forward to having you J

To confirm: Monday 1st April – please be here for 08.50 am and the assembly last for about 20 minutes.

Kind regards

Penny Bowers

Head

Prince Andrew School

Francis Plain St Pauls

St Helena Island

South Atlantic Ocean

www.pas.edu.sh

Hello Ms Bowers.

Thank you for giving me the awesome opportunity to deliver my speech to motivate PAS students to achieve their dreams -

The Title of my 10 minute speech was: "The Ultimate Key To Success"

The students listened intently & attention was focused. The thunderous applause was music to my ears. I received a lot of precious comments.

There was mention that PAS will give a token of appreciation to be brought to Hazel of Consulate Hotel. It would be a treasure to receive one.

Photos saved: Have a great day!

- Odette

Copy of my Speech:

Thank you, thank you to Ms. Pamela Bowers for inviting me to speak. Wow! Am here at the remote of St. Helena. I see beautiful eager faces, curious. Perhaps you are thinking: What will this lady talk about?

Let's begin with a short exercise, for audience participation: "Let's all stand up, face the student on your right, say "Good morning! Welcome to a lovely day!" Applause, Please sit down.

Today, I will share a speech that I won, First prize awardee as Motivational speaker.

The title: "The Ultimate key to Success".

It is not talent, it is not brains, it is not luck. It is a simple trait anyone can master.

Let me tell you a story, about a presser in an industrial laundry. He lived in a trailer and earned $60. a week. His wife worked nights, but even with both jobs they barely made ends meet. When their baby developed an ear infection, they had to give up their telephone to pay for antibiotics.

The laundry worker wanted to be a writer. Night and day you can hear the clack-clack of his typewriter. He spent all his spare money sending his manuscripts to publishers. Every manuscript was rejected. The form letters were short. He could not even be sure if his work was being read.

One day, the laundry worker sent his manuscript to Double Day Publishers. His heart raced only to be disappointed. "The manuscript had too many flaws".

The laundry worker sent his work to more agencies. He began working on a fourth novel. But with bills mounting, he was losing hope.

One night, he threw his manuscript into the trash can. The next day, his wife fished it out. " You should not be quitting now. Not when you're so close."

The laundry worker stared at the pages. Perhaps he no longer believed in himself, but his wife did. So every day he wrote another 1,500 words. When he finished, he sent the novel to the publisher, but he was sure it would not sell.

The laundry worker was wrong! The Publishing house handed over a $2,500. advance, and Stephen King's horror classic, Carrie was born. It went on to sell five million copies and was made into one of the top grossing films. Today, Stephen King is the MacDonald's of writers. Every book is a best seller, almost every book is made into a film.

Let me tell you another story. As a little girl, she read books to her sister. Then she began to write short stories in school. After graduation from college she moved to Portugal and got married. The marriage ended in a divorce. She moved in with her sister.

While struggling to support her daughter and caring for her sickly mother, she worked on her first book. The idea came while she was on a long train ride. After several years of many rejections, she sold her first novel.

The author: J. K. Rowling. Harry Potter, the young wizard and his motley band of cohorts became a best seller, hitting an all time high. She wrote more books hitting fast, flying off the shelves. People were lining up to buy her books.

Stephen King got numerous rejections. J.K. Rowling worked hard as a single mother supporting her daughter, she had meager income. What was their secret?

Perseverance! Persistent people know they can prevail where smarter and talented people fail. Persistent people take advantage of adversaries carving out opportunities from change.

In 1971, we arrived in America with $100.00 in our pocket. We lived with my brother in a two room-apartment in New York. I slept on a folded cot in the living room.

After two weeks of looking for a job, I was hired as a bookkeeper at Gimbels Department Store in Manhattan. But luck was not on my side, I caught the chicken pox and was quarantined for 3 weeks. My boss patiently waited for me to start working. Excited I put my first pay check, $90. per week, as a souvenir in a picture frame.

Life was too fast in New York. It was a rat race riding the subways. We decided to move to Los Angeles. I worked with the Los Angeles Unified School district. started as an accounting clerk. We wanted to buy a house, my salary was not enough, so I worked double jobs. For 3 years, form 4:00PM to 8:00PM, I worked part time for 4 – 5 hours every night at the Garment District in Downtown Los Angeles, California.

Rick on the other hand wanted to be a real estate salesman. He took the exam but failed 3 times. After some time, he passed the exam. We started our own real estate office, called Asian American Realty. One day, Rick asked if I wanted to sell real estate. I was shy then. I said "No way." But after seeing that he had many clients, I took the exam and became the part time troubleshooter. One day I read an article. The title was "SELLING real estate brings PENNIES but INVESTING in real estate brings DOLLARS."

For three months, I woke up at 5:00 o'clock in the morning scouring every newspaper. One Saturday, I saw an ad that said "Hollywood Apartments - 11 units for sale $145,000." I immediately called the number. The broker was shocked to get a call at 6:30 in the morning. He gave me the address of the property.

We drove by and bought our first investment. Rick asked: "Where will you get the money?" I told him " I saved some dollars under my pillow." It was 1976 then, the broker said: "Mrs. Ricasa, one day this will be worth millions". I thought it was a come on. I thought he was pulling my leg.

After this experience, I knew that PERSEVERANCE is the ultimate key to success.

Tonight, I want to share my favorite poem, a dynamic poem with impact. When you leave here tonight, I want you to remember these words:

"Yes, You Can"

If you think you are beaten, you are

If you think you dare not, you don't

If you like to win, but think you cannot

It's almost a cinch you won't

If you think you'll lose, you're lost

For out in this world, you'll find

Success begins with a person's will

It's all in the state of mind

Full many a race is lost

Not even a step is run

And many a coward fails

His work is never begun

Think big and your deeds will grow

Think small and you will fall behind

Think that you can and you will

It's all in the state of mind

If you think you are outclassed, you are

You've got to think high to rise

You've got to be sure of yourself

Before you can win a prize

Life's battle does not always go

To the stronger or faster man

But sooner or later, the man who wins

Is the man who thinks "YES I CAN"

This poem is printed in a bookmark to be distributed tonight. I hope you keep it in a place where you can refer to it. When you are feeling down, it will lift up your spirits.

During one Oscar awards night in Hollywood, famous movie star Whoopie Goldberg said:

"If you have a dream, you better believe it."

All of you, Please stand up, put both hands up in the air, sway it left and right, follow me and say "Perseverance is the Ultimate to Success" and "YES, I CAN."

Applause, Applause. God bless each and every one of you. I love you all. Thank you!

Feel free to ask any questions, take a bookmark and fill up the notebook here for comments.

Motivational Speech: Feedbacks. Prince Andrew School (PAS)

"Great speech….very inspiring. You are very inspirational. We all aspire to do wonderful things to follow your footsteps. We wish all the best for the future. Many Thanks.

---Miss Roxanne Thomas, Teacher Assistant (TA). Joey Beard Year 8, Student 01-04-2019.

I found your assembly very inspirational and motivating. It gave me the impression that even when life lets you down, don't give up. Persevere and things will get better.

Good luck on your travels and keep doing what you do. Best Wishes.

--- Isaac Greeviree, Student Body President

A very inspirational assembly that proves to me that even f you get knocked down, the only way is to get back up and that if you persevere, dreams can be possible.

--- Keira Francs, 6th Form Student.

A truly inspirational assembly from an amazing woman. Thank you for sharing your experiences with us. Good luck and best wishes for your future travels.

--- Kerry Lawrence, Teacher Assistant

Thank you for taking the time to come to Prince Andrew School. The message is so important. Keep passing it on! Bon Voyage!

--- Jean Radcliffe French Advisory teacher, St. Helena.

Thank you so much for the inspirational and uplifting speech.

--- Hazel Wilmot, The Consulate Hotel.

We all need a push in life some days or we succumb to despair or despondency. Life is not always a bed of roses and failure is not falling down but failing to get up. Thank you for the helping hand when I needed it.

- 01 April 2019 Jamestown, St. Helena.

My chest is expanding, still electrified after delivering my motivational speech at Prince Andrew School, I got the above comments. YESSS!!!

After the Big day, I stayed 3 more days to soak in the views and cherish moments.

More sightseeing:

Peter who lives on top of the hill is Hazel's loving assistant at the Consulate Hotel. He has a big family of chickens and goats. He brings fresh eggs to the hotel.

I met Julia Benjamin, a transplant from Orlando, Florida, Mylyn Walton, Daisy Terry, owner of Orange Tree Oriental Restaurant and Fe Scanes, physio therapist at the Senior Center.

Robert Harris, taxi driver is a history buff who took me to where Napoleon died, his final residence with breath taking paths.

We toured the St Helena Distillery. with first-class gin, a coffee liqueur called Midnight Mist and a rum called White Lion, named after the Witte Leeuw shipwreck in James Bay. (Island slang for a rum and Coke is a "shipwreck".)

He explains: That's exactly what Paul did with his friends a few years ago: They harvested and distilled 15 tons of prickly pears to make a delicious drink called "Tungi" Spirit. (Tungi is the local word for prickly pear). Bottles of "Tungi" in every color of spirits were displayed on the store front.

At the coffee stop: The first arabica coffee plants were brought to St Helena from Yemen in 1732 by the British East India Company. Napoleon is said to have enjoyed a few cups a day.

At Rosemary Gate farm 6, owners Bill and Jill Bolton grow their own coffee. Bill will talk you through the whole process: His 1,800 plants flower twice a year and they harvest 2,5 tons of fruit by hand.

It's great fun to watch Bill leaning over the coffee roaster, waiting for the first bean to crack open like a popcorn kernel. When he hears a second pop, the beans are ready, the color and flavor will be perfect. Bags of beans and ground coffee are sold at the Bolton's coffee shop in the harbor.

Get this: Except for Harrods in London, this is the only place in the world where you can buy their coffee. Cost: A coffee tour costs $.00 Sterling Pounds per person. For operating hours, I made arrangements with the tourism office.

I took in the views from the High Knoll Fort, with all its mountains and sea views, St Helena has no shortage of places to watch the sunset. Few sunset spots match High Knoll Fort.

Years ago, there were cannons on the walls to drive a doubt into the mind of a ship captain thinking about attacking. Insubordinate Boer prisoners were also locked up in the Fort. We spent time exploring the moss-covered nooks of the fort. Watched the sun set over the South Atlantic from the parapets.

Basil was my second guide. He is the grandson of Alfred Smith, one of the Boer prisoners of war who remained on the island.

During a historical tour, we walked around the harbor and past some of the oldest buildings in Jamestown, Basil will tell you how the island, which rises more than five thousand (5,000) meters from the sea floor, was formed fifteen (15) million years ago by a series of volcanic eruptions.

He told the story of how the Portuguese admiral João da Nova discovered the island in the year 1502 and kept it a secret for decades until the Dutch and British fleets came upon it.

As we wandered from one historical building to the next, we learned about the island's economic deterioration over the centuries and how the economy has been recovering steadily since the 1970s.

St Helena still faces many challenges.. Once young residents leave the island to study in South Africa or England, there's not much to entice them to move back.

Basil also tells stories about the whalers of the 1800s and that the cathedral built in 1774, It is the oldest Anglican church in the southern hemisphere. He is passionate about St Helena and his tour taught me more about the island. Cost: A tour costs in Sterling Pounds, 35.00 per person and includes a cup of coffee.

Tea time at the Consulate Hotel took me back a century or two to a time when high tea was still an institution. If rainy weather ruins my plans for the day, this is a great place to while away a few hours.

Sit on the veranda or in a comfy chair and admire the collection of paintings and sketches of Napoleon on the walls. Order a mug of hot chocolate (GBP) British Pound 4.00 and a slice of cake (GBP) British Pound 1.50. They usually serve carrot cake, chocolate fudge cake, scones, spinach quiche and milk tart. I had the honor to play the baby grand with Peter Mott and his duckling listened.

I played the grand piano at the bar. Some tunes: "Waltzing Matilde" "Dr. Zhivago's theme from Lara.

Twelve (12) Whale sharks, often congregate around the island. It's a rare privilege to swim with these gentle giants – despite being the biggest sharks on earth, they are harmless plankton feeders. We saw some pantropical spotted dolphins. Tour Cost: British Pounds (GBP) 45.00

One of the structures is *The Cenotaph,* a war memorial resting at the Jamestown seafront etched with the names of islanders killed in World War II, as well as the forty one (41) individuals who lost their lives on the RFA Darkdale.

We visited the museum of St. Helena. The museum is housed in an 18th-century building restored in 2002 to mark the islands 500th anniversary.

It is 47 square miles, roads are very vertical. A lot of up and down the hills driving. The only city on the island, is called Jamestown and that's basically, at the bottom of a valley.

Post cards show the island as a long strip of houses going uphill with enormously steep cliffs on either side of it. The corner roads have huge round mirrors. We blew our horn every time we were on a steep curb to avoid crashing to oncoming cars.

The thing that struck me the most was the people. And to understand what I mean by that you need to understand a little bit of the history of the island. They say there are three S's that are involved in the creation of Saint Helena – Soldiers, Settlers, and Slaves.

So the faces of the Saints… Native American, or Hawaiian, African. Asian, British and Europeanis an intermingling of many people. The island is basically sitting in the middle of the Atlantic Ocean with, nothing around it. And, legally, it is part of the territory called Saint Helena, Ascension, and Tristan da Cunha So, those are three islands, all British territories.

History of the island. It was discovered about 500 years ago by the Portuguese, initially. There were never many native inhabitants on the island. It was uninhabited, settled by the British, and it was originally given to the British East India Company to manage. Basically they would stop there, get fresh water, produce, food before continuing on their journey.

Meet Jonathan, Freddie and Emma, Giant Tortoises of St. Helena

From the sky I could see the view of this charming island located between South Africa and Brazil in the South Atlantic Ocean. Arriving into Jamestown, I was met by Robert, a Saints. "term used for locals born and raised in St Helena. It was sweltering hot, immediately I was swept away to a tour of the city's outskirts. I got on first names with Locals.

Attended services on Sunday Mass at St James Cathedral. It was Mother's Day. The children fashioned bouquets of flowers out of their gardens. I was honored to be given three bouquets!

Met the planet's oldest living land creature, Jonathan. A giant tortoise roamed the green lawn of the Governor's house. Even though, virtually blind from cataracts and has no sense of smell, Jonathan is 188-years-old.

Jonathan may be the oldest land creature currently living on the planet. Television crews, radio announcers, brides to be, people from around the world wants to see Jonathan.

He has trouble finding his food. So Teeny Lucy feeds him, carrots, cabbages, apples and more greens. Tortoises has a sharp tooth that can be a scythe that cuts the grass.

Teeny Lucy wore double rubber gloves to protect her hands. Then the tortoises go to their water shed.

There are two smaller tortoises named Emma and Freddie. As soon as they see Teeny Lucy, they walk closer. They will grab Jonathan's food. But Teeny Lucy makes sure Jonathan finishes his food before they get closer.

Our world is full of weird and wonderful creatures, many of which amaze scientists and non-scientists, alike. But is it true that a living tortoise could have started its life in the first half of the 19th Century?

I have not come to see the governor, nor the large brown hills which dot the pristine lawns. It's only when my charming guide Teeny Lucy, bangs on a large metal bowl, that all becomes clear. The hills rise swiftly towards us…the most beautiful remote island.

Exercises in Writing/ Journaling Class

Pasadena Cancer Society : enrolled in a writing group of 5 or more persons

Nov. 6, 2019 – Assignment: In twenty (20) minutes write a personal manifesto with a Surprise ending.

"I can't eat that, it's smells stinky fish" Mother: "Yes, you Can. Dried fish is Vitamin D. Eat the fried rice with garlic too. Garlic is good for your health." Grumbling, I eat it anyway.

Next day. Dad: "You can't drive the car today. We will use it for important errands." But dad, I have to go to Virginia's house. Our teacher will give us special tutoring classes on Geography and English.

Wiping the beads of perspiration on his forehead with his cotton handkerchief, he scratches his hair. He reluctantly says "Ohhh ok."

When I reached Virginia's house, I jostle through a small crowd, I wade through and Hi-five my friends. There's a cacophony of sounds. The "Victorola" turntable was playing a seventy eight (78) rpm plastic record of Elvis Presley.

Drinks were served in paper cups. Trays of snacks: spicy hot cheese curls, garlic peanuts and fried pork rinds with vinegar were passed around. We hopped skipped and jumped, gyrated our hips. We danced and laughed endlessly. No teacher, no lessons.

Next months to come: "Dad, I can't go to school today, dad. I have a slight tummy ache. I act, my hands, covering my stomach, it really hurts. As soon as dad leaves, I shout to my friend next door. "Pssssst...

Aurora, Danny... Let's play: we kick balls, made of papier-mache. I danced / played the limbo rock and rolled balls in a game of Chinese checkers.

Studying the cobbled stones of our sidewalk for insights, I found solace.

During my twenties, I grew up, and turned a complete round-about from craziness to seriousness.

My brother immigrated to America. He was my sanctuary, my rock. "I will follow you. I want to know how it feels to stand on American soil."

It was early morning. The rising sun bathe me in a golden light.

My knees locked, I cried a river of tears, my soul sighed. I can still feel the feathery touch of his cheeks. He embraced me tightly.

Softly he whispered to my inner ear: "WHITE LIES NO MORE to mom and dad." He knew all along about my weird acts, but stayed mum about it.

Remote Chatham Islands

Fascinated by remote and far away islands. A challenge to reach… Air Chatham flights are only twice a week. The flight took five hours from Wellington, New Zealand.

"One Pub, ONE takeaway shop, one general store," Nelson, a heavy set and solidly built man with a goatee, describes Chatham Islands. We were squeezed in the pub. Packed in the main island's town of Waitangi. It was Ladies' Darts Night. Tattooed men huddled over pints at the bar. Elderly couples in wool coats played slot machines. A group of women in jeans and rubber boots threw darts and high-fived.

North East Rekohu -

I met Cecile, the only Filipina on the island, who works at the Waitangi Fisheries.

She drove me around in her Utility Van. Traveling to the north eastern part of the island, we stopped at Ocean Mail Reserve, took the short walk to see the Chatham Island Aster which is in flower bloom November to March. We visited Hapupu National Historic Reserve—home of the Dendroglyphs (Moriori tree carvings) and in the afternoon we viewed the only accessible seal colony on the island at Point Munning.

Explored the site of an early whaling station, viewed a Sunderland Flying Boat being converted into a museum and visited the fishing settlement of Kaingaroa Village—where the British landed in 1791 on the HM Chatham sail.

North West Rekohu

We traveled northwest to Ohira Pt. to view the five-sided Basalt Columns (one of only two sites in the world). These quite unique slices of Taconic in the Rensselaer Plateau is a must see.

Tholeiitic to transitional alkalic basalt and basaltic tuff form widely separated but distinctive units within the Nassau Formation of late Proterozoic or Early Cambrian age. Then, we continued onto Port Hutt fishing village, explored the Moravian Missionaries stone cottage at Maunganui and stopped at Waitangi West on the coast where the rare Chatham Island Oyster Catchers are often seen wading.

Central Rekohu

Down a very good gravel road, we went to *Lois Croon* at Admiral Farm for a tour of her gardens. We passed a grotto of tall trees and grassland. We were in for a most pleasant surprise, including her extensive vegetable gardens, flowers that survive the fierce winds. We discovered some of the many Chatham Island plants. A variety pf shrubs, flowers, especially the Chatham islands forget-me-nots.

Since I was traveling solo, I arranged a luncheon with a group. The plants in the gardens have been carefully selected to attract butterflies, especially the Admiral butterfly. The gardens also contain old varieties of apples.

At Henga Reserve we took a walk through the bush and interesting Basalt limestone rock formations to a magnificent ocean beach.

North Rekohu

Searched for 30 million year old fossilized shark's teeth on the shores of the Te Whaanga Lagoon. We enjoyed a walk through Nikau Reserve and visit Wharekauri and Splattered Rock - an interesting volcanic rock formation.

South West Rekohu

Exploring the south west coast we stopped at the Chatham Island Parea (wood pigeon) on the edge of Tuku Nature Reserve. Visited the Waitangi shop, museum and River Onion Gallery - a local photographic artist's studio. What a discovery.

Kiribati Travels

Kiribati – celebrated my birthday with Elizabeth and Emmy, my new found friends at the ANZ bank - treated me at their home.

Kiribas people moves me and astonishes me. Most people forgoe the use of shoes or flip flops. They run and walk around with NO shoes, using bare feet over cement roads, stones, shells, at the airport, post office, the bank, market for long distances around town, day in and day out under the burning sun that can TORCH you.

We learn from their simple & undemanding life.

Just came from Fiji (my second time) and the islands of Kiribati, & Christmas island. I had an awesome time.

There are no rental cars, buses or taxis here at Christmas Island. Toroto, our driver with bushy eyebrows positioned a wood block as a step riser so that I can climb to my seat. The adventure continued-- I explored around the island in this truck, the South Pacific wind blowing my hair wildly.

Remote islands are my passion. The innocent students at the Tennessee Primary School in Kiritimati Christmas Island in the South Pacific were thrilled to be interviewed.

Maybe we haven't yet learned to analyze the world we live in. As a result, we are defined by sensation, by awe.

That's exactly what happened with these two ladies who are bank tellers. I was changing money at the ANZ Bank.

Met Emmy Tokia and Elizabeth Teeta Tewareka.

Elizabeth Teeta Tewareka: "What brings you here?

188

"I am an author, I want to write about your country."

Do you know anybody here?

No, I don't, but I know you now. Laughter. Are you alone? Yes, I am by myself.

Wow! Where are you staying?

In front at the Tarawa Boutique hotel.

You came here alone, you don't know anybody. You are very brave! Can we pick you up tomorrow? We will show you the island.

Sure thing, I will pay for gasoline, entrance fees, lunch, snacks, fruit, water. Ohhh and it's my birthday in two days.

The next day, they arrived in two cars with their families, eager to meet this solo crazy traveler.

Meet the Tarawans, Elizabeth, her pretty daughter Jewel & son Jeremiah. & Emmy Tokia her naughty daughter, Beeua. Here I was among them with a languid sense of time in the Gilbert islands.

By a marvelous sense of possibility, they now call me Auntie or Tita Odette. They picked up the term Tita because here in Tarawa they watch Filipino movies at their computer screen. Whoa! Dubbed in Kiribas language.

The next day, Elizabeth and Emmy gave me a birthday party – February 5, and toured me some more around the south island.

Meats usually come in frozen packages. We bought two huge family packs of cut up chicken. Elizabeth generously cooked fried chicken, steamed rice with soy sauce and spices, cut up watermelon, papaya, coconuts and mangoes. Soda drinks and fresh coconut juice. They ordered a birthday cake from a neighbor whose specialty is baked goods.

A huge chocolate cake with pink flowerets, white icing, tall candles were lit. Elizabeth's husband, Bauro strummed his guitar. Everybody sang Happy Birthday in Kiribas language.

What a thrill! Lots of fun, high-fives and laughter. A birthday celebration to remember.

Kiribati, pronounced Kiribas is an independent republic within the Commonwealth of Nations, located in the central Pacific Ocean, about 2,500 miles southwest of Hawaii. It is part of the division of the Pacific islands that is known as Micronesia. Kiribati consists of 33 coral islands divided among three island groups: the Gilbert Islands, the Phoenix Islands, and the Line Islands.

Most of the islands are atolls, ring-shaped islands with central lagoons. Of the 33 islands of Kiribati, only 21 are inhabited. Most of the population is concentrated in the Gilbert Islands and only one of the islands in Phoenix Group, Kanton Island is inhabited and three of the Line Islands are permanently inhabited. The capital of Kiribati is Tarawa, an atoll in the Gilbert Islands. I stayed in Tarawa for five nights.

The majority of the atolls are barely more than six meters above sea level and surrounded by barrier reefs creating picturesque lagoons for fishing, snorkeling, scuba diving, swimming and other water sports.

Year 2017 : I met Emmy Tokia while on a five day tour in the island of Kiribati.

Knowing Emmy's husband is a seaman, when covid-19 struck. I remembered to send text messages hoping to hear, her husband, Tokia Tominiko is safe.

Interview with local
Kiribas, Emmy Tokia

Via Private Messenger

Date: September 19, 2020 – during pandemic times.

Emmy: My husband, Tokia Tomiya is a **bosun**, ship's officer responsible for maintenance of the ship and its equipment. They have been on lockdown for nine months now, since January 2020. They are on their way now to Japan. We communicated via messenger. There are times the wi-fi connection is static and slow, but we always have a chat every day.

We have been married for 19 years, four boys and two girls. They study Math, Science, History and Geography. Our sons attend Sacred Heart college. My elder son is in form 6 and second son is in Form 5, third son went to secondary school TUC1in Form 3.

My elder daughter Beeua is in primary school while the other two are in pre school

She is an expert in climbing coconut trees bare foot.

Tokia's daughter Beeua was only six years old when he left Kiribati and set sail for the Pacific Ocean in January 2020 on an odyssey where his livelihood collided with a pandemic that has kept him adrift at sea and exiled from home.

For more than nine months, Tokia's days have been a monotonous blur of endless fishing on the Bulk Carrier, Nordmosel. They carry copper coil and sometimes timber. As of the interview date, they are in Japan delivering copper from Chile.

As long as there was seafood for their nets, including tuna, crab and squid, the crew members had to haul them in, clean and freeze them.

After Japan, the carrier *Nordmosel* is going to Australia.

Maybe from there, if lucky, the ship will sail back to Kiribati.

- Surely, Emmy and family will be jumping with joy and waving yellow ribbons and balloons.

Four years or so ago, Tokia brought home Filipino movies on compact disks. I played the disks on my laptop. Then the internet became more user friendly. I now download Filipino movies from either youtube or vidmate. I'm a fan of Nadine Resture and James Reid. I love movies and trailers "Bahala Na" "Tslk Back" and "You're Dead."

During my days off I love to spend my day with my kids.

My favorite food is the breadfruit. I prepare it in different ways. I dice it, then toss with oil and salt and bake it until browned. Steam and mash it. Pan fry chunks of breadfruit with oil. Or throw the whole breadfruit into a fire pit and remove it when the skin is black. I love to barbecue the whole fish, or cut into chunks and marinate it raw in vinegar with squeezed lemon. Or cook fish soup with tamarind base sauce. Fish and rice is the main food that we eat every day.

I'm the only daughter in my family with two brothers. We live not too far from each other and often gather for family visits.

I hope more tourists will come to visit my beautiful country, the island of Kiribati. Thank you Odette. Keep in touch!

Christmas Island/Kiritimati

Just came from Fiji (my second time) and the islands of Kiribati, & Christmas island. I had an awesome time.

Flights are only once a week.

Newly met friends, Bengt Enbuske and Gunar Bjork from Sweden also stayed here.

We had a grand time exchanging travel explorations. Bengt has traveled to all the 193 countries in the United Nations list.

Here began our long friendship. Bengt lives in Overtornea, a municipality in Sweden. I visited him twice to experience the Midnight Sun in July. Then by LUCK in late October, I witnessed the dancing Northern Lights, Aurora Borealis right in his back yard. So blessed and how fortunate!

There are no rental cars, buses or taxis here at Christmas Island.

Peter Ignatius Toroto, our driver with bushy eyebrows positioned a wood block as a step riser to his truck so that I can climb to my seat. The adventure continued -- I explored around the island in this van / truck, the South Pacific wind blowing my hair wildly. Stayed at the four star Cook Islands hotel right on the beach.

There is only one gas station, one grocery store owned by a guy from Denmark. He fell in love with the island and has lived here for 28 years.

We drove around the village of Banana, one Catholic church, one coffee store to have a drink.

Beach naupaka, a common shrub dominates the vegetation on much of the island interspersed with tree heliotrope, typical on a Hawaiian island.

I wanted to rent a car, but there were only two cars available and it was being used for scheduled deliveries. So, I went back to the hotel, had drinks by the shore, enjoyed the sunset.

Remote islands are my passion. The innocent students at the TENNESSEE PRIMARY SCHOOL in Kiritimati Christmas Island in the South Pacific were thrilled to be interviewed.

My "Comadre" Perla

I first met Perla in 1974, 43 years ago. "Mare ko" (short for term of endearment "*comadre*" or BFF Best Friends Forever)

We had an instant bond. She had an abounding good nature that was the true mark of her personality.

Over the years, we became closer and closer. We like to think we were twins in our likes with different avenues. When my son Robert was born, I knew she would be the perfect Godmother, "Ninang Perla."

Seven years ago, she proudly announced, I bought my cemetery plot at Forest Lawn complete with services. You will deliver a Eulogy in church. I said What? Eulogy? You must be kidding. You want me to reveal all your secrets?

Eulogy delivered:

Let me tell you our secrets today:

Perla was my personal shrink. Life can be crazy at times. Problems and obstacles I confided to her. She offered heartfelt possible solutions.

We went on many trips and were compatible travelers. She snored so loud, I had to use ear plugs or send her to the next room. On the other hand, I talked and shouted in my sleep, She would get up immediately, cover my mouth and wake me up.

We were daring. In our early thirties, we went to Jamaica. I wanted to write about the nude beach. I told her, if I write about it, I have to experience it, come with me. At first she was shy but finally I convinced her. We had boobs then, not anymore.

195

We dined, danced, name it we did it. One time she was jumping up and down high in the air while dancing to the tune of Kung fu Fighting. In the caldron of loud noises, she shouted, "Call 911 if I have a heart attack here."

We were partners in real estate, bought and sold homes. She had numerous clients with repeated business. She was the only realtor, they trusted completely.

She had a Passion for piano. Perla was the most caring and patient of teachers. Her musical gifts flourished most strongly through her contact with pupils.

I was one of her students. I would come for lessons. We would sit and play, but after five or ten minutes, we began to chat. The piano lesson was forgotten. We preferred to go for Happy Hour in Hollywood and have a good time.

Her legacy will be in the lives of the students she taught and groomed. Some of whom are now concert pianists.

Her community service at St. Dominic's church and other charitable organizations was immeasurable. Legion of Mary, Rosary groups, playing the piano during Wednesday novenas to Our of Mother Help, preparing sandwiches for the homeless and giving communion to the elderly in convalescent homes.

The Love of her life is her family. While hospitalized, Bing, Jovi, Tricia and Joy took off from work and watched her every single day, round the clock attending to her needs, talking to the doctors and checking medications.

She was especially proud of her grandchildren, Alano, Shena, Dominic, Kaili and Maya.

Perla, my darling, I stand here today to give tribute.

During the final hour, Vic stood by your side, caressing your face, touching tenderly your forehead. In a low tune he sung your favorite song "The Shadow of Your Smile."

The whole family were at your bedside. Your favorite piano tunes Debussy, Mozart, "Claire de Lune" was playing background music. The angels came and took you by the hand, somehow easing all your pain and fears. The light was bright Filled with warmth and love.

You were treading through the forests, floating on the clouds as the angels guided you along crossing you over into Paradise, then to heaven, your final resting state.

It was heart breaking to witness all these. The good side is you are no longer in pain. You are now in God's glory.

I love you.

Chapter 9

Day to Dawn

A Letter About Poetry

Dec. 12, 2011

Dear Odette,

Thank you so much for sharing your poems. Poetry is such an intimate glimpse into a person's soul. I want you to know that the one gift I asked my husband to buy me for my birthday, was one of your volumes of poetry. He chose Unguarded Thoughts and I am enjoying one poem at a time whenever I have a spare moment (which isn't nearly as often as I would like).

It's amazing how poetry can evoke the memory of a place so vividly in just a few words. It can truly capture the essence. I just read "A Red Moon in Carcassonne." We were there for Bastille Day in 1984 so I too have vivid memories of Carcassonne at night.

Reading your poems reminded of my 19 year old self when I studied abroad in Mexico City. Everything was so intense for me – my first big adventure in a foreign country and my first exposure to poverty. I was so moved by the plight of the women begging while nursing babies.

I wanted so much to write a poem about that experience. I played around with words in my head for weeks, but never put them in paper. I imagined myself writing a poem about the women in every country I would ever visit.

Alas! My dreams of poetry came to naught. I never even wrote one word down on paper. I'm very happy with Photographic and diary / journal writing, the path I've taken, but your poems make me wistfully remember that budding poet I wanted to be when I was 19.

Happy Holidays to you wherever you maybe during the Christmas season.

Debbie Kightlinger.

Wandering since 1985

Wandering Since1985 –
Every Passport Stamp

Thu, Apr 16, 2020

Riza Rasco mentioned you in a comment in Every Passport Stamp.
Founder: Stefan Krasowski, board member of Travelers Century Club.

Riza Rasco The Philippine Global Explorers has for its members some of the most traveled Filipinos, who travel the world with their Philippine passports, foreign passports, or both. There are now a few who have been to more than 100 UN countries and who are also members of recognized international travelers network such as Travelers Century Club (TCC) and Nomad Mania (NM).

Odette Aquitania Ricasa is currently our top Filipino traveler having traveled to 180+ UN and 290+ TCC countries.

There's AJ Peregrino, Raoul Bernal, Rambi Francisco, Luisa Yu, amongst others who are all here in EPS. PGE members who travel exclusively with their Philippine passports.

Include Andie Andros (112 UN), Jon Opol (135 UN) and Dominador Buhain (~160 UN and 260 TCC), the owner of REX Book Stores and prominent figure in the Philippine publishing industry.

"Starenka" Anna Galikova

Written while in Nitra, Slovakia April 2016

Elegant and graceful
Grandma in relation to my daughter in law Christine
Admirably molded

Indescribable divinity
Within which makes me fall back
Make way for more laughter with her

We sat in the terrace
Her swing with yellow sunflower cushions on our backs
Presented her my books
And purple paisley printed satin scarf as my gift

With fantasies of a massage
She immediately called her masseuse

Few words of English
She made me lay down on the table
Kneaded and pressed her fingers on my back, neck
Ooh! All my tightness released

I slept in the living room of her lovely home
In the village of Nitra

Certain the door was open to let the breeze in

Woke me up "Good morning, Sleep well?"

Her eyes are coin colored
Sometimes green, sometimes blue, at times gray

Wearing her black rubber boots
A smile flashed as she water hosed her garden
So green that I could hide in front of Jack's beanstalk
Cauliflower, tomatoes, basil, green beans, cabbage, onions

Her kitchen, born to bake
Filled with sacks of flour, crystal bottles of preserved peaches,
Strawberry jams, orange peels, pickled onions, name it she preserved
Variety bags of curly pasta, angel hair, tortellini, rigatoni, lasagna

Her garden is unique because it includes a salad or a wrap
Carefully mashing potatoes
Cheeks glowed "Eat, eat, everything is home grown."

Detailed labor of love in her box of crocheted
Needlework and cross stitched
Filled with generosity, she let me choose my present
Doilies she crocheted when fingers had more dexterity

Today is your 93rd birthday, Starenka Anna
To a super grandma who gave us, your family happiness

Now we have grown with the newest addition
A baby doll "Lucy" who makes Richie and all of us
Go crazy

With her newly learned words
Naughty actions as she bounces around
Waves her hand to everybody she shows off

God bless you

Wishing you all the happiness and LOVE

Slovak language: ***Starenka Anna Galikova***

Elegantný a elegantný

Babička vo vzťahu k mojej dcére Christine
Obdivuhodne tvarovaný
Nepopierateľné božstvo

Vďaka ktorému ma spadnem späť
Uvoľnite sa s ňou viac smiechu
Sedeli sme na terase

Jej hojdačka s vankúšmi na chrbte
Ukázala mi moje knihy
Satan šál ako môj darček

S fantáziami masáže
Okamžite zavolala jej masérku
Niekoľko slov v angličtine

Urobila ma ležať na stole
Mihne a prsty prstami na chrbte, na krk
Oh! Všetka moja tesnosť bola prepustená

Spal som vo veľkej miestnosti svojho krásneho domu
V obci Nitra
Niektoré dvere boli otvorené

Prebudila ma "Dobré ráno, spia dobre?"

Má oči s mincami
Niekedy zelená, niekedy modrá, niekedy šedá
S gumovými čižmy

V jej záhrade zazrel úsmev
Tak zelená, že by som sa mohla skrývať pred fazuľou Jackovho
Karfiol, zelené fazuľky, kapusta, cibuľa

Jej kuchyňa, narodil sa na pečenie
Plnené vreckami z múky, kryštálové fľaše z konzervovaných broskýň,
Jahodové džemy, pomarančové šupky, nakladaná
cibuľka, pomenujte to, že si zachovala

Jej záhrada je jedinečná, pretože obsahuje šalát alebo zábal
Opatrne mačiace zemiaky, jej tváre svietili "Jedzte,
jedzte, všetko je doma pestované."
Podrobná práca lásky v krabičke s háčkovanou,
výšivkou a krížovým prešitím

Vyplnená s veľkorysosťou mi umožnila vybrať môj darček.
Čarodejnice, ktoré si háčikovala, keď mali prsty väčšiu šikovnosť
Dnes je vaša 93. narodeniny, Stařenka Anna

Pre super babičku, ktorá nám dala, vaše rodinné šťastie
Teraz sme vyrástli s najnovším prírastkom
Detská bábika "Lucy", ktorá robí Richieho a všetkých nás

Blázni so svojimi novo naučenými slovami
Nezbedné akcie, keď sa odráža

Vláka ruku všetkým, čo ukáže

Boh ti žehnaj
Želám vám všetko šťastie a lásku

Cocos (Keeling) Islands

Cocos islands is in the middle of the Indian Ocean - four hour flight from Perth, Australia by Virgin Atlantic Airways. The airport at Cocos is open only two times a week. During other days, the airport is turned to a golf course. It has only one runway.

Population 240. I waited at the airport. It was a very hot day. Hotels are expensive run $450 per night. No choice because there were only 3 hotels at Cocos. West Island Cocos Keeling (W.I.C.K.) Café serves the finest Cocos Malay cuisines. They had one dining table covered with plastic flowery prints and six steel backed chairs. There were two souvenir kiosks.

The streets were very clean. It takes only 4 hours to tour the whole island, size 6.5 Square miles.

Occasionally small crabs crossed the streets.

There was only one small supermarket, post office, bank and the island's two cafes. In true island style, opening hours are usually a few hours each day, or in the case of the tavern, whenever a plane arrives. opening days and times varied and posted on the front door, open only up to 3:00PM.

Sea Salt is made by passionate artisans who evaporate sea water from the most remote, exotic and pristine island paradises on Earth. 100 % per cent Natural. It is the only sea salt made and exported from Australian Indian Ocean territories.

Breakfast hang out was at "Maxi's by the Sea" restaurant. Specialty: Filipino fried rice.

Home Island: I had to take the fast express boat to reach Home Island approximately forty minute boat ride. On arrival, taxi transportation was by go-truck, similar to golf carts.

At the Pulu Cocos museum I had to knock at the caretaker's door to open the door. Inside the museum. I was the only tourist :). What a surprise! The museum had an impressive collection: bows and arrows, guns and canyon balls, coins from the olden times and intricately embroidered traditional Malay costumes.

There was one gasoline station. We passed by the sign Indian Ocean Group Training Association - Shire of Cocos (Keeling) Island Parks Australia.

Nek Su, is the builder, fisherman, grandfather, imam and elder of Home Island, the only Muslim island in Australia. The link with their Muslin faith is a central part of life on Home Island, for young and old. Nek Su and other elder statesmen teach the boys on the island the ways of their Cocos Malay culture, sailing, dancing and building Jukong traditional boats to maintain a link with their past. He mentions most Home Islanders have been to Mecca.

The Campong life: We Cocos Malay people live in a peaceful family oriented community that evolved, largely isolated from the rest of the world.

We drove around lush palms, serene and quiet. Afternoon tea with Nor and Alsha. They ask "Why are you traveling alone. Are you not afraid?" "Sometimes I am afraid, but I want to travel more."

Walking on the Atolls – Cocos (Keeling) Island

Tropical island
Palm tree lined beaches, aquamarine waters

Sand whiter than snow

Hidden deep in the Indian Ocean
Between Perth, Australia and Sri Lanka
A dream destination for all things aquatic

Twenty seven coral islands that form two atolls
The northern atoll is one single island
A national park and seabird rookery

Horse shoe shaped
At the southern atoll
A picture perfect lagoon

Charles Darwin and his controversial theory
Atolls and coral formation

The only place in the world
Where I walked the entire atoll on foot

Developed for coconut plantations
Due to isolation
Free of commercialism and tourism traps

A jewel in the Indian Ocean
Descendants of original workers
Brought to the island to work on the palm plantations

Life is just too good to leave
Whenever a plane arrives
Golf course is turned into a runway

Simplistic lifestyle

Cocos at a slow pace
Anything but the rush of adrenalin
It happens when it happens

Doors unlocked
Keys left in the ignition

Camping excursions
You organize?

Expect the rest of the island to turn up
"Salam" greeting when entering the outdoor dining tables
"How 'ya going mate? Take a seat."

The clove smell of kretek cigarettes wafts through the air
Mixed with the frying garlic, onions, eggplant, okra, spices
Spitting from the wok

Highlighting the mash of cultures

Zanzibar, To See it Once

Zanzibar island lies in the Indian Ocean, 23 miles off the coast of East Central Africa. Area 600 square miles. Population: 720,000. Can be reached by Ferry from Tanzania or a twenty five minute flight.

It was a pleasantly cool October. I rode a ferry amidst turquoise waters of Zanzibar's Mnemba atoll.

We sailed steadily on a wooden boat (the dhow) with sails the shape of a crescent moon, gently we glided to the harbor. We spotted a school of dolphins.

From Tanzania, us non-residents paid in U.S. dollars for entrance fees. Time tables and prices were displayed on boards outside the office.

Magical place: The mainland Stone Town a maze of narrow alleys leading into secret courtyards, ornate balconies from crumbling manor houses. Oriental bazaars hum with the sounds of locals bargaining.

The carved doors Stone town Zanzibar –You will get lost in the maze of narrow alley ways. Don't worry, everybody does.

To see it once. Zanzibar coffee house serving coffee from its own plantation at the East African Rift Valley. One of the oldest buildings is the Zanzibar coffee house.

Walked to the former slave market. During the Arab rule, the slave trade passed the port of Zanzibar. The dark period in an underground chamber showed chains bolted to the concrete. An insightful tour. On to Emerson Spice Hotel, an ornate tea house.

An Arab archway leading to a white walled square, with the sound, call to prayer were coming from the walls of a mosque.

When the heat is up, we get our daily dose of coconut juice. Admiring the masterful Arabic design of the intricate, colorful front doors to the House of Wonders, a palace built for the Sultan of Zanzibar.

Weather beaten shacks line the roads. Women in bright colorful skirts with matching head scarves pulled bundles of clothing. Watched them swap gossip and jokes, hang out washing and watched the world go by.

Children took our hand to invite us and join their games in the Indian townhouses.

Long bearded old men in white skull caps play the game of *bao* or dominoes with a shy smile.

A simple villa set right on the shore of Page beach, owned by a Japanese lady, Suki. Palms trees shade the white powdery sands. We arrive in the morning, the lagoon is yonder to the reef. In the afternoon, the tide is up and water is deep. A slight rain fell while we took our siesta.

We were served with delicious Swahili cuisine. Katchori fried mashed potato balls with a lot of spices, ginger, chile and lime . Washed down with freshly pressed sugar cane juice.

Crowded Darjani market with symmetrical piles of oranges, woven baskets heaping with spices and enormous chunks of fresh fish arranged under palm thatched canopies is where I shopped.

Imaginings of Zanzibar

Porters maneuvering wheelbarrows
Shout *"Hodi, hodi"* (let me pass)

As dusk falls
Arabic coffee sellers stroll along the streets
Sweaty in their grey blazers
Hanging from a yoke across their shoulder
Swinging bronze coffee pots

Stone Town comes alive
Stalls of fried fish and katchori
Slices of chicken on skewers

Hurricane lamps illuminating piles of squid and octopus
Mounds of spicy toasted or fried chips

Sugar cane pressed through an antique machine
Funneled into glasses
Cool and so refreshing

Young boys strip and leap off the sea

The Palace Museum
House clothing from the days of Sultans

A dedicated room to Princess Salme
Daughter of Sultan
Rumors say, she eloped with a German business man

Anglican church has a crucifix
Where the explorer David Livingstone's heart is buried

The smell of cloves in the old quarter

Swahili people have been welcoming strangers
Whenever ships arrives at the harbor

They regard hospitality to strangers as a sacred duty
Early Arabs came to trade
Ivory, silks, gold, spices, animal skins and horns

A whiff of exhaust fumes
Mixed occasionally with the aroma of spices
Awakens keen sense of smell
Camlur's Indian restaurant
Enjoy the privilege

Pay homage
Freddie Mercury
Influential Rock group "Queen" was born here
Famous song "We are the Champions"
His father worked for the government

Their family moved to England when Freddie was Eighteen
Bohemian Rhapsody important to my musical memories

Chapter 10

Holding Glasses and Clinking

Falala-la Niue

Niue is a tiny island between Samoa and Tonga, three hour flight from Auckland, two hour time difference. Be sure to check your time when booking your flights. Two flights per week. Take a lot of cash or New Zealand dollars. Did not find an ATM machine. Surprisingly okay with internet access. Population: 1,640.

Stayed at an Airbnb: Petite Hatava in Alofi, owner: Tanya

A trip to the Niue Information Centre and I was able to fine tune, book tours and shape my days.

People don't come to Niue for its beaches and resorts—there's only one sandy beach and one resort. There is No Sand – this is no Club Med. If you are looking for sandy beaches, touristy places, Niue is not it. Surely I enjoyed eating on the reef ☺

You are never a stranger. Everyone waves!

Tuapa Village, watch the outriggers come in with fresh fish caught for the day.

Church on Sunday followed by Buffet at Wash Away café.

Visit to Niue National Council of Women Weaving Group, and dinner at Matavi Resort and Ebony carving tours.

Dinner at Talo's Restaurant and Bar with friends made along the way.

Niue has the best Honey, that's why locals are sweet.

You can buy duty free from the Bond Store in Alofi, but don't go overboard.

Have an evening drink in one of the bars looking over the sea. Watch the sun go down at Crazy Uga, Matavi Resort or the Sails Bar at Coral Gardens. It's a chance to meet the locals and to see the whales which are regularly spotted just off the coast.

There's no public transportation on the island except for a shuttle service through the resort ($10. round trips). Otherwise, the island is so small. I walked where I needed to go or hitched a ride.

Locals offer to pick you up on the road sometimes without even putting your thumb out.

The few visitors go to the Rock of Polynesia, fly for its exceptional diving and snorkeling, admiring its unbelievable geography, coastal views, its vibrant culture and friendly people.

The island has no rivers and it filters all rainwater through its limestone coral base. This results in no runoff to cloud up the surrounding waters.

Whether a diver or a snorkeler, you'll get crystal clear displays of colorful reef and marine life at all times.

As a coral atoll, Niue Island has sheer drop-offs underwater within 50 meters out from the shore. This means the water is deep enough for all of the big marine animals to swim within view from the coastline.

I saw whales every single day and heard them singing.

A Sunday service with powerful multi-harmony singing from the congregation at Alatele Ekelesia, where women were all dressed in white.

A morning walk with Dan who shared the spiritual and ecological knowledge of his refuge.

We saw sea snakes over colorful coral.

Enduring memories:

The warm, generous and knowledgeable Tanya and her staff at Hatava Petite airbnb and my neighbor Robert who works in Vanuatu. Exchanged travel stories. He works with the Dept. of Fisheries in Vanuatu.

Old ladies serving arrowroot porridge, pork buns and papaya salad at the early morning market at Alofi opens 6:00 am.

Drink a never-ending supply of the freshest coconut water you'll ever taste

Soon, I was grabbing them out of the trees, Tanya helped chopping them open, and slurping them down like we did in the Philippines.

Every day I had sweet, fresh coconut water bursting from its shell like a fire hydrant.

Coupled with plenty of papaya (called "Paw paw" by the locals), coconut water, and friendly local offerings. I only bought food for two days. Papayas fell off trees!

In addition to the caves, there were plenty of tidal chasms, meandering channels, and coral pools to photo shoot.

If you look around the corner from Avaiki cave, you'll have the chance to feel like royalty snorkeling the aqua blue waters of a lavish cave. As they say Where Ancestor Niuean kings once bathed.

Niue comes with laid back island way of life. You might be familiar with this if you have visited an island country or a state like Hawaii in the past.

Niueans don't need anything new or fancy to be happy. And, in no time, you'll find yourself adapting to this way of life.

O. Ricasa Corona Virus Shock - Oil on canvas - Year 2020

Extraordinary Shock Covid-19

March 18, 2020 – A day the whole world will remember

We faced an invisible beast, Wuhan China
– where it said to have originated

The whole world on Lock down
France, Italy, Spain, Australia, Sudan, Egypt, Indonesia, Singapore
Malaysia, the Philippines, Chad, the Kingdom of Saudi Arabia

In the hospitals
Doctors tested, intubated, extubated patients

Ventilators on the rise
Nurses, front liners risked contamination
But pledged to serve

Personal Protective Equipment (PPE) desperately needed

Schools and Universities closed through the whole country
Continue classes online will be the norm

Work from home moms and dads had to be tech savvy
Four million Unemployment claims
Dr. Fauci, expert on infectious diseases
Covid-19 fast pace contaminating

Churches ordered closed
Easter Sunday masses were online streaming
Drive-in religious rites

Deserted Downtown Los Angeles, Grand Central Market
Fashion District, Staples Center,
Hollywood walk of Fame, empty of crowds

Missed proximity to my fellow Angelenos
Our downtown, China town, Korea town, Mexican Olvera Street

Bustling chaos and endless cacophonous hum have always calmed me
Without it, I am restless, but I stay safe

I turn to my computer
The news is grim
Our world is upside down

Quarantined – total lock down up to May 15, 2020 possibly later
Tech issues plague

Jobless filings, at the same time protesting
Social distancing six feet apart at home but together

In public, urged through summer – that's July 2020!
Theaters, Banquet halls, mom and pop
stores all suffering economically

These days, it seems like almost everything is uncertain

What about your savings, in the long haul
Your retirement, 401-K
Trapped at home

Waiting for the all-clear
You have to wear a mask – no kidding

Move around a little bit
No Open house, no touring of homes, inspection video on line
Buying real estate properties

Good luck!

A Global Pandemic

Compulsory to wear masks even while driving
All travel is a nightmare, even with recycled air filters

Flying is no more, nobody's good time
Hand sanitizers were placed by all door posts

In the hopes that Corona NEVER would come
Caravans to greet Happy Birthday
Happy Anniversary without leaving the car

Blowing their car horns, serenading by saxophone
Holding College classes outside? Maybe

Playful children standing on the back of their dogs

All of a sudden we were creative

Living rooms were turned to imaginary swimming pools

Many gig workers won't get benefits
Broke, desperate and pleading for help

Fruit swaps, produce, seeds of community
Imaginary fitness centers
Hanging on chandeliers

Bands and Orchestras live streaming
Lucky are those holding jobs
Live updates as they stare on their screens

Sneezing or coughing is embarrassing
Leading to a conclusion contracting the corona

Away in a flash to groceries and supermarkets
Hoarded frozen meats, canned goods
Most important of all, the precious toilet paper
Limited to three rolls per customer

Quarantined more than forty-five days or maybe more
Governor Newsome will announce the flattening of the curve

Mayor Garcetti and crew work tirelessly

In the magic of togetherness
Home bound, Shelter in place
Rediscovering connection with our family
Tuning in to Facebook and Instagram

Chat with friends from faraway places
We begin to realize and pray
For Kindness and compassion

Those who lost their loved ones
Waiting in the morgue

Social distancing at the funeral
Bodies lined up against the wall
Buried by the hundreds

President Trump's daily briefings

Dr. Fauci, expert on disease standing by
Next to warn us

A lift on the lock down too soon
Will bring a second wave of Pandemic corona

Dating Guru lays out new rules
Watch Netflix again?

Tough times and tight spaces
Our true colors shine through
Whether we're alone or together
Sacred relationships still together?

Covid-19 restrictions
Leave mourners with grief, guilt and unfinished conversations
Cautionary tale of buying a hotel after lock down lifted?

Craft together, cook together, follow social distancing
Quarolini, vodka mixed with my tears, on a cocktail evening

Visit your closet museum
Found a Nokia flip phone?
Fuji instamatic disposable cameras?
A beep-beep pager, computer diskettes?

Confusion
Even President Trump and the White House are not safe
Looking straight to the moon, I winked

Peace has replaced the impending doom
A potent reminder of what I'm worth
Waiting for an Epiphany out of an Epidemic

O. Ricasa On the Stage Water color 1999

On the Stage

Discover the countries thru the eyes of a local

Not just to write

Live it

The world is my classroom

Still dancing dreamily

Three-four beats of Last Dance

The small repertoire

I can draw expressions of your face

Doodle scenery on a scratch pad

Impulses of century Before Christ (B.C.)

The need to think

Why do we behave carelessly?

Twenty first (21st) Century "GO" vacations

Immersions in language, traditions

Festivals, celebrations, spiritual rituals

Pepe in Guadalajara playing his harp

Laura from Vienna plays the violin

Smell the waft of garlic cuisines

Our throat goes loose with happiness

Words flow

Smile at strangers

Laugh loud with delight

When angry or depressed

Lips freeze into formality

Chest puffed out with self-importance

Spine stiff with offense

Sri Temple

Riotously bright Hindu temple

Viti-Levu island, Fiji offerings

Dravidian style

Wooden carvings of deities speaking in tones

Colorful coat

Impressive ceiling frescos

Devotees flocked

India's best sacred traditions

Recited the Rudra Mantra

Blessings of Lord Shiva

Absorb quietly the beauty

Rejuvenated

Making sense of it all

Bowing with hands folded

Making a wish

You are by my side

Fascination with Caravaggio

With Angela, trailing Michelangelo Merisi da Caravaggio
Die Pinakotheken, museum in Munich

Fascination took over
A turbulent life
Always involved in a brawl
Rome, Naples, Malta and Sicily

Combining a realistic observation of the human state
Physical and emotional, dramatic use of lighting

The Fortune Teller
Mario being cheated on by a gypsy girl
Cheating was regular in the fifteenth century?

The Cardsharps, all sights were fixed
The limits of Art can be its powers
Or an invention
A genre of trickery pictures

Two persons cheats and one deceive
Playing cards with the boys
Another person peeps at the victim's hand
Signals to his accomplice
Palms a concealed card from under his belt

The setting intrigues the viewer
Card games during the time of Van Gogh?

Outlawed from Rome
For killing Ranuccio Tomassoni
A pimp to the prostitutes
Reveals his notorious life

Artists minds can be convoluted
At times mimicked

The Maldives

Pearl of the Indian Ocean

Twenty (26) ring-shaped atolls

More than one thousand coral islands

Turquoise blue waters, swaying palm trees

Rode the shuttle bus to Hulhumale island

Met Irene, a Filipina from Cebu

Charming waitress at the Cinema Paradiso restaurant

Coconut, fish, Chapati, breadfruit, cassava

Heavy rainfall under my yellow parasol

While walking around at Hangnaamedhoo

A small island, finished walking around in twenty minutes

More pounding rains

Stayed at Green Leaf Hotel

Honeymooners in Maui style sarongs

Next day

A speed boat to Olhuveli Beach

Happy hour sipping Long island teas

Clattering of dishes

Chef sweet spicy barbeques, grilled trevally fish

The capital, Malé, has a busy fish market

Sellers in black rubber boots frantic with fly swatters

Continually hosing water

Electronic Shops, Brand name mini malls,
super markets on the main road

Majeedhee Magu, and seventeenth 17th-century

Hukuru Miskiy (Friday Mosque)

Elaborate carved white coral

Hard to say goodbye to fun

The sun baked every inch of my body

Chapter 11

Entering a Reverie

El Nido, Philippines Snake island

El Nido, Philippines

From Puerto Princesa
Took the public van to El Nido
Stopped by so many villages for food and photos

Wow! the Underground Caves
Different and enchanting world
Vibrant coral reefs
Stunning ancient limestone cliffs

I still dream about it
"Welcome to Paradise"
Serene, spectacular, too good to forget
Crystal clear waters
Pure white sandy beaches
Marine and wildlife

Snake island, Helicopter island, Miniloc island
Amazed to share your secret no more

A jeepney was waiting to take us to the Green View Airbnb
Gorgeous beach huts perched over the water

Rustic rural vibes of narrow streets
Humming, roaring with tricycles, motorcycle taxis *(habal habal)*

When I looked up
Lush forests with hundred species of birds
I saw the Last Ecological frontier
El Nido

I love the hectic life but laid-back character
The sea shore at my feet with its thousand shades of blue

Enclosed by ancient limestone mountains
Adoring the orange turning lavender sunsets

Mountains continue to rise
Island's whimsical shapes with razor-sharp edges
The hidden ways as our canoe glided the Underground River

Dark and mysterious forty minute canoe ride
Wearing our protective neon orange life jackets
Bats flew over our orange safety helmets

Befriended two men from Medinaceli, Spain
Joselito and Manolo
Surprised to find out I have traveled to their city

Why not?
I have been to Spain fifty-one times
Believe it or not
Joselito took my friend Gilda's arm
Manolo took my arm, we squirmed, danced the Zumba, Cha-cha-cha

Soft, sun lit and breezy in the afternoons
I still feel the warmth
The sun is your muse

The kind local's hospitality with open arms ready to help
Going about in their daily routine

Selling grilled pork on skewers, fried bananas,
yams in brown sugar syrup
Pineapple slices, yellow ripe mangoes, sour green mangoes
Spanish bread, coconut bread, taro bread

We sipped fresh coconut juice in the open shell, carved out the meat
Men selling plastic pouches to protect
cameras and cell phones from water
Striped sun dresses, straw hats, sunglasses and insect repellants

Backpackers maneuvering their drones chuckle in laughter

Not wanting to leave
Left my low carbon footprint

O. Ricasa Taal Volcano erupted Acrylic on Canvas 2016

242

An A to Z of Planned Travel

From the fine Laderach chocolates of Solothurn, Switzerland
To the narrow twisting lanes of the casbah, Algiers, Algeria

Forget YouTube
Just revisit the bare necessities of crawling
Running into wild affairs around Spain
Cartagena elevates your heart rate

Do some spirit drills in Alcaniz, Spain
Puerto de Beceite with Javier and Ana

Dive into Kanyakumari where the three oceans meet
Bay of Bengal, Indian Ocean and Pacific Ocean

Hit the bar at Alchemikas, Vilnius
The Royal Casino in Belarus

Driving on the left side of the road Hadrian's wall, Scotland
Pick up kudos at the Kamenge Youth center, Bujumbura, Burundi

Slather coconut oil with a Thai massage at Udon Thani

Take on digital culture in Lastarria, Santiago, Chile
How to sound like a film buff

The last morsel of a caldereta with *aliolis*
(garlic) in smoked butter in Gijon

Phenomenal speed crunching data of apps
iPhone manages life with Siri
Having wolfed down chicken Mandi in Xa'naa, Yemen,

Tocino del cielo. roasted suckling pig sliced with a plate in Segovia
Flea markets *rastro* and vintage old world Zaragoza, Spain
Sixty three million years ago
Dinosaur (*iche nites*) foot prints traceable in the Asturias region

Reverting back to a past era
Many times to get lost to find your way is a good thing

I wanted to find the real city
Experience through the eyes of someone who lives there

I wanted to meet Spaniards
Discover the castanets, the twirls of the Flamenco dance
The guitarist Andres Segovia, music beyond the Beatles
The Human Tower (*Castellers*) La Rambla, Barcelona
The vibes of captain caveman beards in the caves of Guadix

Through the forest fields, steep stones
pilgrimage to Medjugorje, Bosnia

Playing the piano, Jupiter Hotel, Addis Ababa, Ethiopia
Palmyra, intense coffee with ground cardamom
Poured from a Syrian metal pot

Devour fried eggs with duck foie gras at Bar Tarragona
Ash reshteh Persian noodle soup in Esfahan, Iran

Oven baked *Takoula* bread in Timbuktu

Hummus and garbanzo beans in Beirut, Lebanon

Cyclists on a vintage bicycle
Sporting a hefty waxed moustache, Dunedin, New Zealand

Star Wars is back with prop light sabers, Berber village Tunisia

Anxiety riding the ferry boat from Dar es
Salaam to Zanzibar, Tanzania

Awww! Pinched by the powerful claws of a coconut crab in Vanuatu

Riding the sailboat, Dal Lake, Srinagar

Dog sledding at Svalbard, Norway

Luck at every traveler's bucket list
Northern lights in Overtornea, Sweden

Dancing lemurs of Madagascar
Color of blue cotton candy, flat footed boobies, Galapagos Islands

Ceremonial burying the dead Tana Toraja, Sulawesi Indonesia

Barefoot walk at Lake Titicaca, La Paz, Bolivia

Grueling bus ride to Olkhon island, Lake Baikal, Siberia

Squat on the floor, Langar food ration at the
Golden Temple, Amritsar, India

Plod erupted Taal volcano, Philippines

Skywalker at the Luke Sky walker ranch
Marin County, California

Am film crazy
Oscar award winning movie " Parasite"
Director Korean Bong Joon-ho

Hollywood is my hometown
The Entertainment capital of the World

Believe in your Dreams

Lalibela, Along Side Saturday Market

Struggling to believe reality

Enchanted, an unseen world

Journey into the Past

Saturday, Sunday market in Lalibela

Local community coming down from their villages

Walking fifteen miles without shoes

Consonants in Amharic sounds

In the middle of the town

Spread out over a big dirt area

Villagers set up tarps overlapping each other

Temporary stalls made of eucalyptus poles and textiles

Spices and heavenly scent of frankincense

Some just sit under umbrellas to hide from the sun.

Others spread out their grains, fruits or vegetables

On tarps or blankets on the ground

Used car tires, basketballs, footballs, sports uniforms

It's hot, dusty and chaotic

Thousands of people as far as your eyes can see

Selling everything imaginable

From firewood to tablet or blocks of precious salt

Art works carved out of wood, on canvas, printed or painted

Coffee pots, tea pots, stainless steel cook wares, ceramics
Blaring drums, guitars and accordions
Dry, dusty, full of donkeys

A living breathing African town
Children encircle us
Any used clothing, shoes, pens, writing pads

Stepped back in time
Thousands of pilgrims in white robes
Biete Maryam, Biete Meskel, Biete Denegal

I have spoken to some of the most welcoming people
Local Afrikaans, that I have met anywhere in the World

Felt as though leaving this city tomorrow
Feels more of a wrench in my stomach

The Nauru Experience

Nauru – the LEAST visited island in the world, because of strict visa entry requirements.

The island is only 16 kilometers long. Annoying because it lacks places to swim. I managed to dip in the waters somehow at the Community Boat Harbor, close to the Menen Hotel, where I stayed. I scraped my right leg bumping to pinnacles.

Happy times: I asked the waitress at a Ruby's fast food: Are there any Filipinos here? She pointed next door: Capelle and Partner Company. Can you imagine a whole troop of Filipinos worked at the company.

It has a supermarket, a bakery, a Digicel office. They work with Information Technology (IT), web design, accounting procedures. We posed for selfies, group pictures, break time of Cassava, bibingka pastries.

All of a sudden, I became their *Tita* (auntie). Fun interviewing them. Some have stayed over sixteen years. When I gave my bookmark, everyone wanted an autograph.

Vicky, Danuba, Lai and Michelle showed me the accounting office, the furniture store, the dress makers shop, rallying the *Pinoy* (Filipino) life.

Nauru, the Smallest Nation

A "moon landscape"
Measuring just eight square miles

No protected areas
No World Heritage Sites

No rivers, slow-paced
Fantasy land of beautiful coral pinnacles
Watching local fishermen bring their catch to land

Anibare Bay amid palm groves
Propped my computer to record the Ring Road
A small stretch of fine white sand

First to see the sun rise
A phosphate-rock island with rich deposits near the surface

Then phosphate reserves were exhausted
Environment seriously harmed by mining

A trust established to manage the island's wealth
Diminished in value

Rolled into a tax haven, illegal money laundering center

Aiwo Harbor, and giant cargo ships
Along the narrow gauge of a railway
Conveyor belts on pylons jutting into the sea
Onto Buada Lagoon, body of fresh water

I walked along the pinnacles to the end
Surrounded by dense palm trees and vegetation

Ruins of continuous Allied air raids
Scattered rusting relics
Disused Japanese pillboxes line the shore

World War II history

A bevy of old artillery emplacements

Six Barrel anti-craft guns pointed towards the blue sky

Ruins of a prison complex interned Nauruan natives

Command Ridge, highest point

Old canons along the roadsides
Or In plain sight between homes

Clutching my lantern in the darkness

Making out Japanese writing on the walls
•

Timbuktu, Alluring Tidbits

Maybe 11 years ago - When I awoke in the Dogon village, I heard the rhythmic chants and drumbeats - hard working village girls trudging to the market.

Timbuktu - Once a byword for the ends of the earth, Mali's desert city feels not as alluring because I was scared. This truck with overload baggage, goats, chickens had to cross the Niger River - INSIDE our vessel. Yikes!!

We waited at the dock for an hour until more cars arrived.

More prayers said - we reached Timbuktu safely.

A yellow fever certificate and a tourist visa to enter Mali was required.

Timbuktu- a mysterious byword towards the end of the earth ! Men from Dogon village and Timbuktu wait for call to prayer.

Tuareg tribes, most men wore blue or purple loose tunics waiting for a hitch hike. People walk for miles.

A woman baking *tacozlu* (millet grain bread) in a traditional cave oven.

Salt is expensive as gold. Sold in slabs or tablets are used to feed animals.

Timbuktu is a UNESCO-listed world heritage site and the spiritual capital of sub-Saharan Africa.

Agonizingly, many of the cultural artefacts that gave the city its identity were destroyed or damaged. Some priceless medieval manuscripts were burnt or stolen from the state archive.

Abdul, our guide, over sweet mint tea tells me the story of the books and tablets form and manuscripts.

Chapter 12

Warm Newsletters

My dad Sixto, owner - Century Pianos Store

Odette Ricasa's Holiday Newsletter 2016

Good and faraway places cast a spell on me. We discover the countries through the eyes of a local. Not just to report it but to **LIVE it.** Still dancing dreamily to the four-four beat of It's a Small World after all.. one of a short repertoire. I can draw doodling on a scratch pad, impulses of centuries, from New Zealand to Algeria.

Forget YouTube just revisit the bare necessities of crawling and running into wild affairs around Chinchon, Spain that elevates your heart rate. The phenomenal speed crunching data of apps and i-Phone manages.

Having wolfed down *tocino del cielo,* (sweet pastry), *lechon* (roasted pig slices) we rush to flea markets in Murcia. I wanted to meet Spaniards to talk about music, music beyond the Beatles. Sharing my travels this year 2016:

Chatham Islands - (2 hour flight from Wellington, New Zealand). Population: 600, the first place in the world to see the new dawn. Ohio Bay, Myths form on mystic isles - Basalt rock columns, actually created by cooling volcanic lava some 80 million years ago. I learned about the Moriori Covenant of Peace. Ate crawfish with risotto and *paua* (edible sea snails). Met Cecile, a Filipina married to the governor. She works at the Waitangi sea foods factory.

Wellington, New Zealand – A fascinating interview with the Island Bay writing group: beautiful ladies: arranged by Ingrid and Miles Lowrie. Topic was about my books and travels. "Did you ever have a frightening experience, what is your favorite country?"

Thank you, Angela Werren. We drove around the Beehive Parliament Supreme Court, new and old Te Papa museum, Oriental Bay, Evans Bay over the hill through Kilbirnie. Famous for very windy weather, houses cling to the slopes. Fun at the Beautiful Opera house concert. Enjoyed outside concert, played the piano at the Waitangi Park, Wellington, New Zealand.

Perth & Sydney, Australia - Thank you, Valma Nelson in the vibrant city of Fremantle. Hopped on the ferry from Barrack Street for a cruise down the Swan River with beautiful beaches. Thank you to Mary Gregory and Rod McLarren, fellow Lions members. We exchanged ideas about community service while dining at the Fishing Boat Harbor and a pleasant walk at the River Park.

Village of *Bassendean* – Thank you, Anne Begg. She gave an awesome tour of The Rail Transport Museum, the Sandy Beach Reserve, and a movie night at the Success Hill Reserve.

To Coral Walsh who organized a Women Welcome Women World Wide afternoon tea get together at the Castlereagh Boutique Hotel. We were a big group of twelve ladies from different cities of North and South Sydney.

Cocos island – 2 hour flight from Perth, Australia. Breathtakingly beautiful sunsets and admired the kaleidoscope colors of the lagoon and fringing reef. Imagine yourself swimming with the dolphins or snorkeling with the manta rays. I took a Ferry to Home Island, a unique way of life of the Cocos Malay kampong.

Christmas Island - island of the Australian Indian Ocean Territories. Population: 2,000 residents, who live mainly in settlements. Regarded as true land crabs, Robber crabs / coconut crabs, are in large numbers. The annual red crab mass migration (around 100 million animals) to the sea to spawn has been called one of the wonders of the natural world.

Leuven, Belgium - Thank you to Vera Haezart, who showed Leuven's beautiful béguinage (an architect's complex to house lay religious women). Hundreds of béguines once lived a simple, nun-like existence, is the town's most enchanting area. Naamsestraat is the Oude Markt, the bustling old square of the city. The entire plaza hums with energy. Holy Trinity College with a glorious Baroque facade dating to 1657. The ornate City Hall is the town's most distinguishing landmark.

Vilnius, Lithuania - Classic French bistro serves potato creations. About a dozen people are silently looking upward. They face us as we walk through the Gate of Dawn. Everyone is so piously focused on a black and gold Virgin Mary icon that glimmers in a Chapel that is built into the top of the gate.

A day tour to the top of the Hill of Crosses. Hundreds of crosses in different shapes and materials piled one on top of the other. A window railing, the only barrier between this "miracle-working" icon and the street. UNESCO named - this the largest Baroque Old Town.

Chisinau, Moldova - Orheil Vechi carved into a massive limestone cliff in a rocky remote spot. We danced the night away at City Club, near Sheraton hotel.

I saw you in the afternoon sun in a position as timeless as the curve of a bone, the air conditioned room hummed and chatted like a friendly drunk. Cicadas chuckled the sky dark, as if blackened by fire. The odor of hibiscus with a sweet smell and my heart beat against my chest like a paddle.

Transdniester is the narrow sliver of land, along the Ukrainian border. Naturally separated from the rest of Moldova. Passports and visas were stamped upon entry. Most roofs of houses were covered with grass. The capital is Tiraspol.

Belarus - A setting for the senses. It begins with the taste. Then MINSK, Belarus drenches you in its magic: incredible cuisine with a blue-heaven backdrop. There I was, left mesmerized by the sun bleached churches, the blue sky, and dazzling white National Academic Bolshoi Opera, the neo-Gothic Red Church, white and gold gilded domes of the church of Saint Simon.

No street food. *smazhanka* a Belarusian pizza at the train station.

Belarussians are proud: Irving Berlin, legendary composer and lyricist "God bless America" was born here.

Valencia, Spain - Step into the labyrinth of Valencia's old district and you will feel like you've been transported back in time. Thank you to Susan Kaplan. We let ourselves get lost in this beautiful city, with the overflowing history and culture.

This efficiently compact history lesson tips you off the city's secrets I love the Silk merchant's market's surprises and the Old market. The historical district will blow your socks off.

Barcelona – My 52nd time to Spain. ODETTE'S Birthday celebration. Our whole family, nine persons in all stayed for eight nights. We rented a four bedroom apartment in la Rambla, the center of night life.

We watched my grandson play football at the famous Kaptiva Sports Academy in Javier Cant Cugat del Valles. Congratulations Riley! We celebrated at the Cafeteria, Jamon Iberico sandwich cost $1.00 Euro, while a giant cup of draft beer cost a whopping $0.50 Euro cents. Whoa!

Barcelona is a cryptic Mediterranean metropolis, with haunted flats that overlook leafy squares and feline temptresses lurk in bars at La Raval. A city where you don't need a plan.

Without fail I would spend days just wandering around the streets, getting lost in the Barri Gòtic. I still have recurring dreams of sitting at the terrace of a CULTURE bar. A Senor just might have the courage to ask me for a date: "Can I invite you for a glass of wine?" he..he..he...

I have been to Barcelona with my mother, with friends, relatives & SOLO at least 38 times. This city never leaves me. I can go back another 38 times.

Basel, Switzerland - The best "Laderach" Swiss chocolates Alley ways to the Rhine river weather was a cold 37 Fahrenheit degrees.

My friend, Ursula recommended Hotel Eleur at the city center. I played the piano at the Bar, alive with running voices. Little faint winds playing chase on the tops of windows out at the doors, the sunflowers and lilies were radiant and alive.

At Café Five, the desserts looked so attractive. I ate delightfully, shaking off the extra icing sugar that looked light & feathery, licking from my fingers whipped cream.

Solothurn, Switzerland - Thank you Cleo Gressly, my high school classmate and husband, Paul, who took us to the colorful Saturday market in full activity. Numerous fountains with figures, on the small squares in the old town.

St. Ursen's Cathedral, the Clock Tower, We had lunch at the oldest restaurant La Couronne Hotel, then Swiss coffee and dessert at her beautiful home.

Puerto de Mazarron, Cartagena and Murcia cathedral and casino Bar Vegas, ensalada de Murcia. Thank you, Jukka and Liisa Kujala who took us to Bar Angel and around, El Faro and Playa del Castellar, Costa Calida, The warm weather, sunshine, and beaches make it a holiday destination.

Bolnuevo is a short bus ride from Puerto de Mazarrón. Here we found an extension of the beautiful coast line and beaches. It's most popular attraction is what I like to call Murcia's "mini Grand Canyon".

Erosions are natural sand sculptures caused by centuries of water and wind erosion. Late lunch at Club Náutico de Santa Lucía. *Caldereta,* rice in fish sauce w garlic.

Alcaniz, Spain - «LIVE IT FEEL IT «. Secret passageways, with century old paintings on the walls fortresses. Ana wanted to know why I travel to so many countries. We had fun preparing English vocabularies for Halloween games.

Living joyfully Life is all about love & friendship. Javier, the husband of Ana loves to cook. Uhumm...I should find a Spanish husband who loves to cook? We explored Puerto de Beceite.

La Fresneda. A municipality located in the province of Teruel, Aragon. We roamed around Casa Consistorial de la Fresneda. Drank more beer, more night life at the old town Lo Coscell de la Freixneda and Restaurant El Convent 1613. Went hiking around the clear lakes at Matarranya.

Algiers, Algeria - Enjoyed *bhourek* at the old kasbah traditional cafe Algerian people very welcoming. The colorful markets of Algiers and the Ottoman style palaces. Remains of the citadel, old mosques, a traditional urban structure associated with a deep-rooted sense of community.

The heart of the city is its ancient Casbah, a steep and narrow maze of streets. It is in one of the finest coastal sites on the Mediterranean, where a Carthaginian trading-post was established in the 4th century BC. The Royal Mausoleum of Mauritania was built with giant rocks WITHOUT using cement.

TIPAZA, an extraordinary mix of Phoenician, Roman, early Christian and Byzantine ruins beautifully set overlooking the Mediterranean. The walls of the arena still describe the area where, in the fourth centuries, gladiator fights were held. The La Mola lighthouse still stands proudly. The blue Mediterranean Sea is stunning!

Asmara, Eritrea - What a discovery. Eritrea is very safe to travel. I attended a holy mass at the cathedral of Asmara. Played with children at Asmara catholic school.

Took painting lessons at the Satreb Art Institute.

Thank you to Philemon Kesete who took me around the magnificent hills view of Durfa hills. Medebar market -the rhythmic banging filled the air, where men with protective masks and goggles, solder pieces of metal together. Hundreds of locals engage in recycling anything: electric Copper combs for the hair; horse carriages can be hired to transport goods. Eritreans are creatively fashioning anything from discarded scrap metals.

Stopped for coffee ceremony & macchiato at La Dolce Vita Café. Philemon is the best guide, customary Erithrean greeting with a kiss on each cheek three times.

Sun Valley, Idaho – Spent 5 nights at this ski resort. Flocked in a frosty coat of white and adorned with shimmering lights, wreaths, and a passionate reverence for time honored tradition, a place that is magical. Thank you to Terry Manglicmot's invite to stay at her lovely condominium. Met her neighbor, Jose Maria, a native of Oviedo, Spain. He loves and prefers to live in Idaho.

Boracay islands, Philippines. For several years, the powdery white sands and turquoise waters has landed Boracay at the top of countless lists, proclaiming it, *the world's best beach.*

Bar Hopping at Hennan Beach resort ate fresh seafood at D'Talipapa, Epic restaurant and Tito's.

Let me tell you, Boracay is just as beautiful in person as it is on postcards. Fancy me!

A perverse kick of the heart a flicker of naughtiness. In the warmth, my feet uncurled and expanded like sea anemones. I stretched my legs out, propped my heels and wiggled my toes.

LIVE, LOVE, LAUGH **A real good time always lasts. You have it all with your nature and all your nature stays with it.** *HAPPYHOL IDAYS!!! ODETTE RICASA, World traveler, has traveled to 276 countries. Platinum member: www.travelerscenturyclub.org Author of five books, www.authorhouse.com www.odettericasatravels.com.*

-end

Teacher Ms. Kessia and Grade 2 Students
Delap Elementary School

Odette Ricasa's Holiday Newsletter 2017

Capture Different to embrace the unexpected.

Finding insight dawn to dusk to dawn hour by the hour odyssey.

From the sun scorched streets of Angola to the streets of Kiruna in the Arctic where the sun is brilliant for 24 straight hours. Along the way we visited Viking families in Norbotten, tried moose heart and elk delicacy.

Twirl until dawn in Lisbon. Weaving a tale or snack attack or soul food fuel - memory lanes – stick around we are going to unspoiled sandy island. - celebrate nature's grandest spectacles, share life in a meaningful way.

My trips for the year 2017:

Nadi, Fiji - After dinner at the Hilton Fiji, I fell asleep like a blanket, within moments of lying down. Before the first glimmer of light touched the sky, I heard Villame sing again... my heart beat soared -- Fijians take their singing seriously with Breezy jokes, greeting everybody with Bula! and a flurry of flowery pleasantries.

Fiji with alabaster beaches and kaleidoscopic reefs. The embodiment of the Pacific Ocean, sun induced coma under a shady palm, over 300 islands where do I lay my beach towel? Volley ball courts with languid sense of time. Saginaw *kava* drink or grog muddy tea made from a root. My third time here and am still amazed.

Kiribati – February - celebrated my birthday with Elizabeth & Emmy, my new found friends at the ANZ bank - treated me at their home, a feast of roasted chicken, fresh fish and a huge birthday cake.

Kiritimati, Christmas Island – Captain Cook hotel. The village of London, the Tennessee primary school, 3 windmills for electricity. Church interviewed teacher and children. Oral story-telling is a popular and important pastime here.

It helps to keep alive the history, myths from the past, as well as legends about more modern figures. So we convene, here with Bengt and Gunar from Sweden, just enjoy jokes and laughter.

Finding a piece of simple happiness – at the Banana village, mixing with locals at the community center where all are welcome. -- There are only 2 gasoline stations in this remote Christmas islands located almost near the equator in the Middle of the South Pacific Ocean.

Often exciting, it is not relatively easy. I love this Church in the town of London. No pews, no chairs to sit, we sit on the floor to pray & listen to services

Lisbon – staying at Bairro Alto, night life, the Fado music plus the sounds of the city serenaded us. Belem Tower, the medieval defensive tower the iconic landmark.

Arenas de San Pedro, Spain - A long hike around the *Pantano* and the Monasterio with beautiful wildflowers.... Refreshing to walk around. Thank you to my new found friends, Teresa, Lucia, Isabel & Rosita, having tapas, orejas n sepia at Asador de Villa Patrimonio.

Luanda & Cabinda, Angola - one of the most expensive city in the world—by far. Forget Tokyo, Moscow. Monthly Apartment Rental: $10,000-15,000, Mediocre Hotel Room: U.S. $650/night; Hotel Breakfast: $75; Non-Alcoholic Drink: $10; Watermelon $35.00, mangoes $2.00 each.

When in Luanda, travelers must try "*funge*", a cassava or corn flour paste which has a sticky texture but does not have much flavor, so it is eaten with different sauces made of fish, meat, chicken or beans and vegetables, often use extra spicy condiment called *gindungo*.

One of the most important Angolan instruments is the Marimba, a kind of xylophone made from wood with different sizes of gourds attached, which produce a highly recognizable sound. Sweet music to my ears.

I met a lot of Filipinos working here as architects, engineers, contractors and accountants.

New found friend, Levi Obidos, invited me to their place three nights in a row for dinner, karaoke singing and good times reminiscing our nostalgic experiences about our original home. Came to say "So long my friend" on my last day with a basket of papaya cubes and mango slices for breakfast.

I was honored to have an interview with Mr. Brechet, honorary consul of the Philippine Embassy about my books and why I travel so much J

Amsterdam – a favorite stop for 2 or 3 nights. Amstel park Food fair. Mooreah & Jergoen were at the bar, serving wine. Drank a little too much.

Enjoyed the music, the saxophonist playing on top of the truck roof. Had polenta fries dipped in special sauce with shredded beef prosciutto and salmon, and of course Waldo's famous chocolates. Awww! The Dutch sure love music and food.

Oxford, England – Dinner at the Bulls Inn, Hughenden valley north west London with Kathie Parkinson, fish plaice grilled and Shepherd's pie, real English menu, at western range Church farm valley Road Tudor style houses.

Harrow School founded 1572 where Sir Winston Churchill & prime minister Nehru studied, is located in a leafy 300 acre estate in north west London.

Entertained by Kumud Banarse and Valerie White, women welcome women worldwide members.

We visited our founder, Frances Alexander who proudly showed her showcase of memorabilia. Reminisced her one year saga about meeting women in the United Kingdom.

Lulea, Sweden - Bengt Enbuske showed me the beauty of the midnight sun in the Arctic Circle. Hearts beat for art. I had to completely close the sun blocked curtains and don my night mask to get some sleep during noon time. The sun shone continuously bright for twenty four hours.

Ice hotel is the world's first hotel made of ice and snow in the Swedish village of Jukkasjärvi – 200 kilometers north of the Arctic Circle.

I will never forget. summer outside, winter inside made of ice from the River Tome -- a life enriching moment of this long trip, a place to discover silence.

The Sami people, an indigenous Finno-Ugric people inhabiting Sapmi where Bengt took me. Traditionally known Laplanders is an indigenous group. Their livelihood is semi-Nomadic connected to reindeer herding, trapping, fishing. The museum exhibits *Duodji* (crafts) such as hunting knives, beaded belts, bone antler needle cases and buri caps.

I had a taste of *Sorstrumm* Herring. When we opened the can, I almost fainted with the pungent of bad eggs with hydrogen sulfide. I had to run but tasted it anyway so I can describe it. It had a salt base line, creamy, crunchy and herbal taste. Bengt burst to wild laughter.

Kiruna in the Lapland – has the largest and most modern underground ore mine in the world. Was so surprised! I took a lot of pictures.

The Swedish government is moving 20 significant buildings from the old town to the new location, including its church, which was voted Sweden's most beautiful building. Each one is being completely dismantled and reconstructed to prevent it slowly being swallowed by the Underground Mine.

Most homes were sitting on trailer trucks with wheels ready to be rolled away.

Oslo Norway – my fourth time to Norway - Thank you to Unn Andersen. We hopped all around the new restaurants, having some ale, sweet breads, moose delicacy, fish and chips with another friend, Vanessa at the Horse & Jockey pub.

The Oslo city hall is where The Nobel PEACE prize winner is awarded. The building has been decorated by great Norwegian art with motifs from Norwegian history. Carillon concerts are held here.

San Clemente pier, CA – Network for Travel club had our yearly potluck. Sixty travelers brought an array of dishes. Quynh NGUYEN, and his wife Hannah, shared fascinating stories about life in Vietnam. Afterwards, most of us strolled at the pier, stopped for drinks and watched the sunset.

Lourdes, France – *my fourth time* - pilgrimage to the holy waters of Our Lady of Lourdes.

Our Lady of Lourdes and Our Lady of Fatima, we prayed, God bless us. Took a swim at the miraculous baths.

Barcelona – never tiring of Andalusian memories, this must be my 38th[th] time to visit the most dangerous pickpocketing place in the world. But then the culinary arts, the electricity at La Rambla, the formation of a human tower and the magic of Gaudi pulls me again and again.

Republic of Marshall Islands - Went to visit a school -- grade two children at nearby Delap Elementary school. Teacher, Miss Keesia

Latvrik was thrilled to show her classroom and her students. She teaches Math, Science, Social Studies, Grammar and Health.

** Photo image (19) school students of Delap Elementary. She was proud to announce to her students they will be featured in my sixth book.

Conversations with the former President of Marshall Islands from 2012 to 2016. He was jovial, sincere and passionate about the Republic of Marshall Islands honorable @Christpher Loeak. Thank you for giving me the opportunity of an amazing exchange of stories.

Aerial view of Majuro islands endless blue green waters - a parade of soft clouds view from my balcony - awesome here slow pace life no stress no crime people are not allowed to have weapons.

Streets are safe to walk. No public busses only taxis. Each ride is U.S. $0.75 cents to anywhere. Their currency is US dollars. They have an agreement with USA. Marshallese citizens can enter USA as non-immigrants. We learn something everyday ;) The best fresh seafood here.

Tokyo & Nagoya, Japan Junko Shinoda and Tamiko Suzuki - Enjoying sake with some of the locals-- all of Tokyo's nooks. -- the breathtaking temples and shrines. Where we gathered for a peaceful moment- gold gray morning --sparkle of intelligence. -- unique personality traits.

About personalities, talk to individuals and about character about emotions our patterns our ideas. About the mind the thoughts these are unique to us - share life in a meaningful way.

My long-time friend Soichiro Fuji over 30 years of friendship across the ocean. We show off and communicate in Spanish, hablamos Español. We exchange visits Los Angeles - Tokyo. Every time he plays the viola -- especially in a concert -- a full string chord explodes into the air and just seems to shimmer from the inside out. That's him, playing a beautiful melody, and dominates symphonic music, leaves me teary eyed.

Congratulations Fujii !!! Ensemble *de cuerdas soloistas* (stringed instruments) México -Japón.

Macau, Hong Kong – Macau – Hong Kong - Around every corner of Hong Kong is something new and unique, whether it›s an ancient temple, a shop selling the latest electronic gadget, or a man taking his bird in a cage for a walk. I love the small corners of Macau.

Just enjoying the Moon cake festival. Tried a variety of dried meats, salted Fish, Chinese cookies. Took the ferry from Hong Kong to Macau, a one hour ride and needed to pass immigration / customs procedures.

Met Marjorie Corpuz Cariaga who showed me around. It was Mid-Autumn Festival - Feast of Hungry Ghosts. Appease the restless spirits by burning paper and food offering by the roadsides for it is said that during this month, the ghosts are freed from the underworld and are free to roam the world every year for a lunar month. Featured in Chinese operas.

Santiago, Chile – An Astronomer's Paradise, Chile May Be the Best Place on Earth to enjoy a Starry Sky. Chile's northern coast offers an ideal star-gazing environment with its lack of precipitation, clear skies and low-to-zero light pollution. Stayed at Henry Ganga airbnb at the center of town,

Stayed near Barrio Lastarria Santiago - feels almost European at times - loving it here near Plaza Italia and El Cerro Santa Lucía -- charming coffee houses. Visited the Philippine Consulate, conversations with honorable Mr. Marcos A S Punsalang.

Robinson Crusoe Islands - Far away from it all -. Patricio is a composer and a famous guitarist entertaining us with comical songs, mixing with the friendly locals Marcela, Maria, Lydia, and Lupita.

Just over 400 miles west of Chile, in an otherwise barren stretch of the southern Pacific, lie three islands, together totaling some 100 square kilometers. Volcanic, vertiginously mountainous, swept by chill currents and buffeted by -- nowadays there are fewer than 600 people living here, and they work chiefly in the lobster industry in the Oorinoque River flowing to the Pacific.

Population: 600, number of cars = 25, number of motorcycles = 3 river, no car rentals, no buses, no taxis, I walked everywhere.

LAUGH **A real good time always lasts.** *H A P P Y H O L I D A Y S !!!* *ODETTE RICASA, World traveler, has traveled to 285 countries. Platinum member: www.travelerscenturyclub.org Author of five books, www.authorhouse.com. – end.*

www.odettericasatravels.com.

Odette Ricasa's Holiday Newsletter 2018

Traveling forces you to trust strangers and to lose sight of all that familiar comfort of home and friends. You are constantly off balance.

Trips for the year 2018:

My fourth time to **Finland** and am still amazed. Thank you to Tim and Outi Vihmo for hosting a day tour of **Helsinki.** Tim drove his car though the main streets near the banks of the Gulf of Finland and dropped us at Kamppi.

We stopped at Cafeteria Roastery - they serve the best coffee in Helsinki. They import and roast the coffee themselves, so the quality is high - even an ordinary cup of filtered coffee is excellent. Kammpi in the neighborhood – we walked around the Market Square, the Chapel of Silence - open to all faiths, the leafy Esplanade Park the Sibelius Monument & Park the Uspenski cathedral, the Ateneum, the impressive huge Finlandia Hall, the marvelous **Rock church**!

Wowwowiee !!! Luck was on our side!!! The **Northern Lights in Overtornea, Sweden-** a quintessential bucket list item. Seeing the impressive display swirling overhead while we watched is an incredible experience !!!

Fortunately we had the rare opportunity to see the display as early as 10:00PM - lights began with a white wisp then changing to bright yellow and Green! So thrilled!!! Viewing these rare moments for 3 -1/2 hours. YES!!! A BIG thank you "Tack" to Bengt Enbuske and Gunnar Björk for inviting Raili Seppala and me to see this geomagnetic storm, due to a positive polarity coronal hole high.

Reus in Spain with Ana Anusk - a picturesque town that was once famous for the production of Brandy and Vermuth. Today it is a busy town that spans 120,000 inhabitants. One of them was Gaudi's birthplace. — had an interesting and varied history, as it was used as a port by the Greeks and Romans. Later it became a haven for pirates evolving into nearby fishing village. speed stream. Still feeling Electrified !!!

Cambrils, Spain is known as the culinary capital of the Costa Dorada. There is a cornucopia of fresh local ingredients, ranging from fish and other seafood to the internationally acclaimed DO Siurana olive oil. Between the historic population center and the ports, life in Cambrils unfurls peacefully around beaches and promenades.

Looking on, as fishing boats glide into the harbor and discovering the Old Quarter are the many pleasures that we explored the port - the best fresh seafood, octopus, lobsters, tuna and salmon.

My third time to Valencia - still amazes me a city overlooked gem of Spain. the third-largest city has enough surprises- urban beaches, a bafflingly futuristic arts complex and even its own Holy Grail. **Valencia, Spain** parties as hard as anywhere on the Iberian Peninsula. The 13ᵗʰ-century Catedral de Valencia is the city's architectural past, incorporates Romanesque, Gothic. Valencia is a great choice when it comes to beaches. Playa de la Malvarrosa and Playa de las Arenas.

More photos, magical Balearic island **Palma de Mallorca, Iberia.** There's a rhythm on the shores of Palma the waves makes a slap roar sound as it rolls back the blue waters.

My own sanctuary- the rising sun bathes me with golden light from the hidden patio along narrow lanes where I see smiling faces. Bar Bosch a legendary place has the best tapas. Muchas gracias Connie for a lovely afternoon.

Palma de Mallorca! Get a taste of Roman, Arab, and Catalan influences in this Mediterranean destination, where you will be forgiven for wanting to stay forever. amazing hidden patios along narrow streets, panoramic views out to the sea, gothic cathedrals and sailing traditions.

Love Spanish cuisine Dinner with longtime friend architect and artist Isabel Ruiz Cano in Madrid. La Caprichosa restaurante - Best Spanish cuisine in the town of Barrajas. Known for jamón a variety of cuts - waiting at airport flying to Palma de Mallorca. Sign says "Am a foodie."

Recife Pernambuco, Brazil, The cuisine is a set of cooking and is characterized by African, Amerindian, Asian and European influences. It varies greatly by region, reflecting the country's mix of native and immigrant populations, and its continental size as well - i gained weight trying it all

Everything in Brazil pulses faster and beats harder - went to Ricardo Brennand Institute a cultural institution located in the city of Recife, Brazil. It is a not-for-profit private organization, owned by the Brazilian collector and businessman Ricardo Brennand. It comprises a museum, an art gallery, a library and a large park. Then Victor showed more spectacular places of his home, Recife. Victor Azevedo is the best guide and taxi driver. Obrigado Victor!

This is my FOURTH time to Brazil and yet everything amazes me.

The island's luxuriously warm unsullied emerald waters are, it was widely agreed, teeming with turtles and dolphins. the area is, in fact, friendly. What's more, the consensus assured us that every type of shark common to the swimmers Ayayayayyyy!!! Joke! Joke! bwahaha !!

I had to pay $35.00 per day at the airport whoa ! Entrance fee to Paradise Beach ! Its pristine beaches, landscapes and wildlife attract tourists worldwide. Ask about Fernando de Noronha when you're in

Sao Paulo, and your enquiry will invariably meet with a combination of wonderment, national pride, jealousy and misinformation.

Fernando de Noronha is an island – named after a 16th-century Portuguese nobleman who may never have actually set foot there – that exists in the Brazilian imagination somewhere not far from Shangri-la, Atlantis and paradise.

People glaze over when you mention it: eyeballs tend to roll upwards in that universal gesture to expect the most spectacular beaches in all of Brazil. Naomi Campbell, popular fashion model, we were informed, goes here to unwind after Sao Paulo Fashion Week. Far from being just a bolt-hole for the wealthy – it is also amazing.

Almost everybody runs around in swim suits up and down the sidewalk to the market to the restaurant to the park wet suits dry easily because it's very windy. together we go to the bus stop free by the way for all. I hop on a bus to go to all of the 18 beaches

Fernando de Noronha is an archipelago in Brazil and a UNESCO Natural World Heritage Site. Its pristine beaches, landscapes and wildlife attract tourists worldwide. Endless beaches. Whole day tour of amazing sceneries, beaches- Uhumm!! I brought 10 gallons of sun tan lotion hehehe to protect my soft skin.

Recife, capital of Pernambuco, lively capital, founded by Dutch colonizers, is brimming with a vibrant culture, an interesting old town (which includes the oldest synagogue in the America's and some nice beaches and LOTS of sharks is one of those special places where you can feel the distinct culture the minute you step off the plane. The climate is warm, the beach is everywhere, and the people are friendly, open, and fun!

On the Hill Gang - a fun afternoon "**Simply Socializing**" in Palos Verdes Estates. View of the ocean was fantastic and so is precious company. We Kayak, bike, hike, ski, snow shoeing and many more activities. Drink and be merry with members Gayle, Mary, Rose Marie, Lois, Linda, Harold, Stan, Charlene, Jackie, Barbara, Medrano - unending blah blah updates, laughter - good times rolling.

VISIT SAN CLEMENTE - A BIG Thank you to Ruby Guerrero Josie Inacay, Luchie Juatco, Nini Maldonado Carolina Cotter Mark Cotter, Femy Wagas and Armando for coming to visit me in San Clemente. We strolled along the pier for hot chocolate greeting the many fishermen. We had an early lunch at the Fishermen's Wharf all the time exchanging jokes, slapping each other's shoulder blah and blah. Then to my home played the piano sung my favorite "Besa Me Mucho" more laughter until we fell off our chairs.

JAPANESE TOWN in Los Angeles – one of the many Family times: Richie, Christine, Lucy, Rica Riley Joe and Rachel, Robert and Chrissy. We walked in downtown drunk Boba teas - shopped around then rode the free Trolley. Dinner by the seaside at Maranouchi Sushi Bar. Took a quick stop at the wine cellar with piano and singing entertainment plus the Big Bonus. Two years old Cutie Lucy danced with the tune of It's a Small World.

The **BAPS Shri Swaminarayan Mandir** is a Hindu temple complex in Chino Hills, California. The Mandir is primarily Hindu but open to all faiths.

We went on a tour to the intricately and spectacular designed temple. What a holy and peaceful place. After the tour we reminisced recent adventures at the Golden Temple in Amritsar, India. Then we ate at the cafe, had mango lassi, spicy samosas, gulab jamun dessert and Indian cookies. Thank you Annette Mann, our president. We all had a fantastic time.

Probably the true joy of traveling in Bangladesh is it's people - beautiful, courteous, proud and warm attitude . They looked and sometimes followed us to satisfy their curiosity, to learn from a foreigner passing through their streets

After an adventure in Pakistan, Meg Pipo - in **Bangladesh** – is often represented negatively in the international media. Very few western travelers actually know about this amazing country except some myths, which makes it the least known travel destination in the world.

The national flower "Shapla" resting on water, having on each side an ear of paddy and being surmounted by three connected leaves of jute with two stars on each side of the leaves.

I have a fascination for the colorful rickshaws and the pedal pushers chaotic maneuvering thru the crowded city of Dhaka.

Meg Pipo and I successfully crossed from **Wagah border India** by taxi trolley. Then to Lahore Pakistan. It took 2-1/2 hours for documentation check. Thanks to Abubakr, Tess Nufable's boss who recommended this Five Star Hotel - man! Check it out a heritage Faletti's hotel **Lahore, Pakistan** since 1880 There is a suite called Hollywood's famous star Ava Gardner. I preferred to check in at Ava's suite but cost much $$$ hahaha!. Marlon Brandon, Duke Ellington, and Aga Khan stayed here.

Pakistan is a country which is often depicted in the media as being a place of religious intolerance. This is far from true, you can find Muslims, Christians and Hindus living side by side in many of the cities. there are many tribal groups still living, largely undisturbed.

When I first told family and friends that I plan to travel to Pakistan as part of my adventure they were somewhat skeptical. Pakistan is a country which is often portrayed in the media as a war-torn hellhole and tourism in Pakistan is almost non-existent.

Every year, only a very small number of tourists arrive, my friend Meg Pipo and I were determined to be one of them. Travelling in Pakistan is a truly unique experience, it can be frustrating, enlightening, and more often life changing. We have been lucky enough to make friends on our travels but the friendships forged in Pakistan were some of the most genuine ever made, the people simply cannot do enough for you.

Thursday, August 2, 2018 early morning yoga in **Jallianwala Bagh** garden...Amritsar. After yoga meditation / exercises, we ventured to the city center. We ordered a fresh potato paratha breakfast menu straight out of the tandoori oven. Not spicy please.

There is something about the sights and sounds of **Amritsar, India** which tugs at your inner spirituality. The market area surrounding the temple premises was chaotic.

The only way to reach here is through a cycle rickshaw, auto or a motorcycle taxi but we managed a private taxi because No cars can enter these narrow lanes. We checked in to a four star Hotel Coy Heart located right in front of McDonalds. Thanks to Gulshan Mehra – the engaging manager who shared his grandfather's harrowing experience during the Partition period of India and Pakistan and travel tips.

Dining in communal style at the Langar sas a lif-time experience. We sat on the floor and scooped food with our hands, helped in the washing of pots and pans.

Indian traditions :

The person who bows down, lets go off his ego and becomes more humble in this act.

The person who acknowledges the gesture with a blessing, becomes a well-wisher and would refrain from developing hatred. A vermilion mark in the parting of the hair just above the forehead is worn by married women as commitment to long-life and well-being of their husbands.

During all Hindu marriage ceremonies, the groom applies indoor and part the bride's hair.

Soaking daily life in India:

Bells from echo in the hills Life is a vacation The Kangra Valley in Himachal Pradesh is known for its beautiful natural landscapes.

Spread over acres of land, the tea gardens are a scenic site. One can easily spend hours here just soaking in the peaceful environment. Meg Pipo and I picked up some fresh mountain tea leaves.

On to Bhagsu Village, a quaint but highly picturesque 'Gaddi' (a shepherd tribe) Tribal village where traditional livelihood was herding and farming.

It lies at an elevation of 6,700 feet. Over the years, this quaint little village has emerged as the hub of tourist activity at McLeod These falls are 30 feet high. From the Shiva Temple, the only way to reach these falls is by walking. The trek is easy as proper walking trails are paved in between the hilly walk. I did not reach the top LOL.

The Himachal Pradesh Cricket Association (HPCA) stadium is the highest cricket stadium in the world high in the Himalayas.

SMILE, tell stories, listen more. H A P P Y H O L I D A Y S !!! ODETTE RICASA, World traveler, has traveled to 295 countries. Platinum member: www.travelerscenturyclub.org Author of five books authorhouse.com www.odettericasatravels.com.

Chapter 13

Apparent Spontaneity

Odette's Travel Club - No Membership Dues

Networking our adventures. Before the show, we pass the microphone around. Each person gets to talk about where he/she has been or dream of going, with the goal of traveling to amazing places. An ORGANIZED EVENT, a Volunteer work of Odette Ricasa, who has been putting together meetings for 14 years.

Date of EVENT: SUNDAY, March 8, 2020.

Time: 12:00 – 3:00 PM -- Social time then Lunch is served at 12:15 noon. Travel presentation immediately follows.

Place: El Floridita Restaurant (Cuban cuisine) 1253 N. Vine Street # 3 (in a mini mall, corner Vine & Fountain St.) Hollywood, CA 90038 Tel (323) 871-8612 Fax (323) 871-0968. Parking in front of the restaurant and side streets available.

Cost: $ 29.00 – this EVENT includes lunch, drinks, tax and tip included. Pls. pay at the door, preferably by check pay to Odette Ricasa.

**This an organized EVENT. We receive inquiries asking if it is possible to attend the presentation only and skip the lunch. Our primary goal is to meet & network. We use the place for 3-1/2 hours, menu is discounted. It is a policy of the restaurant to count PER HEAD. In order to avoid unpleasant issues, it is our policy to charge ONE PRICE for the EVENT (with or without lunch).

Menu: Pollo Asado (juicy & tender baked chicken marinated with lemon and garlic sauce). Served w/ white rice, black beans & plantains. Vegetarian: Salad, white rice, black beans, sweet & green plantains &

yucca w/ mojo sauce. Pls. indicate if you are vegetarian when making the reservation. Includes soft drinks or iced tea. Dessert: ice cream,

SPEAKER: FERIDE BUYURAN

Feride is a native of Azerbaijan. She will share with you the culinary and cultural treasures of her homeland including a very short culinary tour.

Topic: Discover cozy little towns along Azerbaijan and Georgia, eccentric large cities, and far-flung villages nestled along the way in the Caucasus Mountains. Along Meet local artisans engaged in art and crafts unique to the region. Savor lively market visits in the countryside,

A unique tour that goes off the beaten path, where a traveler gets to take in the sights, tastes, and rich history of the Caucasus region while learning about a culture through connecting with everyday people. At the same time, she wanted to positively contribute to the lives of the locals.

Rsvp: ODETTE RICASA – has traveled to 295 countries

Travelers Century Club (TCC) Worldwide Meeting in Barcelona, Spain

T CC - International meeting Barcelona - at Hotel 1898 a restored 19th century building with a rooftop pool and sun terrace. We had afternoon tea, tapas, dinner with members introduction.

Tim and Lana Skeet, JoAnn Schwarz – we ventured to Andorra and Llivia having the most delightful picture poses, tapas in traditional bars.

Met with David Langham from Ireland who shared the secrets of going to Tokelau. We explored the enclave of Llivia an old pharmacy since the fourteenth century.

We had an excursion and returned from a visit to Poblet Monastery, a fantastic lunch arranged by our Mediterranean Chapter, and time to explore Roman Tarragona, Spain. It was great touring together with other like-minded travelers.

Our farewell dinner was at the PLA Restaurant on the last night. We had an amazing time as we closed the restaurant. I would not be true to myself if I didn't say there is a touch of sadness that this weekend has come to a close. Can you believe we had over 55 members who attended.

I truly believe we all accomplished the fundamental TCC goal of connecting with each other this weekend by sharing travel accomplishments, reviewing goals, discussing countries and learning from our peers. All of these worked towards building on our unified passion of helping each other and celebrating world travel.

The Mediterranean Chapter did it right! They have passion, warmth, and genuinely cared about our well-being. To Martin and the Mediterranean Chapter: Thank you very much!! We leave Barcelona with many new friends, opportunities to revisit and future possibilities to travel with your group. We truly hope we can meet and return the opportunity to host our club some time.

Year 2019 ENTREPRENEUR & CULTURAL
HERITAGE AWARD

Sinag Lahi Cultural Awards
– BOCI Charities

Fantastic News from: Odette Ricasa
– Save: Sat. September 28, 2019

Dear Family and friends:

It is with honor and great pride to invite you to the Awards night of BOCI Charities. Exciting! I was chosen as one of the awardees by Ms. Olivia Lopez, Chairman / Founder. I met Olivia in January of this year. She was inviting me to join a real estate firm. I mentioned I have my Brokers license with Midtowne Realty. In May, she recommended that I check out Beverly & Co. Luxury Properties. We have been interacting since then.

Yeah! Hope you all come to this event, jostle, shout, whistle, give a wild applause when my name is called ☺

Invitation:

Dear Ms/Mrs. Odette Aquitania Ricasa- Author of 5 books; traveled to 294 countries, territories & islands. Current mission: Interviewing Filipinos all over the world, Lebanon, Cyprus, Angola, Somaliland, Chatham islands, Christmas island, island of St. Helena, Senegal, the Gambia, Copenhagen, Chile, Majuro islands, Papua New Guinea, and the Solomon islands. Photos & stories to be included in my sixth book. Release date: January 2021.

Re: 2019 ENTREPRENEUR & CULTURAL HERITAGE AWARD.

On behalf of Sinag Lahi USA 2019 board panel, we would like to extend our warmest congratulations to you for being chosen as one of the awardees.

Your success and remarkable achievements have been recognized not only by this organization but most of all by our Filipino-American communities. We are proud of you and hope you will continue your sincere commitment in all your future endeavors.

AWARDS NIGHT: Date: Saturday, September 28, 2019, Time: 3:00 to 7:00 PM; venue: Hall of Crucifixion-Resurrection, Glendale Forest Lawn, 1712 Glendale Ave. Glendale, CA 91205

Together, we will inspire the world and create the future!.

Sincerely yours,

OLIVIA LOPEZ

BOCI CHARITIES INC.

Chairman/Founder

PROGRAM:

3:00 PM – Opening of Doors

4:00 PM – Introduction

Star Spangled Banner – Michael Keith

4:06 PM – Lupang Hinirang

4:10 PM – Invocation by Father Roger Balagtas

4:11 PM – Drama Dance by Lilia Lao

4:20 PM – Introduction of Founders and Sinag Lahi officcrs

4:28 PM – Acknowledgement of VIPs and Honoraries

4:34 PM – Cecil and Magic Show

4:40 PM – Sinag Lahi USA 2019 Presentation of the Awardees
First Group
(Religious Group) Song by Tanya Varona - Ikaw

5:52 PM – Folk Dance – National Institute of Philippine Arts
and Culture (NIPAC)
Salakot and Tinikling

5:59 PM – Sinag Lahi USA 2019 Presentation of the Awardees
Second Group
(Entertainers, Art and Music)

6:28 PM – Serenading of the Awardees – Adrian Manuel and
Band

6:38 PM – Sinag Lahi USA 2019 Presentation of the Awardees
Third Group
(Community Leaders and Entrepreneurs)

7:21 PM – Serenading of the Awardees – John and Roselle

7:31 PM – Fashion Show by Carl Andrada

7:41 PM – Dance Moms – Dahil Sa Iyo

- End -

A very successful event! Feeling high – Unforgettable moments. All family and friends attended. The auditorium was packed with 600 persons.

Berber Villages, Matmata, Tunisia

Berber villages, Star Wars Location under the desert in Tunisia (my second time to Tunisia).

Saturday, March 10: DJERBA – CHENINI – KSAR HADDADA – OPTIONAL SUNSET CAMEL TREK - KSAR GHILANE: overnight in a camp in the Sahara Desert.

Early departure from Djerba this morning. We drive to the mainland via the 6.7 km Phoenician causeway. We continue to the area known as the Berber South or the Land of the Ksars. This mountainous area is dotted with medieval *ksour* – monumental fortified granaries. Local tribes used these for storage and defense right up until the mid 20th century.

Similar to beehives, each *ksar* is composed of a series of individual cells – *ghorfas* – superimposed on one another - some as high as 8 stories ! The region is scattered with these strange but magnificent monumental ksour from ancient times.

This morning we visit the ancient Berber hilltop village of Chenini. Some time to explore the village with its rock-cut homes, olive presses, ancient mosques and enjoy the splendid views.

We continue to Ksar Haddada – a "ksar of the plain" of 3 storeys, constructed between the late 28th to early 19th century (but has had numerous restorations over the last 60 years). It is the most famous ksar in the region, since it was an important filming location for *Star Wars: The Phantom Menace* (1997).

We continue across the desert to the small oasis of Ksar Ghilane. Nearby in the dunes is the **Roman fort of Tisavar**. This was the southernmost military outpost of the Roman empire, and was just one fort along the

Roman line of defense. Some time at leisure to explore the oasis, perhaps swim in the thermal springs.

Schedule a trek over the dunes, either by foot, camel or quad. Excursions usually last just over one hour, or you may do a longer trip into the dunes to see the Roman fort - by camel or dune buggy.

If available, a local family can prepare for us mint tea and "cinder bread" or *milla* – bread cooked in ashes in the sand. Overnight in a desert camp on the edge of the dunes, in Ksar Ghilane.

MEALS: Breakfast in your Djerba hotel, Dinner included at the camp tonight

Basic Choice of Desert Camps. Please tell us which one you prefer. Camp: Campement Paradis, Ksar Ghilane Tents are equipped with 2 beds and some furniture. Shared shower and Wash Closets (WC) blocks. 60 DT per person, including dinner.

Luxury Camp: Yadis Campement, Ksar Ghilane : Tents are equipped with electricity, air conditioning / heating units, en suite WC with shower, 2 beds and furniture. 200 DT per tent for 2 persons (or more in high season), including dinner. (Price for a single is less).

START THE TOUR DAY 3 Sunday, March 11: Ksar Ghilane – Douz – Salt Lake - Tozeur

Enjoy the sunrise over the desert; this morning you may wish to take a quick dip in the thermal springs or explore the oasis of Ksar Ghilane before we depart.

Our first stop is in Douz - the Gateway of the Sahara; we visit the small ethnographic Museum of the Sahara (closed on Mondays) before taking a break for lunch. We drive across the Chott el Jerid, the Great Salt Lake that serves as a barrier between the fertile north and the Sahara desert. If we are lucky, we might see a mirage or two.

We continue to the oasis town of Tozeur. In medieval times, Tozeur was an important cultural & market center, due to its strategic location on the caravan routes. Merchants from North and West Africa gathered in this thriving oasis, trade such goods as wool, dates, gold, ivory, salt and slaves.

Some of the finest dates of the world are grown in the region, the deglat nour or finger of light. Medieval accounts state that over 1,000 camels used to leave here per day, laden only with dates.

We walk through *Ouled el Hadef,* the historic old town of Tozeur. We wander the narrow lanes to admire its 14th century architecture and distinctive decorative brickwork (found only in Tozeur & nearby Nefta), and wander through the colourful souks and date market.

We enter the oasis and visit the *Eden Palm Museum*, where we will learn about the culture and traditions of the oasis, visit a plantation to learn about the date harvest, and sample some local delicacies made from dates. MEALS: Breakfast at the hotel.

Hotel: Residence L'Oued, Tozeur 76 463 https://www.facebook.com/ residenceloued/ 80 DT per double room, with breakfast

DAY 4 Monday, March 12: TOZEUR: The Mountain Oases, Nefta & Star Wars film locations

We start the day with a trip to the Mountain Oases of Chebika, Mides & Tamerza.

Located amidst the rugged outcrops of the Atlas mountains, not far from the Algerian frontier, these date back to Roman times when they served as military outposts to control the caravan trade. In Chebika, we take walk to see the abandoned village and source of the springs. To Mides – with a spectacular canyon – made famous in the film, The English Patient.

We continue to Tamerza, where we walk through the picturesque ghost village of the oasis.

Return to Tozeur and meet our 4x4 for our excursion to Ong El Jemal where you can explore the Mos Espa film set of the original Star Wars movie (1977) & Camel's Neck Rock.

Overnight in Tozeur Meals: Breakfast at the Hotel, Hotel: Residence L'Oued, Tozeur 463 036 https://www.facebook.com/residenceloued/ 80 DT per double room, with breakfast

DAY 5 Tuesday, March 13 TOZEUR - MATMATA – TOUJANE – DJERBA

Our drive takes us back across the Salt Lake to the Matmata mountains, named after the Berber tribe which inhabited this area since at least the 16th century.

The people here have traditionally lived in circular, underground pit dwellings carved out of the rock, complete with courtyards, kitchens and bedrooms.

We visit a troglodyte home belonging to a local family and the most famous troglodyte dwelling (now Hotel Sidi Driss) which was used as a film set in the original Star Wars movie (1977).

Ascending a pass of 585 meters above the plains, we arrive at the village of Toujane, scattered across two sides of a deep gorge – the road flanked by 2 looming fortresses (kala'a) which once protected the medieval caravans.

Return to Djerba via the ferry at Jorf / Ajim.

HOTEL: Ras dar Sema

DAY 6 Wednesday March 14: CLASSIC DJERBA: Half Day Tour of the Island

A half day tour of the main sites and attractions of the island of Djerba, designed for the first-time visitor. Duration: about 4 hours. Today we will see and explore the following places:

· The El Ghriba Synagogue: the most ancient & important functioning synagogue in North Africa, and the spiritual focus of the ancient community of Djerbian Jews.

· ErRiadh Village & the Djerbahood Project: walk the narrow lanes of the charming village of ErRiadh, home to Jews, Muslims and Europeans. See the marvelous street murals of the Djerbahood project – a project which was undertaken in 2015, involving over 150 artists from 30 different countries.

· Guellala & Le Musée du Patrimoine: Because of the rich clay deposits in the area, Guellala was the sole pottery producer and exporter in southern Tunisia for most of its history.

Visit a traditional kiln, meet a local artisan, and learn about the pottery which is still produced today. Visit the superb ethnographic Museum in Guellala: a private museum dedicated to the unique customs & traditions of the different peoples of Djerba.

· Houmt Souk, a commune in Djerba: a walking tour of the oldest quarter of Houmt Souk. See: the historic mosques, the Greek Orthodox & Maltese churches, the fondouks (caravanserays), traditional weavers workshops, covered souks, the daily fish auction (a curiosity – ask us why it is unique to Djerba) & the central market.

Meet traditional artisans and go to a weekly market in one of the towns or villages. We end with a visit of the picturesque fishing port, with its fine views of the traditional fishing boats, octopus pots and the historic

16th century fortress of Borj el Kebir (Borj Ghazi Mustapha) – the site of famous Battle of Djerba between the so-called Pirates of Barbary, the Ottomans and the Spanish Armada.

Overnight in Resa Dar Sema, Djerba.

ISRAEL was My Dream Destination Since High School –

Travel memories Year 1985

Photos are saved in plastic albums some taken by polaroid, other photos by instamatic camera . I was only 38 years old then, young, fired up with energy! Nine years ago I returned and explored the Dead Sea area. A lot has changed.

We joined a tour for 16 days. The Western Wall, or Wailing Wall, is the most religious site in the world for the Jewish people, located in the Old City of Jerusalem.

The site of the Church of the Holy Sepulcher in Jerusalem is identified as the place both of the crucifixion and the tomb of Jesus of Nazareth.

I sweat profusely walking up Masada, a rugged natural fortress, of majestic beauty, in the Judaean Desert overlooking the Dead Sea. It is a natural defensive site.

It is said that the Milk Grotto was the place where the Holy Family found shelter . If they are Catholics, they should pray the Holy Rosary together.

Nazareth is a city in Israel with biblical history. In the old city, the domed Basilica of the Annunciation is, some believe, where the angel Gabriel told Mary she would bear a child.

St. Joseph's Church is said to be the site of Joseph's carpentry workshop.

The underground Synagogue Church is reputedly where Jesus studied and prayed. Nazareth Village, an open-air museum, reconstructs daily life in Jesus' era.

The Jerusalem Market is a great place to rub shoulders with locals and experience the unique Middle Eastern market culture. Smell the spices and find anything. To catch and / or protect yourself from over powering purse snatchers, I kept ready large safety pins to prick their fingers or hands.

An open-air museum in Nazareth, Israel, that reconstructs and reenacts village life in the Galilee in the time of Jesus. Donkeys cross-crossed the alleys.

It was my first camel ride. The camel was not cooperative. I almost fell.

The Golan Heights a rocky plateau in south-western Syria, has a political and strategic significance which belies its size. Israel seized the territory.

Israel in the Mediterranean Sea, is regarded by Jews, Christians and Muslims as the biblical Holy Land. It's most sacred sites are in Jerusalem. Within its Old City, the Temple Mount complex includes the Dome of the Rock shrine, the historic Western Wall, Al-Aqsa Mosque and the Church of the Holy Sepulcher. Tel Aviv, is known for its Bauhaus architecture and beaches.

The salt concentration of the Dead Sea is unusually high. Anyone can easily float in the Dead Sea because of natural buoyancy. No need to swim. I just floated. Made a mistake and opened my eyes underwater Ouch!!! It stinged!!! My eyes were red for one hour.

Jericho is a Palestinian city in the West Bank. It is located in the Jordan Valley, with the Jordan River to the east and Jerusalem to the west. It is the administrative seat of the Jericho Governorate, and is governed by the Palestinians.

There was no conflict then. Palestinians and Israelites were in friendly terms. They helped us get a taxi.

Tel-Aviv, a city on Israel's Mediterranean coast, is marked by stark 1930s buildings, thousands of which are clustered in the White City architectural area. We went to the Beit museum and other museums.

Qumran Caves are a series of caves, some natural, some artificial, found around the archaeological site of Qumran in the Judaean Desert of the West Bank.

It is in the Qumran caves that the Dead Sea Scrolls were discovered. We visited the Yad Vashem Museum.

Love Israel cuisine eggplant tabouli and falafel balls made out of ground chick peas.

We stayed three days in a kibbutz - a collective community in Israel traditionally based on agriculture. During this time, Lebanon were firing bombs to Jerusalem. The lady in charge showed us the bomb shelter area down below the building, in case of emergency.

At 4:00am the next morning I heard loud whizzing sounds I ran to go to the bomb shelter. Then my friend said "No, Oh…No it's a low flying airplane spraying fertilizers " whew! A sigh ☺ of relief .

Every year, Leon Gork, our tour guide sends a Christmas newsletter by mail. I kept one of them. After all these years, during quarantine I found this:

My Dream since High School was to go to Israel, see Bethlehem, Nazareth, Cedars of Sinai, the Golan Heights, the Red sea where Jesus performed miracles with Moses. Fast forward to the 20th century – During the quarantine, one day in July 2020, after 27 years!!! I found this letter mailed by Leon Gork, our tour guide.

Many events has transpired thru all the years. I tried to trace Leon in Facebook to connect again.

Maybe time will be in our favor, I might be surprised one day and hear from him.

Sharing the meaningful letter I found:

- The whole contents of the two page letter and aerogramme envelope is included in my blog link : odettericasatravels.com.

Date: 17ᵗʰ Sept. 1993

From: Leon Gork, Tour Guide

Jerusalem, Israel 91042

Dear Mr. & Mrs. Ricasa & Family:

Thank you very much for your letter, which I received some time ago.

I hope that this letter finds you well. I 'm sure you appreciate that we in Israel have had a very exciting week, and we're in for some big changes in the future.

Only three days have passed since the signing of the declaration of mutual acknowledgement between Israel and the Palestine Liberation Organization (PLO) and the celebrations amongst the Arabs are still continuing.

The Jewish people can't quite get used to the idea of the PLO flag waving throughout Jerusalem, side by side with the Israel flag.

Many people are very worried about the peace agreement with the Arabs, especially with the the PLO. Don't forget that there are many families who have tragically lost loved ones in quite a few terrorist attacks, most of them led by the PLO.

We live in the land where the great miracles were performed.

I believe that this will be a miracle if it really works.

Next time you visit Israel I may take you for a tour of Damascus, or Amman or we might go to Petra and from there to Eliat.

Tonight is Jewish New Year. It'll be wonderful to start 5724 in the spirit of prospect for peace.

I'd like to take this opportunity of wishing you and your family a very happy, healthy and prosperous New Year.

Yours sincerely,

Leon, Ettie, Boaz, ariel, Avishai and Itamar.

Sent by: Aerogramme, Israel. Date: 17th Sept. 1993

Café Baghdad in Syria

Year 1989 - This was the last place I'd expect to find an inn in the desert, yet here lies a ramshackle, shape of different stone that has become a magnet for international travelers over the past years.

Inside, the walls were plastered with photos and currencies, monies of countless visitors from all over the globe.

We've had people from Taiwan, Italy, Holland, France and America, as well as British guests, said the owner, Mohammed, while showing me to a table surrounded by big piles of seat cushions.

The menu consists of just one dish: Omelets and sheep's cheese served with flatbread baked in an old oven. It is tasty and organic. If accompanied by coffee strong enough, you can't' sleep for three nights. The real reason tourists flock here is because, as far as travelers' outposts go, this place is the real deal. It is isolated and exposed against land mines.

I did not know we were just three hours away to Iraq.

The tour guide said we will try to go to the Upper Mesopotamia.

We got to the border, arranged permits, paid quite a big sum. Stepped our foot in and out. The post near the Al-Furat River was heavily guarded. We were not allowed to take photos.

Chapter 14

Terrain Relentlessly Rolling

Monasterio de Albarracin en Veruela Spain

Albarracin to Veruela

Josito, show me your plumes
A universal peacock in a cloister
Proud mama with her hair tied to a bun
A hair net over her face as she tended to baking cookies

Was I a Postulant for six months?,
Bible scriptures become a Novice

There it was
Challenging assignments from the community

Breakfast early six o'clock in the early dawn
The wafted smell of garlic on toasted *pan* (bread)
Ripe red tomatoes and two fried eggs
Wash laboriously the giant pots and pans

After every joyous meal
There is always an annoying piece left
No complaints

I do not remember the name of the wine we pressed
But it had a taste that I liked

If one cannot say something nice
Say something clever in our Lord's name

We cannot refuse to serve
Let's take a look
Attend a retreat
Prayer and fasting
My body needed nothing more

Then Love hovered
Romance was in the air

Above in Albarracin
The crest of the blue Guadalaviar River
Between the verdant hills, the myriad olive trees

Your name "M"
Etched on a wooden post beneath the beams
In the cafeteria

Rhymes and Legends

A Dream
Loved for many years

Here to enjoy your live-green eyes for a long time
Sus Ojos Verdes

Albarracin a Veruela

Josito, muéstrame tus plumas
Un pavo real universal en un claustro

Orgullosa mamá con el pelo atado a un moño
Una redecilla sobre su rostro mientras tendía a hornear galletas

¿Fui postulante durante seis meses?
Las escrituras bíblicas se convierten en novicios
Allí estaba Tareas desafiantes de la comunidad

Desayuno temprano a las seis de la madrugada
El olor a ajo flotando en una sartén tostada
Tomates rojos maduros y dos huevos fritos

Lave las ollas y sartenes gigantes
Después de cada comida alegre
Siempre queda una pieza molesta

Sin quejas
No recuerdo el nombre del vino que presionamos
Pero tenía un sabor que me gusto

Si uno no puede decir algo bueno
Di algo inteligente en el nombre de nuestro Señor

No podemos negarnos a servir
Vamos a ver
Asiste a un retiro Oración y ayuno

Mi cuerpo no necesitaba nada más
Entonces el amor se cernía
El romance estaba en el aire

Arriba en Albarracin
La cresta del azul del río Guadalaviar
Entre las verdes colinas, la miríada de olivos

Su nombre "M"
Grabado en un poste de madera debajo de las vigas

En la cafeteria Rimas y Leyendas
Un sueño
Amado por muchos años

Aquí para disfrutar sus ojos verde oliva por mucho tiempo
"Sus Ojos Verdes"

Memoria para foto en Albarracin

Albarracín, a Small Town

Albarracin is on the hills of east-central Spain, above a curve of the Guadalaviar River. Towering medieval walls, the Murallas de Albarracín, dominate the adjacent hillside. At their crest is the 10th-century Andador Tower. The ruins of a Moorish castle, stands on a clifftop in the old town.

The 16th-century Catedral del Salvador features a bell tower built on the remains of a Romanesque temple.

Veruela is a very nice and well maintained monastery. A peaceful place to stroll and admire the architecture. There is a cafeteria where the poet, Gustavo Alfredo Becquer's quotes are inscribed on the walls.

Apparently in the eighteenth century it was a popular place for gothic novel writers.

Monasterio de Veruela is a religious building, a cloister, located near the town located in Vera de Moncayo, the West part of Aragon province. It is a romantic and gothic building, where one can learn about the history of the wine in the region, Campo de Borja in the cloister. We walked in the surroundings and enjoyed with nature.

These are essential to the study of Spanish literature.

Albarracín es un Pequeño Pueblo

En las colinas del este-centro de España, sobre una curva del río Guadalaviar.

Las altas murallas medievales, las Murallas de Albarracín, dominan la ladera adyacente. En su cresta se encuentra la Torre Andador del siglo Diez. Las ruinas de un castillo árabe se alzan sobre un acantilado en el casco antiguo.

La Catedral del Salvador del siglo Diez y seis presenta un campanario construido sobre los restos de un templo románico.

Veruela es un monasterio muy bonito y bien mantenido. Un lugar tranquilo para pasear y admirar la arquitectura.

Hay una cafetería donde las citas del poeta Gustavo Adolfo Becquer están inscritas en las paredes. Aparentemente en el siglo Diez y ocho fue un lugar popular para los escritores de novelas góticas.

Monasterio de Veruela es un edificio religioso, un claustro, ubicado cerca de la ciudad ubicada en Vera de Moncayo, la parte oeste de la provincia de Aragón.

Es un edificio romántico y gótico, donde se puede aprender sobre la historia del vino en la región. Campo de Borja en el claustro. Caminamos por los alrededores y disfrutamos de la naturaleza.

Estos cuentos son esenciales para el estudio de la literatura Española.

Siempre

Le daré tu teléfono
Si ella tiene una emergencia
Para llamarte

Cuida tu salud
Yo siempre pienso en ti

Mi hija me envió este recorte de periódico
Te he amado en secreto durante muchos años
En mis suenos

Ayer las montañas de Formigal
Estaban cubiertos de nieve de arriba a abajo

El mismo lugar
Donde la luna dar besos

Por siempre agradable
Eso fue todo
Besos por supuesto

Always

I will give her your telephone
If she has an emergency
To call you

Take care of your health
I always think of you

My daughter sent me this newspaper clipping
In my dreams
I have secretly adored you for many years

Yesterday the ski resort of Formigal
Were covered with snow
From the top to the bottom of the mountains

The same place
Where the moon blows kisses

Forever nice
It was all

Chapter 15

So in Love with Lucy and Kai

Cutie Lucy, Super Girl

Cutie Lucy

A granddaughter is like a special book

You are a beautiful girl
With love to share

Treasuring a special bond
Your love so bright with excitement

Lucky to have you

When you were two years old
You were jumping at the seat cushion
To the back edge of the living room sofa

At times, my protecting angel
Holding my hand, leading me
As we go down step by step on the stairs
At the duplex on Garfield Street, Pasadena

You ask "Mama O - Ok step up...Are you ok?"
or I should be the one to ask.. Are you ok?

Christmas program in school
You were a group of angels with white wings
Red tutus with a red and white sash around the waist

Forming a merry go round, jumping with excitement
Holding hands circling the multi-colored lit Christmas tree
Singing loud and clear "Jingle Bells, Jingle bells, jingle all the way"

Your hair growing longer
Braided or pony tails held with colored ribbons or hair ties

During the pandemic
Stay at home orders
We received love, kisses through videos

Your molding Play doh
Kitchen spinning
Food play in shapes of watermelon, bananas, potatoes and eggs

With arms waving describing the steps of your creations
Using a cookie cutter purple, yellow, green and rainbow colors
Pretend pies, bread, bottled drinks and flower vases

Sitting on mommy's lap or daddy's tummy
Reading books: "Once upon a time, a princess and a frog ..."

Cooking lessons, preparing home-made ice cream
Churning milk and butter
Ice cream topped with "Oreo" chocolate cookies

Wearing an orange chiffon dress
Matching the color with the bags of oranges
You washed oranges one at a time
Ready for the juice squeezer machine

Your wavy, shiny black hair down past your shoulders

Dressed as Super Woman for Halloween Eve
Red top with an eagle emblem
Blue flair skirt
Silver sandals with knee high silver dust socks

Cape flapped with the cool wind pinned on both shoulders
Gold arm bands

Studded gold waxed cardboard tiara with a red star in front
A lasso, a sword and a shield

You were ready to charge and save "Lois"

Woohh..woohh..Hooohh…

Up, up and Away
It's a bird, it's a plane, its Super Woman!

Then, joyously counting the basket of trick or treats

Your ballet could tell a story
Stretch, turn and glide
Splice, split, rotation of a spin pirouette

Accompaniment of Arabesque, La Traviata opera song

Wearing glittering black three-layered tulle
Tutu springing upward, downward
Your demi-pointe could win a place in the Royal Academy of Dancing

In front of a big mirror of the bedroom wardrobe cabinet
You watched your movements
Your dance interpreted music
Created a song

Social Distancing during the pandemic
Caravan parade for Baby shower

In front of the house you watched us wave
Clutched firmly the blue ribbon of Mylar balloons
"Welcome Baby Boy"
As you bounced on the front yard
Played hide and seek with cousins

Board signs in neon green and orange
Taped, tied to our cars
Streamers, silver and blue cheerleader pom poms

A spread of party favors
Pizza pie, sandwich bites, donut holes, cookies were served
We took family pictures

A video in your pink dress with white hearts singing
Recognizing the rhythm

Footwork Upper body, step touch
Hip-hop your legs, crisscross arms, wave with happy feet

Turning twice, three times
"How many wonder, he's got everything
I jay jay walk...
But who cares, how they feel, I want more"

With cupped fingers of a singer
Lips pout, crooning *"Woooo..."* *"Woooo..."*

In your light blue summer dress,
For the first time
Overwhelmed
Cradling with astonishment baby brother Kai Christopher

My precious little angel
You always made me laugh

I cherish precious times spent with you

They are worth more than anything else

All the happy ties we have
When your daddy was a child

Years passed by
He met beautiful mommy

Long before you were born
You owned a piece of my heart
I thank God each day for you

Above all this
There is a deep contentment within

Knowing that a part of me
Will go on without end

Grandma O loves you
To the moon and back!

Baby Kai "Victory" with Bunny Rabbit

Kai Stole my Heart

I will always remember the day in July you were born
Pandemic times we could not go to the hospital
Clear digital photos sent by dad through our cell phones
Mom showed you proudly
Our whole family was elated, shouted and cheered
Jumped with joy, ecstasy
Texting messages, calling, spreading the news

Bundled in a light blue soft woolen blanket
With a blue and yellow beanie
Precious and warm

We said a prayer of thanks for a dream come true
A healthy baby boy Kai Christopher

In Hawaiian language, Kai means "Sea"
In Japan and China, Kai means "Victory"

Your dark eyes peeping
Cute little fingers

God bless your hands
Helping out is what they are for
Foretells a bright future

Your life is waiting for a scrapbook to be filled
With memories of love and family

The first day you came home
"Ate" Lucy beamed with cheerfulness
Softly cradled you in her arms

You are a star about to shine
Lolo and I are so happy we have you in our lives

A gift much awaited for
Your smile lights up the world

My greatest wish is that my grandkids always know
How much I love them
And they walk thru their lives
Knowing that I will always be there for them
Whenever they need me

Chapter 16

Rocks Rising Above

Fez, Morocco

A place for my spiritual heart
Strong ties to religious
Steeped in tradition

Oldest market in the world

A peek behind the walls
The oldest medina

Life of spices
Paprika, cloves, coriander, cumin, cinnamon
Smell buffet pyramids of gold, green red and brown
For the body amber, musk, verbena, eucalyptus

Adrenaline pumping
Uncovering the secretiveness of the blank walls,
Walking, eyes rolling

Through the maze of narrow twisting streets
People gathered, shopped, ate
Flaky chicken pastilla, spicy *harira* (lentil soup)

Listening to the last chants of the day
We Prayed

Buildings evoke exotic art deco

Fishermen, girls and goats ran up the trees

From the city's rooftops
Medina part discord, cacophony, part harmony

Looking over the streets
Many appear so narrow
Hammers bang on metal
Shrieks, voices, shout to each other
Children cry

Hand-drawn carts rattle over
Talaa Kebira, world renowned medina

Between modern satellite dishes
Muezzin calls to prayer, minarets
Pierced the clouds beneath the blue sky

Laundry hangs from clothesline
Flap with the short breeze
Black street cats prowled the roofs for food

Foods proximity to the earth
Represents our closeness
We come from the earth
From the ground up
The freshest is said to be sold
Vendors leave produce on the ground of cafes
Fried fish marinated in *charmoula,* a traditional Moroccan marinade
Thick *bissara,* a soup with fava beans
Smoke billows, a grill cooking meat kebabs
We crammed around a small table at Café Clock restaurant
Eating meat and bread with our hands, Berber Whiskey
Time honored tradition

Dharamshala - McLeod Ganj

Feeling light headed, ears ached
About to lose my breath, thinning air
Breathtaking scenery, vibrant mood
Generous sun, at least for a few days
Other times I wore my red rain jacket

My room with a view
Clouds would come floating by close to my balcony
Painting a fairytale picture?

Dharamshala became more touristy
Getting many more tourists than a village hamlet should
Learn Yoga and progress on the path of spirituality

Climbing up the Spectacular cricket ground
Where bowlers seem to run in the majestic Himalayas

At times I couldn't stop smiling for serendipity unfolded
The best footprints of life
Nirvana searching souls
Understand my body

An elder woman in the middle of amazing people
No English, she pointed to go see the Monastery over there
High in the Kangra valley, the McLeod Ganj

Walls with inscriptions of Alexander the Great on the door ways
Take Vipassana meditation course on the path of spirituality

Eat paneer butter masala and roti for lunch
Drink masala chai to warm my hands and soul

Rum and coke for a change
Walked to lower Bhagsu village

Fun tattoos on my arms that can be erased
Intermittent colorful prayer flags
Rich café culture

Gentle rustling of the monk's red robes
In seclusion nuns get their daily cuppa (British for cup of coffee)

Turning the prayer wheels in the never-ending halls
Nagmyal and Nechung open monasteries
Made me feel more content and peaceful

Short hikes to the Kareri village
Paused for free butter cup tea, but bring your own cup
Admired the caravan of nature
Then I became a part of it

But this migration and the exponential growth
Dharamshala tourism has its own disadvantages

Occasionally playing loud music in the night
Or wake up to almost-naked men sun-basking

Smoking, puffing a light MJ
Not wanting to smoke did not make me uncool

Exploring tiny trails amongst garlic fields
Goats and sheep climb up and down
Chatting away with the farmer ladies picking tea leaves

Feeding the cows freshly-cut grass
Children walking on treacherous paths
Listening to loud streams gushing close by

Fragrant Deodar and pine trees at St. John's church
A splendid library filled with history books
Geography of the region, colonial era photographs

Smelling the blood-red rose bushes and closing my eyes
I often tucked up on the sofa bed with a piece of *Bhagsu* cake
Short bread but more buttery crumbly base

Breathing in fresh air wafting from the pea fields
Mcleod Ganj obscure paths through the middle of the jungle

Devoured bowls of mushroom soups in local Tibetan stalls
Gorged on *paranthas* (fried donut bread loaded with butter).

Tiny birds flew
While a young monk practiced playing the flute

Chapter 17

Is it True ?

Whispers in La Junquera, Catalonia

A border town
Just below the main pass in the Pyrenees
Separates France from Spain
Driving a Toyota Fore Runner

Ixsatsu Bar with Mar Gomol
Art Gallery collections with quality
"Your paintings will be on exhibit" someone whispered

Nacional de l'Albera
Carved Heart with letters "M" "O" on the trunk
Little village of Ochre colored houses
Tabletas, tapas de Martin's Jamon

Paratge Natural d'Intereles
MUME Museu Memorial de l'Exill
Eros Center

Maison or Brothel bordels
Cheap Cigarettes, Cheap Sex
We rolled eyes and laughed

We sat at the patio
Fire furnace burning with desire
Where do I go now?

Dreams Continue

Susurros en La Junquera, Catalonia

Una ciudad fronteriza
Justo debajo del paso principal en los Pirineos
Separa Francia de España
Conducir un Toyota Fore Runner

Bar Ixsatsu con Senor Mar Gomol
Colecciones de galerías de arte con calidad
"Tus pinturas estarán en exhibición" alguien susurró

Nacional de l'Albera
Corazón Tallado con "O" en el tronco

Pequeño pueblo de casas de colores ocres
Tabletas, tapas de Jamón de Martin

Paratge Natural d'Intereles
MUME Museu Memorial de l'Exill
Centro Eros Maison burdeles
Cigarrillos baratos, sexo barato

Rodando nuestros ojos y nos reímos
Nos sentamos en el patio
Horno de fuego ardiendo de deseo
¿A dónde voy ahora?
Los sueños continúan

Concerts, Salient de Gallego

Pyrenees Sur in Spain
Summer open air concerts
You were looking for your friend Ashma from Lebanon

She was nowhere to be found
Perhaps traveled back to Beirut

Soema Montenegro passionately
Crooning Don't Cry for Me Argentina

We sat on padded Moroccan stools
Walls of the tents
Hanging bright colorful carpets Rabat, Morocco
Istanbul, Turkey vapor smoke pipes

Beer and wine, tapas morcilla, longaniza, cetas
Pastel de bakhlava and tocino del cielo

Aragonese Huesca, a must stop
Park Miguel Servet for strawberry shaved ice
Like children we hopped on the swing

Punto de Roma
Reservoir of Lanuza
Aguas Limpias
Separates España from France

Loarre Castle
Late dinner Restaurant Casa Marton
Tena Valley

Photos of Sunsets at Village of Benasque
Highest mountain peaks
Graus, People speaking the preserved Aragonese language
We sat on the wall of the River Esera
Roda de Isabena
Barbastro Cathedral
Bodega Sommons wine tasting

On to San Juan de la Peña
Canfranc International railway Station
How can one forget
Turning the wrong way dreaming

Conciertos, Salient de Gallego

Pirineos Sur en España

Conciertos de verano al aire libre

Estabas buscando a tu amiga Ashma del Líbano
Ella no estaba por ningún lado
Quizás viajó de regreso a Beirut

Soema Montenegro apasionadamente
Canturreando No llores por mí Argentina

Nos sentamos en taburetes marroquíes
Paredes de las carpas
Colgar alfombras de colores brillantes Rabat, Marruecos

Tubos de humo de vapor de Estambul, Turquía
Cerveza y vino, tapas morcilla, longaniza, cetas
Pastel de bakhlava y tocino del cielo

La Huesca Aragonesa debe parar
Parque Miguel Servet
Para helado gratinazados de fresa

Como niños, nos subimos al columpio
Punto de Roma
Embalse de Lanuza

Aguas Limpias
Separa España de Francia
Castillo de Loarre Restaurante

Cenamos en Casa Marton
Tena Valley
Fotos, recuerdos atardeceres en el Pueblo de Benasque

Los picos de las montañas más altas
Graus Personas que hablan el idioma aragonés conservado

Nos sentamos en el muro del río Esera Roda de Isabena
Catedral de Barbastro
Paramos en vinos Bodega Sommons

A San Juan de la Peña
Estación de tren Internacional de Canfranc

Como se puede olvidar

Girando por el camino equivocado soñando

My Friend's Prologue

Writing my book, Joseph from Albarracin sent this interesting suggestion.

A muchos libros les espera un destino desgraciado. Cuando son jovenes limpios y bien impresos. Esperan meses y anos en una estanteria para interesar o alguien, sin consiguerlo.

A veces, cuando son viejos, el polvo y la mugre de los anos, los van encarrillando poco y poco al trapero, pasando antes por la libreria de lanza y chamarilero de feria.

Es una muerte lenta, de degradacion en degradacion que dura, en ocasiones, un siglo.

Muere, finalmente, a manos de un ignorante para quien no fue escrito. Sin leerlo sirve para encender la chiminea.

Deseo que no sea me destino." - *Joseph*

An unfortunate fate awaits many books. It is clean and well printed. Young people, wait many months and years on a shelf to interest someone, without getting it.

Sometimes, when they are old, the dust and dirt of the years, little by little sticks on the rag, passing first through the bookstore of freelance and flea market.

It is a slow death, from degradation to degradation that lasts, sometimes, a century.

It dies, finally, at the hands of an ignorant person for whom it was not written. Without reading it, the book is burned and used to light the chimney.

I wish it is not my destiny.

- Joseph

¿Nos conocimos en Ginebra? (Geneva)

Recostada en un Lago transparente
Sembradas sus riberas de colores
Esparce el sol aureos fulgores
Sobre cisnes que nadan mansamente

Te veo aun durmiendo sosegada
esperando el nacer del nuevo dia
No quise despertarte alma mia
Pose mis labios en tu frente amada

Yo creo que en aquella hora, Bella
Soñando al besarte a ti

Ame a Ginebra

Did we meet in Ginebra (Geneva)?

Lying on a transparent lake sown with its colored banks
The sun scatters golden glows on swans that swim meekly

I see you still sleeping peacefully
Waiting for the birth of the new day

I did not want to wake you up, my soul
Softly, I put my lips on your forehead, beloved,
I think that at that hour, Beautiful Bella

Dreaming when kissing you

I loved Ginebra

Chapter 18

Sailing in the Wind

Si Tú Alejas

Antes que tu, ya no existe nada,
Ni despues lo habra, si tu me dejas
Aurora Boreal con colores sol de mi Alma
Me penara vivir si tu te alejas

Ahogare las horas en mis cuadernos
Renunciare a sentir otras caricias
Ire soñandote en todos los caminos de España

Nunca mas tendre paz
Mi dulce dicha

Como yo te esperaba y tu llegaste
Fue muy facil tejer nuestras dos vidas
Pero, amor, si quieres separarme
Tu Tambien quedaras un poco herida

If You Walk Away

Before you came, nothing existed anymore
Nor will there be later
If you leave me Aurora Borealis, colorful sun of my Soul
I would be sorry to live anymore
If you walk away
I will drown the hours in my notebooks
I will give up feeling other caresses
I will dream of you in all the roads of Spain
I will never have peace again
My sweet bliss
I expected you and you arrived
It was very easy to weave two lives
But, love, if you want to separate
You will endure a small wound

¿Eres poeta?

No es poeta quien dices de sus penas
No es poeta quien habla de alegrias
No es poeta quien canta ajenas glorias
No es poeta quien lee poeisias

Es poeta ama a todas horas
Es poeta quien llora con la lluvia
Es poeta quien con pasión, estudia
- Por que nuestra alma vibra

Are you a Poet?

It is not a poet who you say about his sorrows
It is not a poet who speaks about the joy of others
It is not a poet who sings other people's glories
It is not a poet who reads poems

He is a poet who loves hours of the day
He is a poet who cries with the rain
He is a poet who with passion, studies
Because our souls vibrate

Tú Llamada Por Telefono

Tu voz, sin odio, mansa
Mi voz con pena, intensa
Tu dolida y serena
Yo temblando hasta el alma
Asi fue tu llamada!

No se y que dijiste
No esparaba ya nada
Pero el oirte humilde
Llore mientras hablabas
Sueños de separarse

Your Telephone Call

Your voice, without hatred, meek
My voice with sorrow, intense
You hurt and was serene
I, trembling to the soul
So was your call!

I don't know and what you said
I no longer expected anything
But hearing you humble
I cried while you spoke
Dreams of parting ways

¿Por Qué Envías Poemas de Ensueño?

Velare tu Ventana Oscura
Duerme mientras yo velare
Tu Ventana oscura, hasta el sol
Y cuando tu despiertes feliz
Lo sabe sin verte
Mi Tesoro escondido

Why Do You Send Dream Poems?

I will watch your dark window
Sleep while I watch your blocked window
Until the sun shines
And when you wake up happy
You will not know I was looking
My hidden gem

Chapter 19

Like Mirroring a Sky

Odile

Roses into the California Sea

To my fathers who wait for me
To my wife and sons, loved, who remain
To all those who have for me a feeling

A memory or one praise
And why not?

Odile, an inspiration and first actress of this tale

"Yo solo se de mi que sufro
Que as amaba
Y que me numero
No es el estilo de los tiempos modernos

I only know that I suffer that you loved that way
And what is my number

It is not the style of modern times
Now people don't try

But certainly, life is difficult
You are always loved

Signals from the Spanish Skies

I received a signal back
From the gated gardens
Where are you now ?

On O Principe Street the walls of Vigo
Or in Puerta de San Vicente walls of Avila

In Sacromonte and caves of Guadix
Or Cuevas de Drach in Palma de Mallorca

The olive trees of Nerja
Or the orange trees of Seville

The bullring of Pamplona
Or the unique Square Bull Ring Of Chinchón

Picking cherimoyas in Úbeda
Or *moras* (black berries) in Cervera

Military parade in Murcia
Or beating the drums in Torrevieja

Drinking San Miguel de Manila beer in Bar Lanuza
Or Pilsner German lager beer in Bar de Toros

Chasing the sunset in Alicante
Or sunrise in Balcón de Europa
A piano concert in Reus
Or melodic chords of harp on the Hanging hills of Cuenca

Weather too hot?
Are you in Playa de Cadaques
Or in Castellon Playa Peniscola

Dunking churros con chocolate in Gijon
Or Crema Catalana in Madrid
Tablas de Jamon Iberico in Serrano
Or tapas of morcilla in the oldest theater of Almagro

Wearing the shell of St James Santiago de Compostela
Or the blessed medal from the cloister of Burgos

The soft winds blowing the Red poppies in the fields of Trujillo
Or the yellow sunflowers in the orchards of Medinacelli

In the museum of Salvador Dali in Figueras
Or Joan Miro in Barcelona

In the wash basins of Santillana del Mar
Or La Concha in San Sebastian

The Lovers of Teruel statue
Or the statue of El Cid in Burgos

In the hot springs of Ourense
Or hot Spas in Balneario de Panticosa

Wading your feet in the River Ebro in Tortosa
Or the Duoro River in Valladolid

Joining the procession of Virgen del Rocio in Almonte
Or Cristianos y Moros in Elche

Canning fish in Cambrils
Or my favorite sardines in Antequerra

Procession of Semana Santa in Cartegena
Or candle lit procession to Virgen del Pilar in Zaragoza

You are moving too fast
Following you dreams wherever you go

Señales de los Cielos Españoles

Recibí una señal de regreso
De los jardines cerrados
Donde estas ahora ?

En la calle O Principe las murallas de Vigo
O en las murallas de la Puerta de San Vicente de Ávila

En Sacromonte y Cuevas de Guadix
O Cuevas de Drach en Palma de Mallorca

En los arboles de olivos en Nerja
O los arboles de naranjas en Sevilla

La plaza de toros de Pamplona
O la singular Plaza de Toros de Chinchón

Recogiendo cheremoyas en Úbeda
O moras en Cervera

Desfile militar en Murcia
O tocando los tambores en Torrevieja

Beber cerveza San Miguel de Manila en Bar Lanuza
O cerveza lager alemana Pilsner en la Jonquera

Persiguiendo el atardecer en Alicante
O amanecer en Balcón de Europa

Concierto de piano en Reus
O acordes melódicos de arpa en las Colinas Colgantes de Cuenca

¿Hace demasiado calor? ¿

Estás en playa de Cadaqués?
O en Castellon Playa Peñíscola
Mojar churros con chocolate en Gijón
O Crema catalana en Madrid

Tus tablas de Jamon Ibérico favoritas en Serrano
O tapas de morcilla en el teatro más antiguo de Almagro

Con el caparazón de Santiago de Compostela
O la medalla bendita del claustro de Burgos
Los suaves vientos que soplan las amapolas
rojas en los campos de Trujillo
O los girasoles amarillos en los huertos de Medinacelli

En el museo de Salvador Dali en Figueras
O museo de Joan Miro en Barcelona

En los lavabos de Santillana del Mar
O La Concha en San Sebastián

Estas en Estatua de los Amantes de Teruel
O la estatua del Cid en Burgos

En las termas de Ourense
O Spas calientes en Balneario de Panticosa
Vadeando los pies en el río Ebro en Tortosa
O el río Duoro en Valladolid

Uniéndose a la procesión de la Virgen del Rocío en Almonte
O Christianos y Moros en Elche

Conservas de pescado en Cambrils
O mis sardinas favoritas en Antequerra

Procesión de Semana Santa en Cartagena
O procesión con velas a la Virgen del Pilar en Zaragoza

Te estás moviendo demasiado rápido
Siguiendo sueños donde quiera que vayas

By the River Piedra

It is midnight
The moon is a sliver of light
I am still typing
I cannot sleep

Reading the famous novel of Paul Coelho
Down by the River Piedra, I sat down and Wept

All love stories are the same
Maybe so
I write mine anyway

The first time I ever saw your face
I threw a pebble in the waters of the River Piedra
There you were, grinning
We were young then

I was with my mother
You were lonely

Some waterfalls
We took the narrow path
Up, down wet steps
Even behind the waterfalls

Green moss covered rocks
Winding through caves, double cascades
Past tranquil lakes

After twenty five minutes we stopped
We rested
Mother could hardly follow

Multiple small ponds with very large fish
Monks were making wine
Entered the peaceful Monasterio de Piedra

While my heartbeat was erratic
Not knowing I will be a prisoner

Ramon de Campoamor y Camposorio
The Palace of Truth

I believed it

Por el Río Piedra

Es media noche
La luna es un rayo de luz
Sigo escribiendo
No puedo dormir

Leyendo la famosa novela de Paul Coelho
"Junto al río Piedra, me senté y lloré"
Dice que
Todas las historias de amor son iguales
Tal vez sea así

Yo escribo el mío de todos modos
La primera vez que vi tu cara
Tiré un guijarro a las aguas del Río Piedra

Allí estabas sonriendo
Éramos jóvenes entonces

Yo estaba con mi madre
Estabas solto

Algunas cascadas
Tomamos el camino angosto sriba

Abajo escalones mojados
Incluso detrás de las cascadas
Rocas cubiertas de musgo verde

Serpenteando a través de cuevas
Cascadas dobles Pasados
Lagos tranquilos

Después de veinticinco minutos paramos
Descansamos Mamá apenas podía seguir

Múltiples estanques pequeños
Con peces muy grandes

En los monjes estaban haciendo vino
Ingresó al pacífico Monasterio de Piedra
Mientras mis latidos eran erráticos

Sin saber que seré un prisionero
Ramon de Campoamor y Camposorio
El Palacio de la Verdad
Por extraño que parezca

Chapter 20

Whatever is Hilarious

Ethiopian Coffee on Loose Grass

City Park on Harnet Avenue in Asmara
Getting together with Philemon and German friend, Douglas
Fatemah considered it an honor

Loose grass was scattered on the floor
Decorated with small yellow Asteraceae flowers
Bluetooth music played Elvis Presley's
Love me tender, love me sweet, Never let me go

We gossiped, discussed politics, life in Africa
Abundant praises

Building a small bonfire with coal
Fatemah starts to fan the flames
Manually roasts green coffee beans

Followed by grinding with a wooden mortar and pestle
Her delicate fingers, coffee must be boiled again

Decanted in another container through the second nozzle
Coffee is returned to the jebena by the top nozzle
Remains on the coal for a couple more minutes

Scraping the grounds with a ceramic ladle
Put into a special vessel with boiling water
Left on an open flame

Coffee grounds are mixed with the boiling water
Passed into a sieve, six or seven times more

Served in a clay pot
Jebena buna (pottery with a spherical base, neck and spout)

Does not consist of tasting a single cup of coffee
Drink three rounds is the tradition

Flavor varies due to reuse of the beans
First cup is Abol, the strongest drink
Second cup is Tona, reusing the coffee ground
Third is the Baraka or the Caminera, the weakest

Too strong? Drown in cubes of sugar
Each pass of ceremony received a different name
Enjoyed munching crunchy yellow, sea salted popcorn
History with Islam and Christianity
A transformation of the spirit

Meskel holiday commemorates discovery of the True Cross
Yegeniyeley (thank you) to the coffee's spiritual properties

Lahore, Pakistan

Our excitement unbridled
Floating in the freedom of crossing to Pakistan

Badshahi mosque
Lahore fort
Hazuri Bagh
Minar-e-Pakistan -
Wazi mosque

Images of Pakistan far more positive
Despite news of terror attacks
Relations with India

Hospitality beyond measures
Pakistanis friends by internet
Abubakr, lovely Andleeb with deep set eyes and Ahmad

As travelers we narrate tales
Locals invite us over to dinner
Offer to pay our bill
Of course we refuse
Give us free rides
Even invite us to stay in their homes

The affections, kindness, and hospitality
Pakistani people offered have a lasting impression

Heat and polluted air had stung our eyes
As we walked around guided by Aziz
Waving hands sharing the history
Splendor of the walled fort Lahore

Life now, the many mosques, prayer times

We entered one of the great cities of the East
Lahore! Heart of Pakistan,
Garden of the Mughals
Prince of the Punjab

On the rooftop
A ladder led to a 12 foot-square
Strewn broken-bricks
Sheets of corrugated tin
Provided some shade

Soft breeze blowing in
Felt delicious

On the plastic covering
We sat with women and men
Felt like a deep comfortable couch
Rewards of a wanderer

"This is called the 'tribal area,'" said Aziz smiling
He reached out his hand

"Why is it called the tribal area?"
"Because there are no laws here,"

We grinned and squatted
Barefoot in a small mountain of cigarette butts
Matches, rolling papers and dust

A story tellers ritual
Began the familiar sizing-up

How long have you been traveling?
Where are you from?
Where have you been?
Where are you headed?

"We don't know"

Santorini, Greece

Santorini is a summer dream. The noisy classic tavernas everyone is talking about. The white walls with blue domes, world mass wineries and more to see. The best island everyone is talking about.

The Akrotiri is a Minoan Bronze Age settlement on the volcanic Greek island of Santorini. The settlement was destroyed in the eruption sometime in the 16th century BC and buried in volcanic ash, which preserved the remains of fine frescoes, many objects and artworks.

With Yota and Efi, my Greek Friends -- loved watching the sunsets at Le Ceil Restaurant.

The street scenes: batteries and accessories for cell phones, Vendors selling sun glasses,

Fresh fish and vegetables weighed in old weighing scale - Greek cuisine served in classic tavernas.

Most winding streets have culinary gastronomy and roof tops with stunning views of the forever blue Aegean Sea - fortunate to have traveled to Greece several times in my life.

Even so, this charismatic island never ceases to amaze me. No matter how many times I visit Greece, there are always interesting novelties and surprising places to discover. Hellenic Seaways ferry Highspeed 5, and right after morning tea and traditional Greek pie with cheese, we are ready to go.

Blue-white houses, calm skies and our memory cards on the cameras filled up quickly. We saw a few churches, talked to a couple of tourists and finally met our friend's local acquaintance, who took care of us.

We went to eat amazingly tasty waffles in a terrace café, met the rest of his friends and were told what we - Coming back we really appreciated the view – thousands of lights turning on in the different sides of the island, owners of cafes and restaurants calling everyone in to appreciate the seafood, souvenir shop, asking "Where are you from?"

Large cruise ships stop here, full of American tourists, visit this place on a one-day excursion. During the summer there are so many people that you have to squeeze in the crowd.

We did not to go see the volcano and the hot springs. We sat in our guide, Luigi's tiny car (as the rest of the islanders, he drives an Opel), and went to see the old capital of the Santorini. We saw ruins from the earthquake of 1956, old forts, castles, churches and houses. There were many more cats than stray dogs in Santorini.

.

Later, grabbing our swimsuits and towels, we headed to the black beach. There are three types of beaches in Santorini, black, white and red.

White is the usual kinds we know, the ordinary sand. Black looks like dust or dirt, because of the volcanic rocks. The red one is due to iron and volcanic rocks mixing water. It was 87 degrees Fahrenheit.

It was too hot to go sunbathing, probably because the black sand attracts more heat. There were some very interesting cliff formations near the beach, full of hollow holes. The cliffs are made of sand and small stones, so are susceptible to nature forces. We swam, we sunbathed, and we also saw the red beach which unfortunately was covered in seaweed on that day.

We decided to go to Oia right away not to miss the sunset. The sun sets at 6:30 pm, and since we wanted to have a look at the town, we wanted to be on time. OIA is famous for its beauty, the narrow streets and houses even more beautiful than in Thira. At high season it's impossible to get a spot at the viewing tower in Oia to get the best look at the sunset. We got lucky, there were only a couple of people.

We saw the amazing view – windmills, tiny houses, ships and sunset. On the way back we were mesmerized by the beauty of the serpentine roads, and the view, when the airplane and moon were all in one line.

We dined at really elegant Le Ciel restaurant almost on the top of the mountain, where you could see the whole island. We ate chicken kebab chicken and beef kebabs, had Santorini Retsanos red wine and ate bakhlava with pistachios and sliced candied oranges.

Speaking of Santorini wine, we noticed the unusual way the vineyards grow, they have been braided into basket-like constructions, and the grapes grow on the inside, where it's warmer and less windy, so they ripen better. After the dinner we went to the center, Perissa black sand beach.

The next day we had Wine Tasting at the famous Venetsanos winery.

<   Riza Rasco ▶ Philippine Global Explorers   •••
May 6 at 3:39 AM · 📷

EVENT REMINDER: Get to meet our most traveled Filipino **Odette Aquitania Ricasa** in a live Zoom video chat on May 7 Thursday 9:30 PM Manila Time. Odette has been to 185+ UN Countries and 295+ TCC Countries and Territories. Call in information are provided in the member Event invite. — with **Odette Aquitania Ricasa**.

Zoom Interview – Most Traveled Filipino - by Riza Rasco

Zoom Interview by Riza Rasco

Riza Rasco is a Biological Scientist/Engineer, Intellectual Property IP/ Tech Venture Pro, Founder Explore Africa for Impact, World Traveler.

Former Research Scientist – Plant Bioengineering at Du Pont Company.

She is on a sabbatical from her job as a biotech executive in the United States to travel full time.

May 8, 2020 6:30 PHT Zoom interview By Riza Rasco of Philippine Global Explorers

Hello Odette, Attorney Jimmy Buhain will be attending your Interview.

Interview Questions and Answers:

1. **Riza; What inspires you to travel? Odette:** I's a never ending cycle see more - live more - travel more. Optimize movement. people we meet on the journey are the best images. Met Filipinos all over the world except in **Olkhon island in Siberia, Russia** –8 hours by bus n ferry, back ached. Maybe I did not stay long enough ☺. Current mission is to interview Filipinos (from low incomes to high incomes $14,000 plus per month!. Will be included in my Sixth Book.

Plus discovered remote places, way of life. **Qinghai ("blue/green lake") in the Tibetan plateau.**

Riza: What was your worst experience with transport, customs or immigration? – Odette:

Xing hai China, I was pushed out of a taxi because a group flagged the driver. I did not speak a word of Chinese, so I stepped out - they were hurling words, I did not understand.

Also, my camera stolen in **Gabaronne Botswana,**

Calcutta, India, exiting at the airport, passport control, the officer asked me to go inside a room all alone. No choice, he was holding my passport. not a single soul around at midnight. His question? I see your passport has so many stamps, you have been to so many places. What do you do? I showed my bookmark – I'm a writer. Eventually, we laughed. ---

Remote tiny islands, I have traveled:

Island of St Helena

Aland Islands

Isle of Man

Kiritimati islands

Kiribati Islands

- **Cocos keeling islands** land area: 6.7 miles
- **Nauru island** land area : 8 miles
- **Lord Howe island** 6.2 miles
- **Robinson Crusoe islands** – flies only early November to end February. Love it speak Spanish. No public transportation. Population: 240

3. Riza: If you were to personally nominate the 7 Wonders of the World, what would these be?

Odette:

A - the boroughs of Gijón, Ribadesella. **Asturias region of Spain.** Ichnites foot prints of dinosaurs in the Jurassic World coasts La Griega. (*Ichnites* Over 150 million years ago in the Jurassic period, dinosaurs

376

roamed the Earth. Some 63 million years were still to pass before man appeared. Many tracks still remain, even today, marking the passage of these creatures through Asturian lands).

B - **Ha-il** - **Saudi Arabia** rock art in dazzling desert landscape, petroglyphs carved on the rock's surface 10,000 years of history.

C – **Lalibela, Ethiopa** - St George cathedral built downward from a single tuft of rock. Visited twice, fortunate to experience church drum beats and chanting - performance every 3rd Sunday of the month.

D - Great mosque of Djenne Mali in the Dogon Village largest mudbrick structure in the world, kneading by hand - mud plaster clay from the Niger River.

E - **Samarkand, Bukhara and Khiva Uzbekistan** – these are whole towns of UNESCO World Heritage sites.

F - Las Geel caves **Somaliland** – paintings on rocks – 3rd century

G - Nawala Gabarnmung Australia Arnhem Land 24,000years old archaeological and rock art next destination archaeological rock art in **Arnhem Australia**. Dated 44,000 years ago.

H Coliboaia Cave 35,000 years old **Romania Bihor County** – oldest cave paintings in Europe - next destination

2. **Riza: What place was the most challenging for you to travel to and why?**

Odette: Freetown Sierra Leone – I arrived 2:00AM heavy pouring rain. There was only one small light bulb, very dark inside the airport. I had to take a water taxi. On reaching mainland, my friend who was supposed to pick me up was not at the airport. A guy with tattoo on both arms offered to go in his van. I was afraid to take the taxi alone. '*Kagat sa patalim*" (bite the bullet). In the van, I started a conversation.

377

I am a writer, I have written five books, showed my book mark. Wow! Congratulations, shook my hand asked me to autograph the bookmark ☺. He said my driver will bring me home.

He lives in a mansion, 7 cars parked. - Then he will bring you to your hotel. He will pick you up tomorrow – I will show you around. He is from Lebanon assigned to **Freetown, Sierra Leone**, chief of logistics of a diamond mining company ☺. He did show me around for 3 days. Introduced me to friends, "Be careful what you say, she's a writer." He made sure I was safe texting me everywhere until exit at airport because he knows airport personnel give tourists a hard time. Mentioned their chief Accounting manager, field operations is Pinay – Aww! did not get to meet her.

--Another experience, I was invited to speak at the

Kamenge Youth Center in Bujumubra, Burundi After delivering my speech, we took pictures. I gave my camera to Oscar, a student. I was autographing their notebooks, all of a sudden I remembered I gave my camera to Niyameh. Ohh My God! - He disappeared! Nowhere to be found. We traced his footsteps. We went to his home, to the police, no trace. I was so dumbstruck!!! Broken hearted! Then after 3 days, we received news. The police found my camera, but I had to pay US$120. Can you believe that? I gave in and paid US$120. At least I have my photos back.

More scary situation – No money during early travels saw an ad – need couriers free flight. Volunteered to be a DHL courier to **Madrid** 1987. I checked into Hotel Gran Via.

After dinner, I went up to my room. A handsome Espanol follows.. After a few minutes there were knocks on my door. I did not open, continuous knock 10 minutes, not saying a word. My room had no telephone. Was so scared. I blocked the door with the desk and chair. Thinking now, I should have opened the door, Yes? Need a date..hahaha. In th 80's DHL did not have their own planes. I flew by courier to Bangkok, Sydney, Tokyo, Singapore on courier trips. In 1989, DHL bought their own planes. NO MORE FREE FLIGHTS.

5. Riza: Describe a remarkable person you've met during your travels.

Odette: Serge Ondon Titan, president of Servas in **Brazzaville, Republic of Congo**. He was so impressed I had traveled to 247 countries. Impromptu, he scheduled a television interview, complete with a make-up artist who dolled me up. The Interviewer was James Ahou of the Top Matin show for 40 minutes. He also scheduled a Servas meeting – I was the guest speaker at the Pierre Savorgnan Memorial / Museum.

Anatoly Ionesov, President of Servas **Samarkand, Uzbekistan.** I stayed with a family arranged by Anatoly. He arranged a 16 days tour with Dr. Ilhom who operates a travel agency. The tour included Tajikistan. Samarkand, Caravan of Silk Route. I wrote a poem "Samarkand, the Garden of my Soul", published at the Uzbekistan News. Rajasthan Square is the front cover of my third book "Pieces of Dreams".

Riza: In which country do you feel most at home –

Odette : Spain I love vibrant Barcelona. For solitude, I drive to the Pyrenees mountains. – I visit Spain twice a year - 60 times. Spain has 47 UNESCO World heritage sites. I have been to all UNESCO sites except the Altamira caves – need a permit. Tried 3 times, no success --. Have been to most fiestas, Feria de Sevile, Virgen del Pliar, Holy week in Zaragoza, Christianas y Morros in Elche and La Romeria Fiesta del Virgen de Rocio in Asturias.

7. ADDED **Filipino hospitality**: Arrived **Gaborone, Botswana** next day I was picked by the vice president of the association – invited me to parties, met a Filipino whose passion is photography. He loves to take photos of animals in the game park reserve. Every weekend, we

had a barbeque picnic, then we would photograph, gazelles, giraffes, flamingos in the wild.

In **Namibia** I met Jean who gave me a tour of Windhoek and Swakopmund. She also introduced me to Benilda who took me on a tour around **Swaziland** - where I was met by more Filipinos. This is early year 2000 – they ask if I am not afraid to travel alone.

Equatorial Guinea was equally interesting. It's a Spanish speaking country, '*hablo Espanol*' I speak Spanish, I enjoyed.

<u>Island of Tonga</u> – Filipinos were surprised I am not on a cruise. I asked the Airbnb where I was staying" Do you know any Filipinos here"? They pointed me to a dress shop. So many Filipinos working in the dress shop. We had afternoon tea with pastries. Then I was invited to spend the whole day Sunday from morning breakfast with dried fish, stir fry noodles, spring rolls, *kare-kare* (ox tail in peanut sauce) in the morning!

After breakfast, the guys went fishing. One of the ladies, Edna gave me a manicure. More food, rice porridge, bibingka, sweet rice cakes, cassava cakes, chicken wings.

I was introduced to an artist – the only Filipino who can go inside the Palace of her majesty. He paints the fabric for their gowns, he painted a portrait of the royal family on the post office stamps.

He owns the dress shop that sews the uniforms for the police force.

The king sends him a truck load of chicken, bananas and fruits as gifts. He has to get permission from the King whenever he goes to the Philippines for a vacation, because he will be missed in the palace.

When I mention my books, they are very proud, introducing me to their employers.

- END

Philippine Global Explorers

From Nolan Tiangco: We actually met on November 19, 2019. I was having breakfast with Toton (Ton Roque) last November 15th, and we were talking about travel (riding the Amtrak, exotic places we've visited.. Then Toton mentions he has a well-traveled friend who has a collection of souvenir stuff in her San Clemente home. The name "Odette" came out in passing.

Since I already knew you visited Attorney Jimmy Buhain's place a few years ago, I asked Toton if Odette is the same Odette Ricasa. True enough, that's you.

So Toton messages you. Today am here with someone who wants to meet you. You reply back, "is this you Toton? Not a joke? Because you usually call me. I thought it was a robo call.

Then he calls you and asks your availability. Next Tuesday is when you're free to meet us at San Clemente. Toton tells me over the weekend to book on the Amtrak train since this is the most convenient way to get there. And then we see each other on Tuesday.

For February, this was your trip to the Philippines after coming from Saudi Arabia. I know you come home yearly because Riza told me in August that you planned to visit in September 2019, but it didn't happen. So I was anticipating that time you'd visit in September. Good thing you stay at BGC. It was very convenient for me so not a problem showing up during a weekday.

We had lunch at Bistro Madrid. It took three hours to update and fill up information on Nomad Mania.

Riza recruited Odette as a Founding member of Philippine Global Explorers.

At a convivial dinner party south of Manila, three members of the newly minted Philippine Global Explorers gathered to talk about their plans.

Once they started swapping travel stories, however, it could have been a gentlemen's club of some bygone age where adventurers gathered before a blazing fireplace to recount tales of going to the farthest reaches of civilization and beyond, encountering wild creatures, roaming the ruins of ancient cities, and experiencing first-hand the truth that all men are brothers.

The Philippine Global Explorers is interested in going beyond, off the beaten track, where the romance of travel still lives and breathes.

This is not snorkeling in the Maldives, a shopping spree in Kuala Lumpur, or a culinary tour of the hawker stalls of Singapore.

For travelers, it could be Cameroon, where wild gorillas thrive; or Christmas Island, overrun by red crabs, where Australia "houses" refugees and asylum seekers;

Togo, where the ancient African religion of vodun, or voodoo, originated; or magical places like Caral in Peru, where you can see 5,000-year-old pyramids unhindered by tourists, who are all at Machu Picchu four hours away—anywhere where one can still have an authentic, unfiltered experience of the world in all its wonderful weirdness.

Most adventure travelers journey by land, where border crossings can pose challenges quite different from the immigration and customs hassles one encounters in major airports.

Each destination is different, and some journeys—say, from Peshawar in the Pakistan tribal areas to Kabul in Afghanistan—can only be done with a reliable local guide.

Accommodations are very basic. It's usually just a bed in someone's home. And sometimes the conditions are not very sanitary at all. But we go through all that to see how people really live in these places.

Knowing beforehand how to navigate the terrain, where to find help, how to get along with the locals—information found only in certain travel forums and websites—could prove critical.

With the Philippine Global Explorers, anyone interested in planning a trip to, say, the Sudanese desert to see the Nubian pyramids, which are older than Egypt's, can find out the best and safest route from other travelers who have been there, where to find a room, what to eat, and so on to the Future of Travel.

Philippineglobalexplorers.com is a global community of Filipino World Travelers. It is a non-stock, non-profit organization. www. philippineglobalexpress.com.

Featuring:

Bucket List ideas, Favorite Places in the World, Memorable Travel Activities, Favorite Travel Events and Festivals, Monday Memory Lane, Tuesdays Travel Experiences, Wednesdays Where in the World, Thursdays Post your visit to one of UNESCO World Heritage sites, Fridays for Pride Day.

Schedule of Events with weekly Zoom meetings. Attendance are Filipinos residing in six continents, not including Antarctica. Meet and Greet every participant. Interviewing Travelers, Games and sessions and More Fun activities.

Board of Directors and Founding Members: Riza Rasco, Rambi Francisco, Nolan Tiangco, Odette Ricasa, Marcelino Mendoza, Jon Opol, Attorney Jimmy Buhain, Dondon Bales.

Interview with Ele Marie Apostol from Riyadh, Kingdom of Saudi Arabia (KSA)

Name: Ele Marie Apostol

1) Married or single?

• Single

2) How did you learn / arrive Saudi Arabia. For example through a friend's recommendation ?

• This is my first work as an OFW. The agency in the Philippines that I was applying for work overseas only offered - bound to KSA.

3) Your present position example: caregiver. Example of chores take care of a baby, or accountant, chef, or mention your husband was hired by... or Information Technology sample only

• Waitress, providing excellent guest service and guest satisfaction. Making menu recommendation, taking orders, delivering food and beverages.

4) You are treated financially well? With benefits ? Days off? Good working conditions?

• Yes, very good working conditions.

5) How often do you go home to the Philippines?

• I do have 42 days, vacation after my 2 years contract. Hopefully next year I will have my first vacation.

6) How long have you been in Riyadh.

• 11 Months

7) Do you meet with co-Filipinos during birthday parties, baptism, for good news.

• Yes, mostly in local market here. The name of the place is Batha, so many Filipinos.

Are you a member of Paris church - name of church? Serve in fund raising?

Yes, we have fund raising events.

9) Do you send financial assistance to family/relatives to the Philippines? Do you support family brothers or sisters going to school.

•Yes, one of my reason why I came this far is to support my family financially.

Anything to add?

Riyadh for me is one of beautiful country, the people are so nice, the foods are amazing and of course the culture of Saudian people. ☺

Interview / Excerpts - Dondon Bales, Jr. with Philippine Global Explorers

"**Donalito**", also nicknamed **Dondon** is one of the Administrators of Philippine Global Explorers (PGE), a private organization. Dondon is a World Traveler at Explore Next Level. He is currently completing a book about the Most Traveled Filipinos. His Question and Answer (Q & A):

Dondon: As member of the Travelers Century Club (TCC), you have been to 295 countries, islands & territories. Can you describe an instance of stressful level,

Odette: From Maputo, Mozambique, I took the public bus. I arrived at the station early to buy a ticket. Turns out, it opens at 7:00AM which in African time is 8:00AM. But, the, we had to wait for the bus to fill up. I had to leave my small luggage in the U-Haul cart. I refused to put it in the back, for fear it might get lost with all the luggage, furniture, live chickens, pets. Finally, after 2 hours, the bus was filled. We drove for one hour, then the bus stalled. We waited in the heat for another hour until a rescue bus arrived.

Dondon: You must have had Terrifying incidents.

Odette: I was on United Airlines flight **from Honolulu to American Samoa Pago Pago** International airport, which takes approximately five hours. After two and a half hours, the captain announces, "The Weather semantics in the cockpit is not working." In other words, he cannot see if it is too cloudy. "We have to return to Honolulu". Passengers looked at each other in disbelief !!

Questions: "We have to fly back another 2-1/2 hours with or without weather determining factor?" " Is it safe?"

Thank God, we reached back Honolulu safely. We stayed overnight with free accommodations and were able to fly after two days.

Another instance: **At the Chatham Islands airport.** Check in early because, the wind is the determining factor if flights will take off that day.

Flights are only six month of the year. So we were able to fly after six hours waiting.

Can you imagine, one of the passengers said he will sit in the cockpit and have a conversation with the pilot. There is no door to the cockpit, only a black curtain. And this was allowed? I asked the flight attendant, she said "it's ok,".

After 10 minutes, I reminded the flight attendant again to tell the pilot, I am nervous because the pilot might get distracted!! The plane was full of boxes of ice crates with cray fish.

In case of emergency, the passengers had to jump over the crates to the nearest exit. We were only 14 passengers. I told the flight attendant "This is it. I am going to write a complaint to Air Chatham." Only then, the talkative passenger return to his seat. We landed safely at Wellington, New Zealand.

Dondon: Some LUXURIOUS STAYS?

Odette: When in Spain, I stay in Paradores, historic buildings such as a monastery or a castle with panoramic views of a monumental city. There are 90 paradores in Spain. I have stayed in 87 paradores. I have the gold card which includes, breakfast, and dinner with open bar and a variety of tapas. I take advantage of free cooking lessons when offered.

Parador de Leon, North of Spain, on the huge San Marcos square. In the XVI century this luxury hotel used to be a San Marcos Monastery and hospital. It has a huge chapel inside. Excellent service and superb architecture represented by epic columns, spacious halls, and historical interior impress all travelers. I lived like a princess, waiting for a Prince?

In the VII century Parador de Alarcón in Cuenca - used to be an Arabian fortress and castle. It is a hotel that combines medieval style and modernistic. Its monumental style made me feel inspired and safe.

Discovering the castle I imagined being shot in a historical film because the spirit of the past is carefully preserved. A museum inside, the interior of the hotel is decorated with a collection of majestic paintings. I enjoyed the amazing view from the top of the fortress.

Near Paris. The Auberge, nestled in the Domaine de Chantilly, between the château gardens and the Grandes Écuries, displays the monumental paintings from the Condé Museum. Its elegant lines echo a very particular French-style art de vivre.

Its restaurant, La Table du Connétable, serves inventive traditional cuisine, and the libraries and the open fire in the Winter Garden Bar create a truly warm and welcoming atmosphere. The spa's subtle lighting and colored mosaics add the finishing touches. It takes an arm and a leg, but I always take the 3 day luxury package.

I went skiing at Santa Maria Cap d' Aran, Spain which is one of King Carlos' favorite spot. The valley runs about 25 miles from the French border to the ski resort of Baqueira Beret.

The main town, Vielha, and a few dozen small villages dot the valley floor, where stone-and-slate houses are clustered along the banks of the Garonne River and around the spires of medieval churches. Stayed at the Eira Ski Lodge.

Chapter 21

We Give Back to the Community

Acknowledgements, Charitable community service mentions:

Thank you to Ruby Guerrero, our leader serving the homeless of Los Angeles, California. Ascencia homes for charity in Glendale. Our mission is to lift people out of homelessness, one person, one family at a time. It is a non- profit organization, where we serve breakfast and lunch. We donate food and essentials.

All Saints Episcopal Church is also a non-profit organization. We cook and serve lunch, 100 to 120 persons. The quarters for the homeless offers clean shower facilities.

Bagong Silang Group, leaders: Carole Cotter and Meg Gutierrez. We send Balikbayan boxes of food, necessities and wire monies especially during the time of covid-19 pandemic.

Thank you to Myrna Aquitania for Weekend Balta News write-ups.

Lydia V. Solis for the Filipino Independence News reporting and National Freedom of

Filipino American Association of greater Los Angeles (NaFAA).

Evelyn Aviado Portugal for the celebration of the Black Nazarene festivities, site of miracles, prayers during Fiesta sa Quiapo, in Torrance California.

To Dante and Cecile Ochoa @ Filipino American Press club, for Writing classes with Peter Remo Bacho. Imagine 23 folks learn how to set up a protagonist, antagonist and more amazing to hear the laughter, the tears, the fondness for literary words.

Writing class held at the building of Larry Itliong also known as Pilipino Workers Center (PAC).

During the pandemic, we gave to numerous GoFundMe causes, eg: Marlene Cagatao, Janet and Jing Quipones, Meg Pipo, Edna Alvarez, Luz Santos, Godeh Silva, Carmen Aniceto, Angelita Aquitania, Rodolfo Perez.

Chapter 22

Tricks of the Wind

Xining Dongguan Monastery, Qinghai Tibetan Plateau

From Beijing, I flew solo to Xining airport. Waiting at the terminal I asked a Chinese lady about public transportation upon arrival. Surprised we"You are alone ? you don't speak Chinese?" "I want to write about Qinghai." "Welkom" my name is Linda (ohhh... my ears flap - a Good Samaritan) - "Come with us we will take you to your hotel." Turns out Linda is a nurse at the Qinghai's People hospital. "Our obstetrician is a Filipino and we have two Filipino nurses. any problem, call me ". ☺ Reflecting On Tibetan Kindness recording wonders of Mongol, Hui and Tu.

Dongguan Mosque is the biggest mosque in Qinghai Province. It was built in 1380, and now boasts a history of more than 600 years. The Mosque is not only famous for its magnificent architecture but also as a religious education center and as the highest learning institution. I walked around this square stopping for Chinese pastries and tea drinks.

With Francoise, who fell in love with China. - has been a resident for 10 years. – we stopped at the bar and pastry shop she owns.

Qing-Hai Hostel - My home - receptionist scrolled my Chinese name -\ pronunciation (PinYin) : ào dài té. QINGHAI is a large, sparsely populated Chinese province spread across the high-altitude Tibetan Plateau. It's a place of strong Tibetan and Mongol cultural traditions.

I have an altitude sickness so I chose this Tibetan plateau with 6,728 feet above sea level in some areas.

By virtue of a high altitude, Qinghai has beautiful plateau landscapes, a dream scape. Its waterscape within Qinghai Lake is the largest inland salt lake in China. has been attracting tourists from all around the lake.

There are numerous creeks and lakes scattered all over the province. As a region where many ethnic minorities dwell, Qinghai has various folk cultures of Tibetan, Hui, Mongol and Tu descendants of the Salur tribe, belonging to the Oghuz Turk tribe..

Xining has long been the meeting point of Han China, Tibet, and the Muslim regions to the west (Gansu & Xinjiang).

This mix is reflected in the Chinese dragons adorning the minarets of some of the city's mosques. There were Tibetans in white shirts with cowboy hats and red-robed monks rubbing elbows with white-capped Hui Chinese in Han Chinese eateries. A combination of Chinese, Tibetan, and Arabic scripts are in use on shop signs around the town.

Pagodas shine outside the Ta-er Monastery also known as Kumbum Monastery - built in a narrow valley.

In the Tibetan language, it is called : Gongben which means 10,000 figures of Buddha, known for its distinct ethnic and native style. It has 9,300 rooms and 52 halls. It is a group of fine buildings in a combination of Han and Tibetan style. It has lofty temples and halls rising one upon another All echo each other enhancing the beauty of the whole area. It was built to commemorate the Tsong Khappa, founder of the Yellow Hat Sect and regarded as a sacred place.

I took many photos - where locals lined to enter the mosque. Foreigners were not allowed to go inside the mosque.

Dongguan street was lined with tea cake shops for take-out. Shops were filled with hanging brown / reddish roasted chickens from the ceiling. Shy Tibetan ladies with their take-out smile. Satisfying curiosity aroused looking into Tibetan medicine culture.

Tibetan cuisine is super spicy hot!! My tongue burned but I ate it all.

Wi-fi connection was weak. Fortunately, Xingjiang also known as (Jack) easier to pronounce, shared his wi-fi password.

With my new found friend, we ate noodles with thin slices of lamb in spicy sauce. I found it hard to twirl the noodles with the wooden thongs, so I asked for a fork and spoon, unheard of in this part of town. He also accompanied me to the Dongguan Chinese Bank to change US dollars to local currency.

I took a taxi to Ta'er Monastery, 35 kilometers away. from Xining, it was built in 1577 in memory of King Ta'er . This is where I found peace.

The Gelugpa (Yellow Hat) order (means positive relativity) is the youngest school of Tibetan Buddhism. It is led by the Dalai Lama. They wore yellow hats fashioned in Tibetan style. Other monks wore red or white hats. When monks wore long, steeple crowned hat monks, it means they attended a special meeting. Sticking up high in the head, these neatly sewed cap resembles the shape of a rooster's comb.

On the way to the airport I asked the taxi driver to stop at this beautiful Sand Island.

The month of May is the best time to enjoy a wide field of wild bright yellow rape flowers around the Qinghai Lake.

Seven Emirates in the Middle East

In the Middle East the United Arab Emirates consists of seven emirates, which were historically known as the Trucial States. I traveled 3 times to complete the seven Emirates.

Abu Dhabi – Flooded with oil money- Yas Island in Abu Dhabi with the Ferrari complex I made three trips to Abu Dhabi.

Nine years ago the Sheik Zayed mosque was about ninety percent done.

The gardens and balconies and the women's Prayer room celebrants from around the world witness the spectacular onion-top domes The reflective pools that engulf the courtyard and the iconic prayer hall overflows with blissful sunlight. The mosque houses the world's biggest chandelier and carpet, both meticulously handmade. The calligraphy encircling the hollows of the domes, etched with verses from the Quran are painted with gold leaves in An-Naskh lettering.

Ajman - Ajman beach and museum - sincerely Emirati, more than a beach or museum – it is an inherited tradition of receiving and providing for guests.

At the museum we were offered free bottles of cold water, bowls of dried dates and square cakes with an almond dot in the middle. We were welcomed in and sincere generosity is everywhere in their daily life. IT IS A TRUE SENSE OF PLACE.

Dubai – an avatar of wealth, quick blooming skyscrapers, opulent hotels a mall with an indoor ski slope and temporary workers shipped from around the globe. Many labor work forces are hired to help build skyscrapers, clean the hotels and serve cold lattes to shoppers in the mall. Workers need to apply for a worker's visa. There are no chances workers can apply for Citizenship. The wealthy own futuristic Lamborghinis and Rolls Royce.

Emirates of Fujerah - I took the public bus from Dubai- as the rugged foothills of the Hajar mountains give way to the coast of Fujerah .

Skyscrapers and office blocks rise up from the arid desert. Hamad Bin is a strip of malls and flashy glass buildings. On the north are vast fields of circular oil storage containers. A taxi ride took me here to see the old fashion museum and its tiny fort. The museum exhibits Bronze age tombs and pre-Islamic forts.

Sharjah - Highlight of my tour was the Sharjah mosque that can accommodate 25,000 worshipers. The Rain room was a unique modern art installation offering a magical experience for visitors. It was an inspirational visit. The Mleiha Visitor Center shows the secrets of the life of early men in the Arabian Peninsula. I had a chance and rode a dune buggy after 6:00PM when the sun was not too hot.

Creative gardens at Al Noor island is all about creating nature art and creativity. We ate at the restaurant that served vegetables grown from within the gardens filled with floating butterflies. We roamed around the bespoke art sculptures, Climbing Stairs at the Maraya Art Park.

Umm al-Quwain - wrapped around an island-dotted lagoon stands in contrast to the glitz of Dubai. Much of it is at King Faisal Road with a few resorts on the peninsula tip. It showcases how the emirates looked like, before it struck oil.

Ras Al Khaimah: Al Marjan a man-made island covers an area of 2.7 million square meters of reclaimed land that extends 4.5 kilometers into the pristine waters of the Arabian Gulf. With a 23 km long water-frontage, the island is home to white sandy beaches, and is a unique holiday destination. Short dip in the waters too hot. Explored the museum and Mohammed bin Salem MOSQUE. Stunning view at the Mountain top: The Dhayah Fort.

Day Light at Faroe Island

Flight from Vagar airport
Jolly taxi driver wore a green flannel plaid shirt

What's your name?
Aggusteinus, madam, you can call me Augustin

It hardly snows here
The wind current so strong, the snow gets blown away
The northern sun
Creeps at almost midnight

"Please drop me off at Torshavn Hotel, Augustin"
Through my window
Wind lashed on the cliff tops
The climate surprisingly mild
Multi colored cottages, grass roofed wooden churches

Arresting landscapes
Treeless moorlands
Patches of farmland
Cairn-marked foot paths

Crisscross craggy layer-cake mountains
Scenic Mykines island with hundreds of puffins

Walking along the coastline in Mulafossur waterfalls
Sumptuous dinner, Faroese puffins with roasted potatoes

Unusual dessert at Koks Restaurant, Faroese concoction
Fresh cream cheese, sour cream foam, raw cucumber and radish

Was there a dash of honey?
It tasted sweet after all

Chapter 23

Dedication to Our Fallen Traveler

An Ode to Ryan de los Reyes

There's so much beauty in the world to see
That you need two lifetimes
But choose what you want to see in your lifetime
To make it worthwhile

Photo posts were Wow!
Replies were instant

But that particular day, sunset arrived
I did not get any text message
Hmmm... he must have stopped to rest, eat, look for a place to sleep

Next day was busy another sunset Hmmm... no text
Next morning "that's strange no texts"

I heard the news
A horrible car accident near the volcanic crater in Boise Idaho
Friends, family Philippine Global Explorers
We stormed the heavens
"Lord, please help Ryan recuperate"

While you were in the hospital
I played over and over your Instagram posts
Teary eyed, clutching my prayer book

Following your road trip
Amazing jaw dropping photo shoots
Attacks of the pigeons at Plaza Catalunya, Barcelona

When in Paris, Moulin Rouge

Strauss and Mozart in Vienna concert

Kids race in Macedonia
Crossing with driver Yuri to Armenia
Sanahin, 10th century monastery

Mandala Ecovillas,
Cascada de Tamanique, El Salvador

Under the Stars, Boracay
Flat tire from Guatemala to Honduras
A wedding day in Perth
Rainy day at Brandenburg Gate, Berlin
Trieste Centrale, Florence
71st country all the way up there to San Marino

A boating spree with family
Back to school days
A must have Karoake nights

Bratislava, Slovakia
Belarus, Transylvania,
Transdniester
Soviet Era Tiraspol

Instagram Wandering Waray with 24,000 followers

Eyes riveted, You have a powerful camera
Use your cell phone and a selfie stick

That certain morning in July
Rapid exchange of texts Changed route plans
Am now in Idaho Tita (Auntie) do this, Tita, do that

From the top of the waterfalls
Falling into the hot springs
Rescuers transported you to Emergency

More than three weeks
Doctors prognosis second and third degree burns
Need skin grafting, more updates

Prayed the rosary, offerings and lighted candles
We were all full of hope

Then the devastating news
A fallen traveler who lived a full life
Doing what he loved best
Gone too soon
Joined mom and dad in heaven

I was up early
Aghast and in disbelief
I pulled my summer blanket
A moth flew by
Did not pay attention

Hundreds and hundreds of friends
All over the World wrote
You were

"AN INSPIRATION"

A man who lived life to the fullest
Every single day with contagious laughter

I believe in after life
Two days after

Can you imagine
I found memory photos year 2016

I forgot all about the time I explored Idaho
The beauty of Redfish lake

Happy hour at Ketchum city
Bear meat burgers, fried venison, long Island teas
July 4th - With friends we sang God Bless America
At the Pioneer saloon

Driving up and down the road
Swinging on a tree trunk
The Bald mountains
Dollar and Stanley slopes

The last place you took photos
Consoling myself, I heaved a sigh

Whispered " Four years ago, I was there Ryan"

In the bedroom
Sun light was a sliver thru the blinds
I sat on my green chair

Admiring, looking over and over at your photos in Idaho
Sobbing, crying a river of tears
A moth flew by
Chased it away

Circled three more times
Strange, moths are usually outside
Fluttering with lights at the porch, at the balcony
Not in bedrooms

I realized
You were saying hello and good-bye
Ryan, is that you?

You left the stories
You told me your life to go by

You held them here
They surface now

.Winged bits of light from a moth
A butterfly, at times a fly

Like the floaters in my left eye
One evening when every time I tried to focus
They sped away

Rainee made a You tube tribute video https://youtu.be/gcV9-zlJNtc

Songs Kung Kailangan Mo Ako (If you need me) - passionately sang
your last song with friends on a karaoke night.

The song speaks about a friend who is always ready to extend a helping
hand and carry your burdens with you. Reflects the person you are –
always there.

The second song, I lived - reflects the way you lived your life - you did
everything that mattered in your life time. – with Reese de los Reyes
and Ate Roche.

In Loving Memory : RYAN CUESPO DE LOS REYES -- April 28,
1979 to August 20, 2020.

Chapter 24

The Essence of the Old

Exceptional Galapagos Islands

Streaked with the golden sun
Waters pristine, breathtaking aqua marine in color

Five million years ago
Underwater volcanoes erupting
Rising above the ocean surface

An incredibly fearless and unique wildlife
Stretched out to the peaceful horizon

Flight from Guayacuil, Ecuador
Puerto Ayora in the island of Santa Cruz
Roads with many speed bumps

Wonder why?
Speed bumps were placed for the drivers to slow down
Birds do not crash on the car windows

Day cruise to the islets of Caamaño, Isla Lobos
Las Grietas and Punta Estrada
Our boat rocked
Lashed away with the giant waves
We tumbled!

Are we going to capsize?
Angel was cool and calm
With a shy Ecuadorian smile

Enthusiastic naturalistic guide
¨»No preocupes» (not to worry)
"No precoupes"!

Clutched the side bar
Hid in my bright orange vest and yellow raincoat
Prayed hard

Soon we stopped
"Ole!" "Ole!"

Three steps beside me
Rare blue footed boobies (species only found in the Galapagos)
Tangerine/red colored sally light foot crabs
Inching their way to the black lava rocks

Angel climbed the sharp like razor blades
Of volcanic rocks with bare feet

How can he do it?
My feet hurt even with my rubber shoes on!

Avoided stepping on a family
Marine iguanas scurrying over the lava rocks

Barren and volcanic
A haunting beauty
Wildlife is truly phenomenal

Like sparrows
Awakened in the middle of the Pacific ocean

Elongated necks
Our chins held high
Darwin finches, swallow tailed gulls,
Pelicans, pink flamingoes, Chatham mocking birds

White checked pintails
Frigate birds that puff their red chests
Attracting females during mating time

411

White tipped reef sharks and sea lions
Just so unforgettable

Early morning market
Locals load their fresh catch

Fisherman slit the innards of the albacore
Feed to a school of pelicans
While three sea lions snatched some of the food away

An early walk through the arid Miconia vegetation
Salt brush, mangroves and prickly pear cacti

Oh.. wow! a deep crack in the lava filled with crystalline sea water

Stood awkwardly on the wooden plank
Arms stretched out for balance

"ONE DAY AT A TIME"
Dreamy letters flowed across the sunrise

Above the water overlooking the cruise ships
Water taxis and small boats plied the vast blue waters

Angermeyer Point dinner cuisine a la Galapagos
Black rice and beans, giant lobsters

Patacones (fried bananas)
Mild Galapagos cheese
Maremoto (tomato soup with fresh fish, shrimps)

Budget hotels and expensive hotels
Feel like Bill Gates
Rent a villa $7,500. per day

Charles Darwin Foundation building
A 150 pound tortoise lumbered through the cactus forest

Turtle Lonesome George
Sixty years old, the last of his species

Lonesome?
No mate
He could be extinct soon

A life span up to 300 years
Hopefully a mate is found

The summer sky began to fade
Into the white of early evening
Took three deep breaths from my diaphragm

From the distance
Memories swirled
Contemplated on the stars
Possibility of cosmic life

Margarita Island

A sun kissed island
The sun blinded my eyes,
Swaying palm trees, parrots
Warm blue sea

I found it delightful in the purple sunset swell
Where pearls the size of eggs were found ages ago

Reaching Punta de Piedras
Surrounded by mountain peaks
Maria Guevara's breasts

Needed to bring adrenaline level down
Have a less intense good time

Strolled the white strips of sand at Porlamar
Quiet fishing towns

Waters sparkled in the sunlight

A short and chubby mestizo
In a red and yellow flowery Hawaiian shirt
Strummed his guitar wildly
Comically sang
El Caballo Viejo (Old Horse)

Sunny Senegal in Africa

Claiming more than 3,000 hours of sunshine yearly

Flagged down a blue and yellow mini-bus
Careened through Dakar streets

Shouted our destination
To the *apprenti* (a person who works with someone to learn their skill)
A boy in charge of collecting bus tickets
Hanging by the steel bar at the rear

Speaking in French or Wolof language
Juno, a scrawny guy with glasses and steel wool hair
Smelled of syrupy alcohol mix that burned my nostrils.

Pushy touts
Exotic music
Cuisine that gives it the right dash of spice

Visa hunters strolled the waterfront
The underworld
Reefs and cays holds a promise of extraordinary sightings

Posed for a picture at the Millennium Door

Needed a hair cut
No problem
Executive Barbing Salon welcomed

Awww! Gorgeuos look
My hair primmed and tinted

Took a ferry to colorful Goree Island
Doomsday darkness
Slave ships headed to the Americas

Entered only for learning and curiosity
Colonial architecture
The landmark House of Slaves museum

More film locations from Dutch Portuguese era

O. Ricasa Axis of the Earth Oil on Canvas 2014

To be an Artist

At times an artist guru

We the artists belong
We all inhabit
Musicians or painters

An art movement
Pop art or contemporary
We look to the bright future

Happy, elated and exulted on sections of walls
Our creations on display
Ordinary to extraordinary stuff

The verdict of the Axis

A crowd basking in glory to admire
Or a sharp critique

To shine a strong light
In the shadows of the art world

Salvador Dali, Pablo Picasso
Rembrandt and Gustav Klimt
Francisco Goya, Diego Velasquez

Catalina Festival of Arts
Sevada Studio Gallery, Japanese town, California

We like to think as
Rising stars
A hopeful wish

We meet in Paris
A tiny landscape by the Seine River
Or at the Broad museum in Los Angeles

Souvenir posters
We speak with our paint brush
The art scene

Cultural and linguistic barriers
Themes connect our work

We live and work everywhere
We come out and tell you

- March 2020 - submitted a work of Art to Jean-luc Turlare
in Paris. Art work display in Samara, Russia. .

O. Ricasa Two Women Oil on canvas 1997

Note: As a student at Mission Renaissance Art School, we had to copy and study the techniques used by masters. I chose one of my favorite Paul Gaugin.

Artistry in Moorea

Adapting a local custom
Wearing a *pareu*
Printed with purple orchids and yellow butterflies
Wrapped around my chest
Driving on the opposite side of the road

Speaking a few French words
Off to Paul Gaugin Museum
Mango trees everywhere
Stopped and picked some
Swimming at Papenoo beach

Fautaua Waterfalls
Part of a keen pleasure
Jumping in a glass bottom boat
To the exotic South Seas
Feeling the salty breeze blow on my face

A bright sunny day, hot and humid
Sky with puffy clouds
Full of dreams in Tahiti
Posing at the foot of Mount Orohena

Pearls from the Papeete Market
A gift from this island
Staying on the right side of the shore
French military men " Bonjour'
Walking barefoot beneath breadfruit trees

Tropical forest speckled with coffee plants
Reaching a jumble of basalt rocks

Dense foliage around Afareaitu waterfalls
Striving to be entirely free

Shadowy Mount Venus
Blue lagoons
Swaying to distinctly Polynesian jazz

The Running Cows of Pinsoro, Spain

At Ejea de los Caballeros
Temporary barricaded fence
Set up all around the plaza

Cows let loose in a sectioned-off subset
Made the locals jump up and down
Avoiding to be swaggered by its horns

Like Running of the Bulls in Pamplona
Closer and closer to the arena
We crouched and labored in a methodical motion

A summer time festival
Colorful banners flapped across the clear blue sky
Playing a trick
The crowd waved their red jackets to attract the cows

Watching carefully in a festive air
The band of Taxarongga di Fustiñana
Played a jazz tune as a salute to us *Americanos*
A patriotic honor

After the show
We sneaked by the back door through the hallway

Took a drink at Casa Rural el Cierzo
With fluttering wings
We drove the car away

Always parting
A single crow cried

Reed Boats in Lake Titicaca

Musicians played guitar and flutes
A wooden hull and a salvaged bus engine
At such a high altitude
We chugged at a brisk five miles per hour

Sacred to the Inca
Manco Capac and Mama Oello, Children of the Sun
Emerged from the lake to the Bolivians
Paying homage by erecting temples

Navigable blue waters that exude potent power
A two ton gold chain from legends is in the lake
Now only the stones talk

Tortora reeds grow in the shallows
My feet sunk a foot down with every step
While Mercedes showed potatoes she cultivated
On this manmade island

Uros Indians selling bright colored blankets and aprons
While the transistor radio blasted Andean music
Vibrant mix of modern and traditional culture

My ear ached from the High Altitude
Drunk seven cups of hot water with coca leaves
Which did not help
My breathing was laborious

Took deep breaths
Sat on a concrete bench on the red earth
Crowned by seven gorgeous stone arches

Mer de Glace, Chamonix

Dressed warmly like Eskimos
We sat on a wooden bench
With exulted admiration watching the sharp cuts of ice
Constantly shifting with the effects of sunlight

Rode the cog wheel train to Monteveners
Glaciers the Druts and the Grandes Jorasses
Blown away by its magnificence

Like fiery stalactites when the wind blows
The mist evaporated on the border of France and Italy
A vast jumble of splintered white snow formations
Wooded hill sides and Alpine meadows

Climbers and skiers
Wind twisted firs
Deep crevassed glaciers

Sheer rock faces and splintered crags
Frightening spears of rocks
Magically towering above it all

Panoramic views mountains rising from either side
Sweeping bits of granite
Now and then obscured by clouds
Our smiles were glistening snow faces

Dreaming about Panticosa, Spain

The ray that does not stop
Songbook and romance absences

The sun still shone at twelve midnight
I had a faint disturbance in my mind
A vision that could float out of sight and yet, not
Arctic desert rose purple, wild along the Russell glacier

Expanse of hills covered with green grass
Shed of pine trees seemed a natural setting
For so festive a welcome in the majestic mountains
La Foratata stood high

La Ripera restaurant was opened
Red wine overflowed from the cave
Rapidly drank a full glass from Ribera del Duero

Amazed at how easy it was
With alcohol to be lost from the bondage of spirits

Hangover the next day seemed mild
Hot water in the cold, high mountains
Baños de Panticosa
I stood by the lake and watched you

Like a wild galloping horse those early days

Half certain I will see you in my dreams
The feeling grew more ominous and persistent

Chapter 25

Finding New Meaning

Loop Around Split in Croatia

A sea of Croatian humanity
Piercing turquoise seas
I chose a bench by the Riva
The blue waters laps the walls of the Diocletian's Palace

Watching life go by
I wandered the labyrinth lanes of the Old Town

At Stari Grad hotel
Sat on a red cushion by the tall windows
Ordered a small glass of red wine
Continued on the People's Square (Narodni Trg)
Dalmatian history imbedded here

A single loop around the park
Grand Old Café (Gradsk Kavarna)
Where everybody meets
Bacvice beach and Tresnik beach

Stopped by Konoba Varos
Near the market
Piles of wriggling fish
Catch of the day

The neon glaze of the signs switched off
Revealing all the charm and color

It looked like the beginning of a thought
The ocean of land
Pulled like a tide
On this side of the Adriatic Sea

El Crucero, the Tapa Bars of Spain

Be it Victor Hugo's Bar
Or Palma de Mallorca Bar
Or Pepe's Bar at Chinchon
Or Palosanto Bar in Barcelona

At ten o'clock in the evening
It is packed
A crowd of faces
Slap their hands
A scrum of bodies
Calling "Hola!!!" Que tal?"

The radios cough with static
With the latest news and gossip
The television screens light up

A flurry of shouted orders
"*Morcilla*, (sausage) *Gambas al ajillo* (Shrimp with garlic)
Berenghena (eggplant)

Calls for service
Loud whistles
Appetizers. more sophisticated cuisine

The noise builds
Shuffling growls
Women's raucous laughter
A dissonance of sounds

Cerveza Negra (Dark beer)
Enrique is behind the bar
Pulls pint after pint

Leaning against the pumps
The beer froths in the glass

Or gets the salt shaker to melt the foam

The battered grandfather clock in the corner
Strikes twelve
Drowns in the noise
Nobody hears it

There is an ongoing sense of excitement
Almost everyone is tipsy, winking and smiling

O. Ricasa Cliff dwellings in Bandiagara Water color - 2002

Cliff Dwellings, the Bandiagara Escarpment

Village of Banani
Moving on further to the ancient Ireli Village
To Tireli for a Dogon mask dance
Some deep rooted revelry
Religious stories

Caves of Deguimbere
Carved into the mountains
The edge of high cliffs
Hot and dusty
Frozen in time small villages

Families in stones and mud houses
Granaries built up high

Moving on to Djenne, millennium city

Arriving at Mopti, the Venice of Mali
Dizzying fishing port
Four drum beats of Cumbia music
Full of commotion market

Ethnic groups
Bambara
Fulani
Bozo
Bobo
Dogon
Songhai
Come trekking by camels to trade

Production of food
Onions and millet
Communal bowl meals

The search for wood and water
Consume enormous human energy
Especially that of the village women

An archaeological exploration

Medieval Skadar, Albania

Driving from Stevi Stephan, Montenegro
High mountain ranges
Zig zag narrow roads
Sometimes not viable
Coastal zone of blue waters

Crossing the Mesi Bridge
No more traces of communist era
Few tourists venture here

Biggest town in the North
We climbed the Medieval Castle of Rozafat
A fine view of Lake Skadar
Stare out across the river Drin

Shut off from the rest of the world for twenty years
No central bus station
Roads not in fair condition
Few speak English

Mosques are all around
Rare to hear a prayer call in the early morning

Although a Muslim country
Very few women wore a Hijab

Logistics of why I came

Not that many adventurers have been here before

Follow the book of travel
Bookish

I heave a sigh

The Albanian flag is everywhere
Not just on government buildings

Difficult mood and experience to explain
Traveling back to centuries in only one day
Grow rich in knowledge

"Pershendetje" Hello in Albanian
Much too lovely a day

Celtic Soria, Spain

Philosophy
You wanted to gulp more beer

Valdelavilla
Siesta time
Ghost town

Complete strangers
In a tiny rural village
A thin sheet of early January frost

Pressing your pointed finger
On the frosted glass of our car's windshield
You spelled "Minnie Mouse"

Traveling along the
Duero River

Occupied in solitude for a whole hour
Numantia Celtic outpost

Iberian resistance to Roman conquest
Indulge
Embrace very tightly or avoid

And so it was
An ordinary encounter
Feelings in a songbook
Your eyes lingered on

Dreaming once more?

Chapter 26

Let the Sunshine In

Clear Skies in the Deep Blue of Tasmania

Setting foot almost to cross Antarctica
In the heart of Hobart
Between Mt. Wellington and the Derwent River
With its magnificent harbor
Sullivan's cove, docks, piers, wharfs

Source of springs
Tassie's famous fresh air
Passing the historic suburb of Battery Point
Slipping under the pier
Roaming around Salamanca market

Listening to Banjo Patterson
And his poetic love for Aussies

There is something about the open sea
The open horizon
An endless space right in front of our eyes
It calms the mind
Let go off some of life's stresses

Serenity!

Dining at the Mecca of fresh fish
Mure's restaurant and Fish Frenzy by the wharf
Helen and I feasted on Salmon with brie cheese salad
And blue eyed Trevala

A good look at the Tasmanian Bridge
And how it came crashing down years ago

Out the blue open space
Right in the middle
Dolphins jumped clear out of the water
Sea eagles with meter long wings flew above

Over and beyond
Finding new meaning

Standing on the Walls
of Avila, Spain

The road was steep and winding
By late October the wind blew sharply
The sun still stroke hard
Nerja appeared behind the white hills

Deeply religious city

The mountains undulated and circled around
The Ebro River splashed on the cliff side weeds
It carried through green terrain
Purple capped thistles descended the way

Driving through cypress trees to the village
The sun had crept to the north and was poking yellow
The wind had eased away

I sat by the road to Avila
Ate pomegranates
Its walls erupted to wide vertical rocks

Ancient Celtiberian culture
Mystic Santa Teresa of Avila
A large bouquet of red roses
The power of spiritual love

Sitting or standing
Intoxicating compassion
Robed priests
Engaged in the massive walls and stone towers
Puerta de Alcazar

We walked on the thick fortified walls
Of saints and angels

Somewhere was an easier ascent
A raven blew the blue skies
I cried softly in joy

Plaza Mercado chico
We bought boxes of famous *yemas* (candied egg yolks)
Hojaldres (butter flaky cookies)

The Pubs at Jersey Island

In search of the ultimate crab sandwich
Jersey crabs
A humble sandwich bulging with tender crab meat
A taste sensation with jersey royal potatoes

Pomme d'Or hotel
The tireless charm of St. Brelade's bay
Rocky headlands, sparkling seas, beach side cafes

Mont Orgueil Castle
Huge fortress hewn into a cliff
One of the Channel Islands in the English Channel

Into a series of giant steps
Above the Gorey harbor
Grassy meadows with coastal paths
Dotted with lavender and white flowers

St. Brelade, a farm devoted
To the growing, harvesting, distillation
And drying of lavender

La Mare state wine and chocolate tasting

Diamond Chinese restaurant
Walking on Hill street and Snow street

Room with a sea view at St. Helier
Battle of the flowers festival

Honey colored jersey cows

Untouched cliffs and coves, La Hogue Bier

Elizabeth's Castle
Accessible only by causeway at low tide
Originally a monastic settlement

Jersey associated with knitting

The sea a sparkling deep blue
That mirrors the complete sign of clouds

From my vantage point at Havre de Pas
A short walk

Grassy headlands and granite cliffs
Suddenly there are abandoned fortifications

Through a mix of ferns, heather and shady woodlands
The island's wildlife, a jersey green lizard

Boats beached in neat rows
At the Hungry Man Cafe
A wild windswept jumble of rocks

Jersey tides rise and fall quickly
Past countless rock pools
Alive with scurrying crabs and marine life

Fisherman's chapel - peaceful and simple
A strange moonscape in the night
Beneath low tide, rocks and gullies

Moon walk to Seymour
Pubs everywhere

Jersey is like the West Country
With a pleasant twist of France
Creamy milk ice cream and La Mare wine festival

Central market in downtown
Mighty ghast of winds
My umbrella turned upside down

Cornish pasties, liver and meat pies
Fried egg, ham and beans
French baguette and Scottish bread

Gestures of your childhood
You whispered *"Mon ami"*

Ohhh…I almost missed my bus ride

O. Ricasa Do You Want Love Water color 1999

Do You Want Love?

Love what you do

Focus on what you are given
Say Aloha again with free coffee
Across the shores of Oahu

The calm waters of the Red Sea as you float
D'Wave restaurant in Riyadh, Kingdom of Saudi Arabia

Namaste in India
Romp in the waters of the Bay of Bengal

The unspoiled coral islands of Lakshadweep

Eat in commune at Amritsar's Golden Palace

Last call for Fall color in Vermont
Flashy foliage shimmering
Maple trees, birch, beech and alders

Just you in a photo safari in Hwange National park
The white rhinoceros, post it on Instagram

Hola Muneca Dance the erotic tango
Calle Florida, Argentina
Create a story on Facebook

Push the tired donkey up the steps of Petra Jordan
Tour guides ride their galloping horses
Their turbans flying
Up high to the Treasury

451

In the pursuit of the Dalai Lama
In front of the stage
I kneeled, clasped my hands and bowed my head

Bow and arrow festivities in Ulanbaatar, Mongolia
Wrestling, horse racing and archery

An Ode to Romance
On a boat ride in Dal Lake Srinagar, North India

Beautiful chinar and deodar trees at the Mughal Gardens
Shasti sweets souvenir store on Residency – too sweet

Senorita in Tlalpan, Mexico
Bended knees planting maize
Flattening, rolling flour and corn tortillas

Discover with new eyes
Just do it
No procrastinators here

Love Echoes

Distinto de la Criatura

Poesia, que ya no me acompanas
Porque no amo lo mismo que ame entonces

Poesia, que mueres cuando al alba
Me agitan, con el dia, mil pasiones

Poesia, belleza, hecha palabra
Poesia, amor hecho belleza

Poesia ensueños que no pasan
Poesia, dolores que se quedan
Poesia, eterna como el alma
Que hace al hombre
Distinto de la criatura

Different From a Creature

Poetry, that you no longer accompany me
Because I don't love the same that I loved then

Poetry, that you die when at dawn
A thousand passions stir me with the day

Poetry, beauty, made into word
Poetry, love made beauty

Dream poetry that does not pass
Poetry, pains that remain

Poetry, eternal as the soul
What is a man
Different from a creature

So that I May Leap Higher

Voila!
I assure you
I am happier, elated

We deserve the right to be happy

No, no, no more tears welled up
No more crying
That makes my eyes swollen like plums

No, no more sadness
Without knowing why

No, no more
Strolling aimlessly

No, no more angriness
In such small matters

No, no more transient joys
Or relying on destiny

I proclaim
With a singing tune of sugar and honey
I will laugh heartily

In the course of my earthly existence
With clear eyes
I shall see the golden lines
The half silver and full moon

In silent contemplation
Though at times obstructed

I will find complete satisfaction
Through these purposeful verses
In the mundane joys of the senses

A Pilgrimage, Chartres Cathedral

Rose of France
Where the Druids once worshiped

Acropolis of France
Finest French Gothic style

Virgin Mary in a garden of Roses
Myriads of stained glass
Marvelous rich deep blue

The ancient wooden Virgin
Figures from the royal portal
The Last Judgment

You held my hand
Near the North transept
Notre Dame de la Belle Verriere
(Our Lady of the Beautiful Glass)

A lily of purity
Violet for humility
Closely linked to the roses we were

Song of Solomon
Unbroken virginity
Queen of Heaven
Stellar Maris, Star of the Sea

Attracted to each other
The Annunciation
The Nativity

The Purification
The Assumption

The gates closed
We continued on to our journey

Chapter 27

Don't Waste, Live It

Sometimes I Am Scared

Ever dissolving a panorama of memory
A sound track that runs and repeats the very words
Most painful to hear
You love me

A film which replays even against my closed eyes
Particularly in the air that I breathe

Drowned in bitterness
Dark experiences of the crucial past
I am afraid to love again

The senses that I long to forget
Wounds that are fresh
Cautious of the moment

One likes to be loved
You profess faithfulness over and over

A gusty wind will fall
The sun will go down
What is my poor soul to do?

Against a pale blue cloudless sky

Kanu, the Bar Man on the Island of St. Kitts

A sprig of black grapes
A twist of lime

He had the obsession drive to prove
To know the alcohol makes us forget

Skin dipped in hot waters of Sugar Bay Club
With a necklace of tiger's teeth

He stole a furtive kiss on my cheek
While we swayed to Bob Marley's rhythm

Until the light faded
Until the music rocked more

My anklets
Slipped into the wet blowing grass

Towering cloud fringed Mount Liamuiga
A dormant volcano
Lush tropical rain forest rose gracefully

Intoxicated by the sunlight
Sea, air and abundant vegetation
We tanned our skin in exotic paradise

Strolling along Basse Terre and Brimstone Hill
Kanu, with his West Indian accent
Laughed at my history buff

Real Nothingness

Needing to get away
I had to stop

Look at what I am doing
Study my potential

Convinced I am doing something important

In an angle, I hear muted voices
A phonograph record playing?

Suddenly I am awake
Laughing

An unusual warmth has settled in
The room was lit by moonlight

No longer hurt
Innovated by an optimistic future

Owing Kudos to Marife

Special mention to **Mafe Leal-Lalonde** who introduced me to her friends with the United Nations around the world, especially in Africa. I first met her dad, Maning Leal during a solo travel in the island of Vanuatu. We clicked, became close friends because we grew up in the same neighborhood of Quiapo, Manila, Philippines.

Maning mentioned, since I love to wander solo, I should meet his daughter, Mafe. We kept in touch. There was no Messenger, Viber, Skype apps then. For communicating, we sent emails. If at the last minute, she remembers a name of a co-worker who can help me at my destination she would even call long distance using her personal phone.

Mafe became my fixer. To name a few countries: Hungary, Switzerland, the Comoros, Haiti, Sierra Leone, Monrovia, island of Timor, Papua, New Guinea, Accra, Togo, Cameroon. Burkina Faso, Ivory Coast, Uganda, Swaziland and Mozambique.

Mafe was single, until she met the love of her life Jean Lalonde. Congratulations for a happy blessed marriage. Thank you for always being there for me.

Satreb Art center, Asmara Ethiopia

Art Lessons While Traveling in Eritrea & Ethiopia

Assuming From the Other Side

A modest thought or belief
Reciting a song

Thinking probably
Intended to be a classic

I frequently dream
Am studying the art of painting
With Vincent Van Gogh or Rembrandt van Rijn
Salvador Dali or Gustav Klimt
Joan Miro and Francisco Goya

Applying the techniques
Visual artist, Michael Adonai

Painting classes
Satreb Art Institute in Asmara, Eritrea

To gather a few gems
Maybe I inherited
Their natural, melancholy
Fits of obsession

To write anywhere
On any piece of blank paper
Shaded with the forceful writings of Shakespeare

Poetry of Emily Dickinson
Literary artists of immense proportions

The great writers, the aura
The wit of prolific Guy de Maupassant

Edgar Allan Poe The Raven
The Grapes of Wrath, John Steinbeck

Rich dreams to exotic places
Ever adventuring and endless curiosity
I fell in love with insatiable travel
In Halliburton's Book of Marvels around the world

Splendors of the Past
Nabataean Aramic Petra, Jordan
Valley of the Stars Persepolis, Iran

Underground Berber villages, Matmata, Tunisia
Unimaginable existence on the other side of the globe
Pictured in olden times and modern days
As Star Wars

Reflecting the sunlight
And procession of the clouds
Remote islands of Lakshadweep in India

Reunion Island, east of Madagascar
Tonga in the Caribbean
The unchanged culture, Dani tribes of Papua

I sat at the piano
And played a few bars

My Way by Frank Sinatra
At Spinney's in Beirut, Lebanon
Made the small crowd teary eyed

Roland Cafe in downtown Slovakia
Elvis Presley Love Me Tender

The music sounded full
And flowed around

The Moments Always Pass By

You looked beautiful in your sleep
For a happy moment
I thought you had been looking at me during the night
Then I realized I fell asleep on the sofa

I had thought you were by my side
With entrancement
I saw the fire in your eyes

As your arms trundled around my shoulders
Dusk flew a flight of late pigeons in the sky

I went out in the semi darkness for a long time
Ministered by thoughts of an angel

Who brought you to my side
And gave me a zenith of contentment

Warm summer dreams

History Unknown Giant Statues of Easter Island

Heads larger than the body
Aquiline long nose

Chins with a pronounced edge
Finishing in a small rectangular beard

Eyes made of coral
With a red volcanic scoria for the pupil
Closed until erected on an *ahu* (platform)

Slightly swollen abdomen and a concave spine
Covered genitals with a loin cloth
Hands with long fine fingers
Thumb carved upwards

Breasts have nipples modeled as spirals
Thick neck with collar bones
Navel is marked

The ephemeral power of man
And the immortal strength of the rock

Hats were red cylinders of stone
Balanced on the head
Positioned a bit askew over the eyes

Eight hundred eighty-seven massive statues
Each statue weighed about two hundred tons
Heads of those in walking position
Lifeless bodies jutting out of the base

Sculptures have secretly had torsos
Buried beneath the earth

Tattoos on its neck
The great Tetokanga
A Maoi with a European ship carved on its chest

South Pacific Oceans Easter Island's enchantment

When and why these people leave their native land
Still a mystery

Winging Strasbourg

That night in Petite France
I felt a throb of lightning

Your hands offered q bouquet of spring flowers
A wanderer, a stranger
You spoke French
I spoke English

Feeling utterly defenseless
What did you say?

Climbing up the spire to the
Cathedral Notre Dame platform
Down below were foot prints and crypts

On to Ponts Couverts
Dominating the sky line
On a boat trip along the water ways
Waddling in the form of a line of yellow ducks
We encircled the old town

A welcome celebration
Surrealism to abstraction

Transported by music
Can Can, Les Toureadors
Habanera

How long will it last?
It might just be a blink away

On to Moselle, Alsace-Loraine
The tide rushed on
Feeling the grains of sand
Falling from the hour glass

A Date During Quarantine

It was in early March
When Corona virus hit the whole world

Entering eight months now
Hanging out with friends and family halted bit by bit

Safety Protocols of wearing masks
Social distancing of six feet
Washing hands, using sanitizers

Conflicts came in
Do not take the risk
Fitness in dancing Zumba

Reminiscing songs of oldies and newbies
Frank Sinatra and The Boyz

Amassing zoom invites, interviews
Smiling faces showed up in little zoom boxes
Television screens lit up in green

At times, zoomed out
Friends on the opposite of the spectrum

Digging Treasure chests
Photos of long ago
Instamatic cameras, analogs, hard drives
Now using drones

Re-arranging closets, spruce up flower beds, décor
Families sent follow-ups text messages
Emojis of love and laughter

Wine Bars, coffee shops
The walk, the brewery

Fancy cocktails, Dine-in Restaurants
Churches were closed
Sharing a secret joke

Sipping wine at home
Dash Door deliveries. Post Mates

World Olympics
Rose Parade of Pasadena postponed

Virtual Lakers, Dodgers, Wrestling games
Tall ships, Carnival, Nordic cruises stranded on open seas

Finding rhythm in yesterdays or days to come
Watching the sunset from my balcony

Blasting votes for Trump or Biden for Presidential election
A dance we did not know that was coming

When will lock down be lifted

Chapter 28

Without Pause, Choosing You

Rolling by the Shores in Algarve

Mediterranean Seas
Every shade of blue beaches
As far as my eyes can see
Bordered by craggy rock cliffs and iconic caves

Flip flops, sun glasses, golden sun in July
Camera on tripod, catch the colors

Bamboo beach mat at São Rafael in Albufeira
Abundant waves Praia da Amoreira

Watching surfers hit the waves
Praia da Marinha in Lagoa

Spa and Sky bars
Sipping wine pressed Negra Mole grapes
Clams bathed in oil and garlic to grill
Fish fillets crisp-skinned sea bass

Algarvian treats, octopus capital of the world
Polvo & Companhia, Santa Luzia

Meet foodie friends
Silver trays of percebes
Café Correia in Vila do Bispo

Kneel in thanksgiving prayers
Sé de Faro cathedral, Portugal

Titanium Scales of the Guggenheim Museum, Bilbao

Look! The building oozes and extrudes
Around the Puente de Salve
A building that extrudes
A curved riverside promenade

Along the Nervion River
We drove, articulated jokes and giggled
There was a slight drizzle
But the sky cooperated with our smiles

Curves of the Building by Frank Gehry
Swirling forms and sensuous materiality
In glass and titanium
Appeared and disappeared here and there

To catch the light
Resembling Fish scales
Or some organic life
Steps gradually narrow like a canyon

Enter the atrium
Dervish whirling volumes
Perpetually changing shadows

Through the lustrous and luminous
Soaring height of a cathedral like space
Stimulated our fanciful free association

Marilyn Monroe's wind-assisted skirts
Willem de Kooning drawings
An exploded artichoke heart

Light is diffused through slashes of glazing

Exhibits were too modern
It was hard to comprehend their beauty
Splashed colors and cans of paints

A huge lobster seated in a vintage Chevrolet

Giant circles of curved varnished plywood
We were lost in a maize

Art from German towns, Italians and Russians
In electronic forms
Depicting different poses of the body
We turned on our headsets for clarity

One of those rare moments
We deciphered everything and anything
Or was it about something?

The Matter of Time
Weathering steel columns

Tulips in shiny neon colors
Sculptor Jeff Kloons

Something different
A floral sculpture of a puppy
A gigantic West Highland terrier
Forty three feet tall
Covered with seventy thousand flowers

You held my camera with care
I posed for more photos

Iran, Echoes of Red Rose Splendor

Immersing myself in the permanent university of traveling
Pulled in myriad ways, curious and intrigued
To the roads less traveled
Red rose is the national flower
Flower of love
Rearrange the words
It is Eros, the God of Love

My loose jogging shoes slapped against the stone roads of Persia
If you like people, you will like Iran

Iranians are endlessly welcoming
They have the human touch
Hooked on anything Western
They opened their hearts to us

They spoke candidly about everything
Internet, Facebook, Iran's relations with the West
Where are you from?
Where do you live?
Why did you come to Iran?

Frustrated by politics
A land and people wanting to change
We weaved a tale through pilgrimages to ancient sites

We walked in sun speckled cloud shapes
To Tehran's Reza Shah Pahlavi's White and Green Palace

The lavish Golestan Palace
Mirrored glass that turned into a prismatic fire
Flashed and glowed in a kaleidoscope of colors

We scaled the slopes of the Alborz Mountains to Velenjak Park
Lined with tall leafy plane trees
People strolled and hiked, some played ball
Others enjoyed the evening's music
Pop Tehrangeles songs
Danced to it

The colossal slightly snow covered Damavand was up ahead
Water from melting snow flowed and lapped the foot of the trees
Paused for Mexican pizza with Al, Jazz, Puran and Shirin

At Ferdowsi Avenue there were men with calculators at the ready
Exchanged money, dollars to toumans, rials

Drank Parsi cola, ate yogurt *sabzi* (soft greens) and soft white cheese
Dizi, lamb stew, highlight of Persian cuisine
Traditionally cooked in a small stone crock pot
Justified Soul food believed to sustain us through a long day

Shrines of medieval poets Hafez and eloquent Saadi in Shiraz
The Quran and a collection of the poems of Hafez, Iranian folk hero
Who transported us back to the magic of Ancient Persia

Amplified tones of muezzins called the faithful for prayer
We basked in the glories of an early civilization
The tomb of Cyrus the Great at the honey colored plains of Pasargad

Explored the sparkling turquoise-tiled domes and minarets of Esfahan
Intricately designed copper lamps
Beautiful boulevards with covered bridges
of the *Zayandeh Rud* River
The life giving river that cuts across the city

The April breeze ballooned out my chador
With the generosity of Fereshte and Marti

We ate *Ashreshte* hearty soup
(Black lentils, kidney beans, garbanzo beans in pomegranate paste)

Old caravanserais
Abbassi Hotel in a lavish setting
Period paintings on the walls

Striking woman with a yellow scarf and red headband
Carrying a red rose in one hand
A massive clay jug on her shoulder
Big brown eyes, smiling red lips
Black hair jutting out from her printed scarf

Lush gardens, palaces, mosques, and minarets
Led to the Persian
Isfahan's beauty is half of the world

The awesome power and beauty of Persopolis
Trees and my umbrella offered cool solace from the midday sun
The size of five football fields
A collection of fraying once luxurious yellow tent suites
With marbled bathrooms from the distance

Nowadays it is has some rocks with graffiti
I love Leonardo di Carpio

Tall columns, stunning example of Pre-Islamic architecture
Mythical Iranian kings and semi divine rulers
Invading armies with their swords
Guests of the King offering sacrifices

Monumental and majestic testament
Splendor of Achaemenian Persia
Attention to the detail
Left us breathless

The mud brick alleys and rooftops of Abyaneh
Zoroastrian women in flowery dresses
Sold dried apricots and mulberries
Young girls in satin and tulle with head veils brought out smiles

The wind swept lanes of Kashan
Flowing water canals and stone walkways
Apple and watermelon carts
Tree shaded shops
Street kids selling Chiclet chewing gum

The golden domes of the holy city of Qom
Politically speaking mustachioed Clerics in turbans
Motorcycles buzzed by
We sat on green benches
Low–spouting fountains kept us cool

We quenched our thirst with
Faludeh (a bowl of frozen sorbet with thin
crispy starch noodles and rose water)

Lost in a maze of twisting bazaars
Exquisite carpets in ever green colors, squares
with landscapes of animals
Weeping willows and sky blue background
Burgundy Oriental medallions, silk and lustrous weaves in detail

Developed meaningful relationships with new friends
Lingered over small cups of hot tea
Stirring with tiny teaspoons
Sharbat, carrot juice shake with vanilla ice cream and walnuts

If your travel decision is based on what people say
You will probably never make it to Iran

However you choose your journey
Iran will change the way you see this part of the world

Soul searching in mysticism

This journey freed me
Of every concept and image
My mind has ever known

Chapter 29

Splash and Mosaics

Battle of Flowers, Cordoba

It sounded like a distant thunder
A steady drumbeat broke through
Louder and louder, more insistent

Requiem-like rhythm out into the darkened street
Huge candelabras in the shape of twisted golden serpents
Stood guard at the corners of the velvet-draped float

Smoke from the candles mingled with clouds of incense
In the center of it all
Serene in her innocent, cobalt dress

Illuminated by flickering candles
Surrounded by lilies, daisies and roses
Assumption of the Virgin Mary

Her slow swaying progress down the narrow street
The float supported
On the shoulders of a phalanx of Andalusian devotees

Córdoba, Spain's the Great Mosque

Inviting squares and lively taverns
Spring time fragrance of jasmine and orange blossom
The Alcázar de los Reyes Cristianos

The Synagogue and the Roman bridge
Christian, Islamic and Jewish cultures
Jewish quarter, the Calahorra tower
Roman theatre, Plaza de la Corredera

Equestrian arts, Andalusian horses Caballerizas Reales
Medina Azahara, Caliphate's former capital

Web and tangle of narrow streets
Callejón de la Luna and Calleja de las Flores
Fountains, mosaics and courtyards, thousands of flowers

The Courtyards Festival, the May Crosses
Battle of Flowers, Railings and Balconies competition
Feria de Córdoba

Tapa bars, San Lorenzo, San Andrés, Santa Marina
Salmorejo (cold tomato soup), *flamenquín* (pork fried in breadcrumbs)
Iberian ham Los Pedroches
Flamenco tablao
Arab baths, hot springs

I can still hear the accordion
Andres Segovia and his guitar

The harmonica and the castanets
Indulged in the delirium of good life

Rumors of a seduced past

Curing the insomniac

To ensure a safe journey

Batalla de Flores, Córdoba

Sonaba como un trueno distante
Un ritmo constante se rompió
Más y más fuerte, más insistente

Ritmo de réquiem en la calle oscura
Candelabros enormes en forma de serpientes doradas retorcidas
Se puso guardia en las esquinas del flotador cubierto de terciopelo

El humo de las velas mezclado con nubes de incienso
En el centro de todo
Serena en su inocente vestido cobalto

Iluminado por velas parpadeantes
Rodeado de lirios, margaritas y rosas
Asunción de la Virgen María

Su lento avance oscilante por la calle estrecha
El flotador apoyado
Sobre los hombros de una falange de devotos andaluces

Córdoba, la Gran Mezquita de España

Plazas acogedoras y tabernas animadas
Fragancia primaveral de jazmín y azahar
El Alcázar de los Reyes Cristianos

La Sinagoga y el Puente Romano
Culturas cristianas, islámicas y judías
Barrio judío, la torre de la Calahorra
Teatro Romano, Plaza de la Corredera

Artes ecuestres, caballos andaluces Caballerizas Reales
Medina Azahara, antigua capital del Califato

Telaraña y maraña de calles estrechas
Callejón de la Luna y Calleja de las Flores
Fuentes, mosaicos y patios, miles de flores

El Festival de los Patios, las Cruces de Mayo
Concurso Batalla de Flores, Barandillas y Balcones
Feria de Córdoba

Bares de tapas, San Lorenzo, San Andrés, Santa Marina
Salmorejo (sopa fría de tomate), flamenquín
(cerdo frito en pan rallado)
Jamón ibérico Los Pedroches
Tablao flamenco
Baños árabes, aguas termales

Todavía puedo escuchar el acordeón
Andrés Segovia y su guitarra

La armónica y las castañuelas
Complacido en el delirio de la buena vida

Rumores de un pasado seducido

Curar el insomne

Para garantizar un viaje seguro

Mount Matutum, Mindanao

Indigenous natives
MunaTo (first people)

Invasion of Sarangani
Belligerents
Imperial Japanese Army

The world renowned
"Ang Galing Mo" (You are good)

Sarangani women face to face
Whsipered and laughed
Wearing sash and belts with bright colored beads

MunaTo Festival in the Philippines
It was like the chatter of dressed up dolls
With men clinking their glasses

Isla Parilla
Invisible creaturs
Ancient burial jars

Ayub Cave
Sagel Cave
Maitum

Mindanao's armed conflicts
Names and sketches
Prehistoric civilization

Caracas, Venezuela

Common greeting *Mi Amor* (my love)
Town of Pampatar

Trudging up the steps
Castle of San Carlos Borromeo
Island's most important pirate defense

Church of the Holy Christ of good Voyage
Facing the port was

Sailors claim
Crucifix over the altar was brought on a passing ship
Found itself unable to lift anchor until this was left behind

Casa de la Aduana (Customs House)
A yellow and white colonial home

Most renowned religious spot, El Valle del Espíritu Santo
Home of the Santuario del Virgen del Valle
A chapel guarding the patron saint of Venezuela

Ornate pink and white neo-Gothic chapel house the revered image
The Virgin dressed in an elegant gown
Covered with *margaritas* (daisies) and a gold crown.

Across the church was the House of Mariño
Santiago Mariño, patriot official in Boca Chica

Sunsets and seafood at El Caracol (The Snail).
Reflection of the golden moon
Danced in the dark night waters of the Caribbean Sea

Fresh fish heaven - fried prawns, giant mahi-mahi, paella
A live band played Salsa and Reggae music

Farewell dinner at Restaurant de Don Pablo

At the airport
I gave my guide, Guillermo, a big hug

Hard to say the words good-bye, so we bade him

"Hasta Luego" until we meet again

Chapter 30

Family is Priority

July 2020 Taken during a Baby shower for coming Baby boy Kai Christopher Ricasa

Our Growing Family

July 2020 - From left: Rachel Rudio, Riley Rudio, Rica Ricasa Rudio, Richie Ricasa (holding sign Welcome Baby Boy), Christine Zalenke Ricasa (expecting mother) and Cutie Lucy Ricasa

Rick Ricasa, Odette Aquitania Ricasa, Robert Ricasa, Chrissy Ulanday Ricasa.

What an exciting Baby shower party!

Banners, Mylar balloons, Pom pom garlands, Streamers, Neon lights decorated the front garden and the walls. Pizza slices, chicken and turkey sandwiches, potato chips, donuts, butter cookies, pecan pie, chocolate cookies – the works. Decorative Souvenir bags and Drinks too – we all wore masks for protection and followed the guide lines of 6 feet social distancing.

More than 21 cars were in a caravan. We honked, blew our horns, hooted, jumped, whistled and waved our hands in a circular motion.

Richie and Christine's friends, all family were present, Tita Onggi Santos and Ambe Kaw, Tita Goody and Tito Rene Silva, Pete and Carmen Santos and family, Tito Ed and Carmen Aniceto and family, Jing, Mikey, Malia and Makoa.

A Big thank you to organizers: Janet Jing and Mikey Quipones, Rica Rudio, Robert and Chrissy Ricasa.

Portrait: From left: My Handsome Brother Reynaldo
(Rey the King), Elegant mom Luz,
Comical and hardworking dad, Sixto.

Sisters: Goodeeh Aquitania Silva, Odette Aquitania
Ricasa, Carmen Aquitania Aniceto,
Luz Aquitania Santos

Nostalgic Family Photo

We all squeezed in our 1954 Ford sedan
Dad drove us to Escolta, Manila
Comadre Georgina Montemayor was the owner
Famous X'or Studios
We wore our Sunday best dresses

The photographer and his camera on a tall
tripod was covered with a black cloth
Holding a bright light bulb with his right hand
He says "One, Two, Three Smile"
The light bulb pops, it's out!

We celebrate
Driving to Dairy Queen
Ordering chocolate cookies
Mountain scoops of ice cream and banana split

Heacock's, an upscale department store for clothing, cosmetics, jewelry, sporting goods on Escolta and David street. The cafe was located on the mezzanine floor that gave a pleasant overlook of the entire store.

M.Y. San Restaurant – for *merienda* (snacks), crackers and biscuits. Gem Gift Shop, for occasional gifts.

The Gregg Shoe Store and Walk-Over Shoe Store was THE place to get shoes. I recall after seeing movies at the Ideal theatre, we went window shopping.

One of the most memorable stores for me in the Fifties, was the <u>Botica Boie</u>. Oh, I loved that store. It smelled clean, disinfectant clean – I guess because it was primarily a drug store but it also had a soda fountain.

We sat on high bar stools and ordered chocolate, vanilla or strawberry ice cream sodas.

Luxurious goods were also found in the area. La Estrella del Norte, Oceanic, La Perla del Oriente stores. The windows usually displayed the most elegant apparel imported from the United States.

For more fine clothing, there was a handful of Indian merchants such as Assandas and Bombay Silk Supply.

The Capitol Theater, depicts Filipina ladies in native costumes set within a tropical landscape. It sat approximately 800 persons and had an unusual double balcony. It run Columbia Pictures because I remember seeing a lot of Western movies there.

The Lyric Theater sat more than 1,500 people. I remember going to more movie houses at the Ideal, Life, Galaxy, and Scala theaters.

We also went to watch pelota players at the old Jai Alai building.

There were many other stores such as Sim's Department Store, Aguinaldo's, Soriente Santos and Berg's.

Syvel's and H. Alonso were at the Dona Regina Building.

Our dentist, Doctor Unding Hernandez's office was near Syvel's.

My mom's good friend, Georgina's studio, the X'or Studios was on David Street, Escolta. On several occasions, we went for portraits bringing the family gifts and goodies.

Some of the other buildings on the Escolta:

Masonic Temple

Meralco Bldg., Escolta and David

Philippine Education Co. Quiapo – our apartment was on the corner of Arlegui and Farnecio Street.

Roxas Bldg., Escolta

Index

About the Author

LOURDES ODETTE AQUITANIA RICASA is an artist, a world traveler and a motivational speaker.

She has written six books. She loves to paint and took painting lessons at the Ecole d Artes in Mauritania, painting instructor Jay T in Fiji, Reverie in Solomon Islands, Satreb Art School in Asmara Eritrea, Escuela de Pinturas de Allue in Zaragoza, Spain. Recently, she submitted her Servas work of Art with Jean-Luc Turlure in Paris, France. She has on display more than one hundred works of Art.

As a motivational speaker, she was invited to speak in various occasions, the Prince Andrew School in Saint Helena island, the Kamenge Youth Center in Bujumbura, Burundi, San Clemente High School, Pasadena Journaling Class, and more.

Wandering from one moment to the next from Zanzibar to Chatham Islands to the Faroe Islands, to Seville, Spain to Olkhon in Siberia and then perhaps she will be back to Spain in Palma de Mallorca with a sudden crisis of the heart.

Spanning a fertile imagination in discovering pre-historical places shows the author is at her concise best. This book is at the very least, ferociously entertaining.

Her books and art flourish and give variety and individuality.

LOVE ECHOES, SHARE AND INSPIRE - is a clear exercise of her talents, a special type of poetry for readers.

Love cannot remain by itself – it has no meaning. Love has to be put into action. Not all of us can do great things. But we can do small things with great love.

Having traveled to two hundred ninety-five (295) countries, islands and territories, her book is a premiere show case, the world on pages of journeys.

Lightning Source UK Ltd.
Milton Keynes UK
UKHW020425301220
376108UK00004B/579